May Mann Jennings

May Mann Jennings

FLORIDA'S
GENTEEL
ACTIVIST

Linda D. Vance

UNIVERSITY PRESSES OF FLORIDA
University of Florida Press
Gainesville

UNIVERSITY PRESSES OF FLORIDA is the central agency for scholarly publishing of the State of Florida's university system, producing books selected for publication by the faculty editorial committees of Florida's nine public universities: Florida A&M University (Tallahassee), Florida Atlantic University (Boca Raton), Florida International University (Miami), Florida State University (Tallahassee), University of Central Florida (Orlando), University of Florida (Gainesville), University of North Florida (Jacksonville), University of South Florida (Tampa), University of West Florida (Pensacola).

ORDERS for books published by all member presses of University Presses of Florida should be addressed to University Presses of Florida, 15 NW 15th Street, Gainesville, FL 32603.

HQ
1413
.J46
V36
1985

Library of Congress Cataloging-in-Publication Data

Vance, Linda D.
May Mann Jennings, Florida's genteel activist.

Bibliography: p.
Includes index.
1. Jennings, May Mann, 1872–1963. 2. Women in
public life—Florida—Biography. 3. Women social
reformers—Florida—Biography. 4. Governors' wives—
Florida—Biography. 5. Conservationists—Florida—
Biography. I. Title.
HQ1413.J46V36 1986   305.4′2′0924   85–17963
ISBN 0–8130–0750–X

Printed in the U.S.A. on acid-free paper   ∞

12552740   *5/14/90 RB*

Acknowledgments

The author is indebted to many people for the completion of this work: first, the staff of the P. K. Yonge Library of Florida History at the University of Florida—Elizabeth Alexander, Ellen Hodges, and Steve Kerber—who were always helpful; second, the Jennings heirs—Dorothy Jennings Sandridge, Gordon Sandridge, Guy Odum, Linda Odum Sweat, S. Bryan Jennings, Jr., and Gordon Sandridge, Jr.—who gave generously of their time and shared family papers, mementoes, and photographs; and Dr. Samuel Proctor, friend and mentor.

Contents

Illustrations

CHAPTER 1

Crystal Grove and Papa

I N 1873 a young family from the North—Austin Mann, his wife, Rachel, and their baby daughter, May—wintered in Ocala. Impressed with Florida's beauty, the business opportunities that seemed available, and the beneficial effects of the warm climate on his wife's health, Austin decided to make the state the family's permanent home. By autumn of the next year he had purchased an established orange grove at Crystal River in Hernando County and had moved his family into the small cottage on the premises. The Manns called the place Crystal Grove, and it became the childhood home of their daughter, who would grow up to be one of Florida's most notable women.[1]

Many people, places, and events shaped May Mann's character and personality, first and foremost her father, whose political ambition and ability to work with people she would share. Austin Mann became a successful businessman and prominent Florida politician. Dynamic and carefree, energetic, imaginative and inventive, his entrepreneurial talents developed early. He was small of stature, feisty, restless by nature, a spellbinding talker, and a natty dresser. A born promoter, what some might call a "wheeler dealer," Mann was also a visionary, often as impractical as he was ahead of his time.[2] A free-thinking nonconformist, he was usually ready to try out new ideas and spent much of his life in economic and politcal pursuits that brought him both notoriety and financial rewards.

Austin Mann was already successful when, at the age of twenty-six, he moved his family to Florida. Born in Delaware County, Ohio, in 1847, he attended local schools and, for three years, Capital University at Columbus.[3] After studying law with his cousin G. L. Converse, a future congressman, he was admitted to the Ohio Bar in 1869. But Mann was ambitious and interested in things other than law, and he moved east where he believed there were more business opportunities. At Mauch Chunk, Pennsylvania, he met and married Rachel Elizabeth Kline, the second of five children of Frederick C. and Marietta Staples Kline, longtime residents of the area. A Methodist who sang in the local church choir, Rachel had thick, dark hair and attractive features and was much admired for her piano playing and her clear soprano voice. Unfortunately, she suffered from poor health and would die in her twenties. She and Austin were married 24 April 1871.[4] A year and a day after the wedding May Elizabeth Austin Mann was born in Centerville, Bayonne Province, New Jersey, where the family then resided.[5]

Austin had developed a new type of metallic heel plate, valuable in the manufacture of shoes, and it brought him a large, steady income.[6] After Austin decided to locate his family in Florida, he returned north to settle his business affairs; with $90,000 from the sale of his heel plate patent, he bought Crystal Grove. Years later, May remembered her parents' first Florida home as a small, crudely built cottage sitting "on pine pillars about eight to ten feet from the ground."[7] Her mother was probably appalled by the primitive and isolated area and disappointed with the house at the grove, since the family had been accustomed to better accommodations. But in those days houses in that part of the state had only one purpose, to provide a high, dry place to eat and sleep. Austin soon built a more appropriate and spacious home for his family.

In the 1870s, Crystal River, scarcely more than a hamlet with a population of less than one hundred people,[8] was cut off both from major highways and from railroad routes. The only practical way in or out was aboard one of the steamers that plied between Cedar Key and Tampa Bay but stopped periodically to discharge freight and to take on firewood. Contemporary descriptions of the area were not flattering. Daniel G. Brinton, in his 1869 guidebook, described the Hernando County coastal lowlands as "rich" but "the most unhealthy part of the peninsula."[9] J. M. Hawks, author of a tourist guide published in 1871 for "those who migrate with the swallows and robins," called Crystal River a "flourishing village" whose inhabitants made their living by farming, fishing, tending citrus groves, and working in the cedar sawmills.[10] The people were described as "peaceable and quiet, frugal and hospitable," not much interested in politics or in the outside world. There were no public schools and few churches, and the nearest newspapers were published in Ocala and Tampa, both a day's journey away.

Why Austin Mann chose this remote spot is not known. While influenced by Florida's tropical beauty and the hope of better health for his wife, he was also obviously afflicted with what one historian has called "orange fever," which swept Florida in the 1870s.[11] Intrigued by tales of quick riches, thousands of wealthy northerners began to move south, investing large sums of money in citrus acreage. How simple it all sounded—money figuratively growing on trees and available just for the picking. One alluring advertisement brought many a northerner and his money to Florida: "Clear off one acre of ground. Plant but one hundred orange trees twenty-one feet apart and in three years one has a capital of $10,000 bringing in an interest of 10 percent. The land will cost but little, Each tree will produce 1,000 oranges each year bringing 1 cent a piece."[12] This promise is more alluring when one remembers that one 1870 dollar was equivalent to approximately ten today. Most of the would-be grove owners who flooded the state bypassed the remote Gulf coast region.

Although David Levy Yulee, former U.S. senator, had had a large and prosperous plantation in Hernando County until the 1860s, few of the area's original settlers had remained after the Civil War. "It was still frontier in the 1870s, its people hacking out a living under primitive conditions."[13] According to one old-timer, "in the early days bear and deer were as common as cattle now,"[14] and turkey, otter, and other wildlife were also abundant. The people lived off the land, which was fertile and productive—and cheap, since most of it was nearly inaccessible. Less isolated than South Florida, the area was still remote enough for its growth to be hindered. Most supplies and mail arrived by water, although weekly stagecoaches ran from Ocala and Brooksville when the weather was good. But such land facilities were not dependable: One of those coaches was described by a visitor to the area as "a little rattletrap sort of affair."[15]

Active and ambitious, Mann soon acquired a reputation in his community as an adroit businessman. His grove proved lucrative and provided capital for him to purchase additional lands for speculative purposes and undertake some innovative agriculture ventures.[16] Florida's west coast needed developers like him; one writer noted that there was not "a single improved farming implement in Hernando County."[17] At one time Mann tried raising sheep, but the venture failed even though he imported high quality merino stock from Spain.[18] Perhaps his neighbors were involved in his failure: the cattlemen in the county resented the intrusion of the new livestock and turned their dogs loose on his flocks. Unbowed, Mann acquired the largest herd of cattle in the area, some two hundred head. In addition to his agricultural business interests he practiced law and entered local politics. By 1881 he had served two terms as a county commissioner, had attended various district and state political conventions, and had been elected to the 1880 Hancock-English presidential electoral ticket.

Mann was able to pursue successful political and business careers simultaneously. His ingenuity and energies were well suited to the post–Civil War era. He held to the belief that progress and the public good were irrevocably linked to the many grand schemes in agriculture, timber, land, and railroad development that promoters and investors were relentlessly pursuing everywhere. Consequently he involved himself in a number of activities that he hoped would attract settlers to Florida and make money for himself at the same time. He became an enthusiastic booster of railroad, canal, and road development in his adopted state.

While Mann had the ideas and the abilities to become a nineteenth-century tycoon, he lacked the necessary ruthlessness. A promoter, he was also a maverick; unlike many entrepreneurs of that period he was too trusting and often misjudged character. He possessed a strong sympathy for poor people and devoted time and energy to provide them with economic opportunities and a measure of social and legal justice. Mann thought of himself first as a farmer, then as a businessman. Although his abilities and personality enabled him to adjust to a time when capitalists were profiting handsomely from the development as well as from the exploitation of America's natural resources, he was never to pull off the coveted "big deal" and make the millions he sought.

If Mann never became a millionaire, he was by most standards financially successful. Unfortunately, he never managed his money well; he was extravagant and spent freely on travel, fine clothes, cigars, horses, and expensive hotels and restaurants. He enjoyed hobnobbing with the rich and famous at their watering holes along the east coast.[19] Mann's wife and children led as comfortable and genteel a life as frontier Florida would permit, even though his business and political activities forced him to spend much time away from home. Though his finances were to fluctuate his family never felt any insecurity, and as far as May ever knew there was always enough money available to live well. She grew up feeling both emotionally and financially secure.

Austin Mann's spendthrift nature sometimes forced him into debt, but mortgages and personal loans helped carry him between harvests, elections, and business deals. On occasion he was on the brink of bankruptcy, but he always managed to recover, relying on little more than his perseverance. He never lost his optimistic outlook. Even in the bleakest of times he believed things would work out well: "I can't make a deal at all. Seems tomorrow I think I will see a ray of light. . . . It is simply almost impossible to get men willing to part with cash and strange to say I have been parting with mine very rapidly but I know how to do once I am busted"; "It takes pluck to make a deal at these times. If I fall down I might as well keep going. . . . I am a fair sample of a gambler or like Napoleon believe in my Lucky Star. Yet even those who have a Lucky Star fail to see it in cloudy weather. Yet I am in good spirits." [20] To his daughter he wrote, "Why worry and make of life so anxious a matter? What you can't help don't worry about." "Dear, you take life too seriously. It is a large joke." [21] May was to inherit her father's positiveness but not his nonchalant fatalism. She would have her feet planted more firmly on the ground.

Austin Mann had a wide-ranging career. Even after arriving in Florida he practiced law, owned and managed several sizable citrus groves and out-of-state peach farms, and operated a newspaper. He was elected to public office and became a leader in his political party. He promoted railroad, canal, and land development schemes, headed the Florida Orange and Vegetable Auction Company, managed the Florida Home Market and the Sub-Tropical Exposition, served as president of the Florida State Agriculture Association, and organized the Florida "Good Roads" movement.[22] Mann's peripatetic life style, together with his active mind, caused one friend to refer to him as a "brainy, rushing man." [23] He himself admitted, "I have to be moving. I hear the rumbling of the [railroad] car and must move on even if it overtakes me." [24] Throughout his life he traveled, politicked, and organized business deals. He was reluctant to stop and rest, although late in life he wrote his family: "I sometimes get tired of rambling always waiting for a deal to close. . . . I am going to get into something else. I am tired of skimming wind." [25] May inherited her father's restlessness and tireless vitality, but she was able to channel her energies into more practical, worthwhile pursuits.

Throughout his career, Mann was undaunted by inconsistencies; for instance, he championed liberal political beliefs while insisting upon a laissez-faire capitalistic economic philosophy. Accused sometimes of being a secret Republican, he was identified over the years as a Democrat, Independent, Allianceman, and Populist. His inconsistencies, combined with the controversies he seemed always to be enmeshed in, led his political opponents to accuse him of erratic and fickle behavior. Enemies labeled him "an aristocrat," "a first-class demagogue," "a land shark," and a "Political Nondescript." [26] Naturally his admirers and friends viewed him differently. If his unconventional hybrid politics defy classification, it is obvious that he was a shrewd politician who possessed superior abilities and seemed to thrive on Florida's rough-and-tumble politics. Regardless of the assessment of Mann by friend or foe, he left his mark on Florida and on its business and political institutions.

During the years that Mann was consolidating his business interests and establishing a political career, his family was growing. Three years after May's birth, a boy, Roy Frederick, was born. In 1876 a second daughter, Nina Lucy, joined the family, and in 1879 Grace Irene was born. [27] A fifth child, Carl, died shortly after birth.

Crystal Grove was an exciting place to live in the 1870s; it was not only the family's homestead but also Mann's political headquarters. During these years May's lifelong fascination with politics began. From early childhood she watched her father's political friends come and go. The lights often burned late in their home while her father and his associates met to talk over political stategy. May was the only one of the Mann children to develop any inclination toward politics.

May's father was the most important personal influence on her during her childhood years. From her mother she inherited artistic talents, but from her father she inherited a zest for life, an optimistic outlook that was never to leave her, and a love of politics. From the beginning Mann's eldest daughter was his favorite. He never excluded her from adult activities or discussions, and he never assumed that there were some things she could not do because she was a girl. This liberating notion was to hold a key place in her philosophy of life. To May, politics was just as legitimate an interest for women as for men. This radical belief, so natural to her, was to thrust her to the forefront of the women's movement just when females were beginning to enter Florida's political arena.

The Crystal River area expanded with the arrival of new settlers. The Manns were recognized as one of the most prosperous and prominent families in the county, and if their life was comparatively simple it was not dull. Children were educated at home or at one of the small private schools in the town. In addition to household and farm chores, there were picnics, church socials, political rallies, fishing trips, blackberry hunts, holiday celebrations, orange harvests, romps in newly cut hay, and buggy rides down shady, moss-draped lanes. May especially enjoyed horseback riding; she liked to perform stunts and acrobatics on her horse and became an expert horsewoman. Years later she hung her girlhood saddle and riding habit in her Jacksonville home as a reminder of those carefree days.[28]

Even Crystal Grove was to have an influence upon her. Growing up in rural Florida's tropical wilderness, in the midst of a citrus grove where the scents and beauty of nature were ever present, would produce in her a life-long love of the outdoors. Plants, trees, flowers, and wildlife became special ingredients in her life. Later she planned and developed award-winning gardens, and because of her attachment to nature she became a recognized leader in the movement to conserve and preserve Florida's tropical wilderness. Of all her public works her unwavering commitment to this cause would at times take precedence over all her other interests. When grown, she remembered Crystal Grove with fondness: "My memory lingers caressingly over the years spent in dear old Hernando. . . . Crystal River is very dear to me."[29]

After 1880 the Mann family was never the same. At the age of four, Nina Lucy died during the summer that year, and Rachel, pregnant and weak from a chronic cough, never recovered from the death of her child. The next winter she came down with what the family believed was a severe cold but was in reality an advanced case of tuberculosis. Unable to recoup strength she traveled to Pennsylvania to live with her parents and try to regain her health as she awaited the birth of her fifth child. Carl Mann was born on 25 March 1881. Rachel's health deteriorated rapidly, and she was weak and unable to care for her baby. He sickened and died only a few months after his birth. Rachel Mann never recovered from this final blow; bedridden and unable to care for herself she lingered little more than a year and died at the age of twenty-eight at her parents' home on 20 August 1882, with Austin at her bedside.[30] The medical cause of her passing was tuberculosis, but grief no doubt played a role. A gentle woman, Rachel was remembered by Florida friends as one who would "mount her horse with her babe and a basket of necessaries in her arms, and ride ten miles through the forest to minister to the sick and poor."[31]

The loss of Nina Lucy affected May deeply, but nothing was to overwhelm her and change her life as much as the death of her mother. Years later, when she was directing the clubwomen of Florida in public health work, she wrote to a colleague who was proposing an antituberculosis campaign: "I do not think there is any more important work. . . . I lost my mother with the disease, when I was a little girl of nine. . . . So you see the matter comes very close to me."[32]

Drastic changes took place in May's life. Becoming the eldest female in the household, she was forced to assume responsibilities beyond her years.[33] Austin Mann faced the serious problem of raising three children alone. There were servants in the house, but they could hardly be expected to provide the necessary supervision and guidance. He had neither the inclination nor the time to take on that responsibility himself, for he was in the midst of an intense political campaign for the state senate.[34] When he won the election, the problem of how to care for his children became even more acute.

Crystal River friends helped out, but a more permanent arrangement was necessary if Mann was to fulfill his public duties and ensure that his children's needs were properly met. He persuaded a cousin and her husband to come from Ohio to live at Crystal Grove and to care for the children while he attended the legislative session at Tallahassee, but the arrangement was temporary for the couple had to return to their own home after a few months. Mann then took the children to Jacksonville where they lived with friends, but this too proved unsatisfactory.[35] In October 1883, he found a solution: Roy went to live with family friends in Brooksville, and May and Grace were enrolled as year-round boarders at St. Joseph's Academy, a convent school in St. Augustine.

Austin Mann continued to cultivate both his citrus groves and his political career. In 1885 he was married again, this time to Susie B. Williams of Nashville, Tennessee. Once more there was a mother in the household but only for a few years. In 1886 she gave birth to Austin, Jr.; in 1888 she died giving birth to a second child, who also succumbed.[36] For a second time Austin was left a widower, and now there was a toddler to care for. The family with which Roy was living agreed to take Austin, Jr. The girls remained at the academy, and a new chapter in May's life began.

CHAPTER 2

"Beyond the Alps Lies Italy"

M AY MANN and her sister remained at the St. Augustine convent for seven years, receiving the personal attention, discipline, and education that they needed.[1] They left St. Joseph's with a strong sense of duty and an understanding of their responsibility to society.

The Mann boys, Roy and Austin, Jr., were less fortunate. They were to become alienated and to develop behavior problems which later brought dismay and grief to the family. It is tempting to attribute the striking contrast between Austin Mann's sons and his daughters to the difference in the quality of their respective upbringings.

The school at St. Augustine was operated by the Sisters of St. Joseph, a Catholic order organized at Le Puy, France, in 1648.[2] The order had come to Florida at the summons of Bishop Augustine Verot after the Civil War to minister to the newly freed slaves. Arriving in St. Augustine in 1866, they had established one of the state's first schools for blacks. A school for white boys was soon added and, in 1877, a school for white girls.[3] From the time the nuns arrived in Florida they raised money to support them-

9

selves and their schools by teaching, by giving private art, music, and French lessons, and by selling their famous delicate, handmade lace. By 1883, when May and Grace enrolled at St. Joseph's, its reputation as a highly respected educational institution was firmly established.[4]

From 1874 until 1982 the convent and academy occupied the same site in St. Augustine. The O'Reilly house, one of the city's oldest structures, and still maintained by the order, once served as the academy. When May entered the school, however, a new three-story building housed the classrooms, chapel, and dormitory. It was of Mediterranean-style architecture, constructed of coquina and brick overlaid with white plaster, and it had a red tile roof. It fronted on St. George Street, two blocks from the waterfront and historic market square. The building still stands and is still used by the order.

During the 1880s the school was surrounded by spacious grounds which contained vegetable, fruit, and flower gardens, grape arbors, and an octagonal gazebo. The entire property of several acres was enclosed by a high rock wall for privacy. Great wooden gates marked the entrances. The tropical vines and flowers that cascaded over the walls provided a friendly, inviting appearance.

Most of the academy's white students came from St. Augustine and the surrounding area. Students of all religious persuasions were admitted, but the majority were Catholics. May and Grace maintained their family's Baptist faith throughout their years at the academy.

St. Joseph's Academy was unique; unlike most institutions in the South, with perhaps the exception of schools in New Orleans, it projected an international aura. The nuns were French, and many of the students came from Spanish, Minorcan, and Italian backgrounds. This diversity may have sparked May's natural inquisitiveness regarding other places and peoples. As an adult she extended her knowledge of different cultures through travel and books. Once, explaining her liberal attitude, she wrote, "I was educated in a convent and I look at life through much broader glasses than the average person does."[5]

When May entered St. Joseph's Academy, the superior was Mother Marie Lazarus Lhostal and the school's principal was Sister Margaret Mary, both pioneer workers in the order. May's mentors and counselors, they were to remain her friends after she left the school. The steadying influence of the nuns at the convent gave May the equanimity and poise that she carried the rest of her life. Further security came from May's close relationship with her sister, which provided a sense of family and prevented them from feeling isolated and forgotten. May not only looked after Grace while they were at St. Joseph's but continued her guardianship until Grace married and established her own home.

At school, the girls lived in a large dormitory room on the top floor.

From the moment young girls arrived at the convent they were struck by the kindness of the sisters, women who wore long black dresses and veils, and white guimpes [collars] starched of linen, which they called holy habits. Almost immediately, the sisters would take the newcomer upstairs to be assigned her place in the dormitory. The first sight that met the eye left an impression of spotless cleanliness; long rows of [iron] beds neatly curtained in white and windows that opened almost to the floor, set in a large room made airy by tall ceilings. Off the dormitory was the lavatory, with several basins, tubs and stalls. Washing one's face in sulphur water was a new experience for some. Supper in the refectory (seldom called the dining room) was served after dark, and then the girls gathered for what the sisters called recreation. Bells sounded for all changes of occupation and when the bell rang, very loudly, for retiring, the rules of the academy were that the girls were to obey immediately. A new girl went through a period of orientation, learning the rules, including early rising, and going through the beautiful grounds of the academy. Students there interchanged the words academy and convent as if they were the same, but the convent was off bounds for the students.[6]

The girls were allowed to take only a few personal items to the school, but each had that omnipresent boarding-school object, the traveling trunk, in which she kept her most personal and prized possessions. Twice each year the school had a "trunk day." The boarders carted the musty trunks, some of which were quite large, to the grounds below, where they opened them and aired out their contents among the roses and fruit trees. Trunk day was looked forward to; fun and laughter and the exchanging and swapping of prized treasures made it seem like a holiday.

Despite the confinement and strict rules, life at St. Joseph's was not gloomy or harsh. The girls received, along with academic courses, a traditional southern finishing-school education. A school prospectus described the offerings; discipline was "mild but firm," and the "young ladies [were] tenderly cared for and trained not only in matters of knowledge, but also in the principles of refined deportment."[7] There was constant emphasis on morals and manners.

Tuition and board were $140 per year. There were no uniforms except on Sundays, when the girls were required to wear black dresses, white shirtwaists, and high-buttoned shoes. Rules and regulations were well enforced and included "strict adherence to correct and refined language, polite deportment, gentle and engaging manners at all times, mandatory attendance at all public exercises, the observance of silence except in the hours of recreation, no visits home during the entire year, the subjection of letters and packages to inspection, and the prohibition of private friendships."[8]

Music, both vocal and instrumental, as well as drawing and painting, received special attention. The latest chemistry apparatus was at the command of the pupils. Boarders were taught, without extra charge, plain sewing, embroidery, different kinds of needle work and the making of French lace. Every means was taken on the part of the sisters to make the academy not only a place where knowledge and manners were acquired, but also to make the institution a happy home for the pupils during their school terms. . . . The academy had some modern conveniences, with water throughout the house and cold and warm sulphur baths available. . . . Convent girls learned to live by group rules.[9]

One boarder left this description of a typical day in the life of a St. Joseph girl:

There are always some sleepy heads among the crowd, so the sister in charge has to shake the lazy ones and tell them the bell has rung. When all are up one of the girls says prayers and some answer. Sometimes I do and sometimes I don't. It depends on how I feel. Then we hurry to dress—not much time for primping but if you do not look neat you are ordered back to the dormitory before school and lose a mark on neatness. Besides you are reprimanded by one of the sisters before the other girls. As we do not enjoy that we try to look our prettiest. The next thing we hear is the clapping of hands. That is another signal and it means that it is time for Mass. We have one little girl who primps so long before the glass that she is never ready to go downstairs with the rest. You can hear her thin voice chirping out, "Please don't lock the door, sister." Sister stood the nonsense as long as she could, but one day she locked the young lady in and the rest of us proceeded on our way. The young lady rushed downstairs on the sister's side of the house and met us on the second landing, and talked indignantly about being closed in. Downstairs this is what we met: "Well, girls, I thought a regiment of soldiers was coming and not a crowd of convent girls." We knew who was the guilty one but said nothing. We went a little farther on when out popped a sister from the chapel: "What do you mean, girls, by talking so loud. You know you are not permitted to talk going to or coming from the chapel." All looked at one another and giggled a little and then proceeded to the chapel. We are expected to be there on time to say morning prayers before Mass, but sometimes we are too late and other times we are too soon. It is very seldom, however, that we fail by being too early.

Mass over we march out to breakfast. Occasionally some girls will laugh or talk so much that we are all called back and made to walk from chapel to the refectory again. By this time we are quite hungry and ready for breakfast so we behave. After breakfast we go upstairs and make our beds; then some go to practice, others to study, at six we go to the chapel to say the beads. When the beads are said, we go to supper. After supper, if it is pleasant, we recreate in the yard; if not we go to the sitting room where the sister reads aloud to us large girls while we work on embroidery. The juniors at their end of the room play games or talk. Sometimes they forget they are in the house and become too boisterous then sister stops reading to say, "Not so loud, girls." At eight-fifteen the bell rings to retire. We go to the chapel and one of the older girls says night prayers. Then we must go in silence and order to the dormitory. Some of us would like to "cut up" but we know that if we do not go up in order, we will be marched down again and again until we do as we are told; as that is not very enjoyable we usually try to behave. Some are noble enough to do right because it is right, but others—well, it takes all kinds of people to make a world.[10]

Life within the confines of St. Joseph's Academy was not completely isolated. During the 1880s, when May was at St. Joseph's, St. Augustine was a lively city. Henry Flagler, one of Standard Oil Company's founders, had become fascinated with the area during his honeymoon in 1883 and had decided to turn the town into a fashionable winter resort for the rich. The excitement of the resulting building boom in St. Augustine permeated all of northern Florida. Northern tourists, many in private railroad cars, arrived to stay in the magnificent local hotels Flagler built, the Ponce de

Leon, the Alcazar, and the Cordova. The winters were filled with parties, fancy-dress balls, lawn tennis, trips to the beach and to historic sites and promenades along the waterfront.[11] May and the other St. Joseph's girls were aware of the exciting happenings taking place just beyond the school walls. They heard about the parties and the social life and about the rich and famous people who were visiting the town. They were not completely isolated but made occasional chaperoned visits to local stores to shop and sometimes even took trips to the beach. According to one school advertisement, parents were advised that "there is a fine bath house situated on the Bay near the Convent [and] the young ladies are frequently taken to bathe."[12] May liked St. Augustine. After leaving St. Joseph's she visited the city each winter for over thirty years.

The academy's scholastic year was divided into two terms, September through January and February through June, with written examinations at the end of each term. The curriculum was divided into primary, junior, and senior courses of study. May was an excellent student. Self-motivated, articulate, and inquisitive, she had an excellent mind, and, as one of the most talented pupils ever to attend the school, she appeared regularly on the honor roll. She became proficient in music, piano, voice, and art and was awarded a gold medal for excellence in class work in her junior year.[13] In her senior year she received gold medals for achievements in music, art, piano, voice, English composition, and French.[14] Her course requirement for her senior program, which took three years to complete, included catechism, church history, etymology, geography, ancient history, Middle Ages history, rhetoric, grammar, science, mental and practical arithmetic, algebra, elocution, modern history, logic, chemistry, botany, geology, literature, astronomy, composition, classics, bookkeeping, mental philosophy, and civic government.[15]

During his daughters' years in St. Augustine, Austin Mann visited them frequently. Undoubtedly he approved of the educational program at the convent, for he publicly supported the school by advertising in its publications.[16] During school holidays and summers May stayed with her father at Crystal Grove and later at Brooksville, where he moved in 1887. She gained valuable political knowledge accompanying him to his political meetings and on his travels around his district.

May graduated valedictorian of her class in 1889. Her valedictory address, entitled "Beyond the Alps Lies Italy," was a poetic and whimsical Victorian composition in which she metaphorically described her years of residence and study at St. Joseph's and her feelings now that she had achieved her goal and was leaving. She had climbed the mountains and overcome all obstacles, she told her audience, and below lay the fair vista of a lovely land which beckoned her onward.[17]

After a year of postgraduate study, May left St. Joseph's, at eighteen an articulate, well-educated young woman ready to take her place in the outside world. Her fellow students wrote of her: "Our esteemed friend and schoolmate, Miss May Mann through her amiable disposition is much regarded and will ever have the fondest love of her teachers and companions. Having entered the academy when a mere child she was placed under the careful guardianship of the sisters. At the expiration of six years [she] was the worthy recipient of the highest honors. She proved herself to be a studious girl, a respectful pupil and a faithful friend."[18]

In January 1891, Austin Mann married Alsina M. Clark of Jacksonville, a woman much younger than he, who would outlive him by many years. Although May was at first distraught that her father had married so young a woman, she soon overcame her feelings and became a good friend of her young stepmother.

Mann's political career had continued while his daughters were at St. Joseph's. From 1883 until 1887 he represented Hernando County and the twenty-second district in the state senate. As a member of the liberal wing of the Democratic party he differed with the business-oriented leadership over the issues of railroad and corporate regulation, agricultural policy, and Negro rights.

In the 1883, 1885, and 1887 legislative sessions, Austin Mann's main interests were agriculture and the promotion and development of the state. He tried without success to get a state bureau and commission of agriculture established, and he sought to promote Florida by urging the state's participation in world and regional fairs. For two sessions he chaired the committees on agriculture and immigration, also serving on committees which investigated the Disston land sale, Indian war claims, and the Internal Improvement Fund. Well known throughout Florida, Mann spurned a move to make him the Independent party's candidate for governor in 1884 and supported the regular Democratic candidate.[19]

In the 1885 session he reluctantly supported Wilkinson Call's election to the U.S. Senate, for he doubted the sincerity of Call's liberalism. During that session Mann served on the organizing committee for the historic state constitution convention, which convened at Tallahassee on 9 June 1885. At the convention he played a prominent role, chairing the committee on suffrage and eligibility, around which swirled several of the meeting's most controversial issues.[20] The 1885 Constitution decentralized state government and stripped the governor of much of his appointive power. Mann favored home rule and local elections, and he clashed with representatives from "black belt" counties who favored a strong executive and a poll tax to disfranchise Negroes. The poll tax was unpopular in predominantly white counties, and Mann, who sided with farmers and labor, believed it to be "unfair to the hard-working laboring class."[21] He was responsible for the articles in the Florida Constitution that made prohibition a matter of local option and authorized construction of a cross-Florida ship canal. He also supported creating an office of state commissioner of agriculture.

In the 1887 legislature, Mann's attempt to wrest the leadership of the antirailroad Democrats from the Call faction failed. Mann withdrew his public endorsement of Call, whom he considered a "windbag" and a "fair weather liberal."[22] His feud with Call would consume much of Mann's attention for many years. In the same session he also supported a bill whose passage was to prove harmful to his career, for it created Pasco and Citrus counties out of parts of Hernando County.

A special election was called to choose representatives for the new counties. The election in Citrus County, Mann's district, turned into a donnybrook. Mann, always a controversial figure, was standing for reelection. He threw his support behind the new town of Mannsfield for county seat; he was one of its developers and had already succeeded in having it designated as the temporary county seat. As the campaign became heated, two factions developed, known as Manns and anti-Manns. Years later May and others told one anecdote of the contest:

The only charge that could be brought against [Mann] was that he was an aristocrat. He denied the charge and said he loved Citrus County and its people, and was a cracker just like the rest of them. But when it came to the political speeches, anti-Manns were loaded for bear. They charged that the senator slept in a nightshirt and was, therefore, an aristocrat. They called his hand when he was making a speech and forced him to admit that he [had] slept in a nightshirt even the night before. So what more did the people want? The candidate himself had admitted that he slept in a nightshirt, and anyone who slept in a nightshirt was an aristocrat, and an aristocrat was not a cracker, and by no stretch of the imagination should an aristocrat be a senator from Citrus County; and if you voted for him, someone might think you had a "tetch" of aristocracy in your own system and might tell someone else. And it was just possible that it would become common knowledge. And that would be a disgrace that you could never live down. On election day the senator was snowed under.[23]

The town of Mannsfield fared little better. In an election to choose the county seat, charges of stuffed ballot boxes resulted in an inconclusive outcome. Catching the Mann forces off guard, the anti-Mann group settled the issue one night by moving all the courthouse records, furniture, and equipment to Inverness. Mannsfield become a ghost town.[24] Angered and humiliated by his defeat and suffering from financial losses sustained during the harsh winter of 1886, Austin Mann left Crystal River. He sold Crystal Grove and most of his other properties in that area and moved to Brooksville, fifty miles away. There he established a new grove, bought the local newspaper, practiced law, and continued his interest in politics.[25]

The 1880s were years of discontent for farmers throughout the South and West. In 1887 the Farmers' Alliance, which had begun in Texas, was organized in Florida. It grew to an estimated 20,000 members in the state by 1889. Mann sympathized with the organization's ideas and aims, some of which he had espoused for years, and he soon became one of its most prominent leaders, referred to by newspaper reporters as the Alliance's "silver-tongued orator."[26] He organized the historic national convention that the Alliance held at Ocala in December 1890, out of which came the radical populist platform known as the "Ocala Demands."[27]

In the fall of 1890 the Alliance entered candidates in all of Florida's political races. Mann ran for the Florida House in what, according to one historian, was a heated and contentious contest. He "had made a number of enemies in [Brooksville] because of the positions he took on the political issues of the day. . . . It was a bitter campaign with mud slinging on both sides."[28] Despite an anti-Mann torchlight parade on election eve, Mann won the election.

Over two-thirds of Florida's 1891 state legislators were Alliance men, and Mann was their leader in a legislative session that proved one of the stormiest on record. Mann's old enemy Wilkinson Call was up for reelection to the U.S. Senate, opposed by the railroad tycoon William D. Chipley and by Alliancemen led by Mann. Chipley and the Alliancemen were uncomfortable allies, united only by their opposition to Call. As the pro- and anti-Call forces actively debated Call's reelection, Mann's harsh laugh was often heard by news reporters as it echoed above the din in the House. One of Mann's speeches was described as "a series of explosions."[29] The pro-Alliance *Daily Floridian* called him "the Hero of Hernando." After weeks of inconclusive wrangling and deadlocked votes,

Call's reelection was finally decided by an episode known as "Babes-in-the-Woods." Seeking to prevent a quorum, Mann persuaded more than a dozen legislators to go on a picnic the day of a crucial vote. They journeyed to Thomasville, Georgia, where they whiled away the time eating lunch and drinking cider. The ploy failed: The pro-Call faction, undaunted by the maneuver, called a joint session, declared a quorum of both houses, and reelected their candidate. This bitter defeat for Mann and his Alliance followers marked the beginning of a decline in his political fortune.

Disillusioned with his fellow Democrats and disappointed when the party did not adopt the Alliance's platform at its 1892 state convention, Mann broke with the Democratic party. He joined the newly formed People's Party, more commonly called the Populist Party, and became its candidate for Congress. The Democrats branded Mann and the Populists as traitors. They were also opposed by almost every major newspaper in the state. The *Jasper News* derisively denounced Mann as "the chief hornblower [of a] scalawag circus." [30] He and the other Populists were defeated in the election. The agrarian movement waned, and so did Austin Mann's political career. Earlier, when the Alliance's co-op programs had gone under, Mann had remarked that "we busted because we failed," [31] a statement just as apt for his own defeat in 1892. Although he continued to voice his unpopular and controversial views, he never again ran for public office. His interests turned toward improving Florida's road system and developing the state's natural resources.

May observed firsthand the last stormy years of her father's political career. In 1890 she left St. Joseph's and joined him in Brooksville, helping him with his political campaign and with the arrangements for the Ocala convention. Late in 1890 her father introduced her to Brooksville's Judge William Sherman Jennings, an ambitious young man beginning to make a name for himself in Democratic party circles. Jennings was attracted to May, a vivacious and charming woman who was his intellectual equal and who enjoyed politics as much as he did. They began to see each other at political rallies, church socials, and cotillion dances. Soon Jennings was calling at the Mann house to court May formally.

Jennings's visits continued in 1891 during the legislative session while May and her father lived at the St. James Hotel in Tallahassee. [32] May attended House sessions, handled Mann's correspondence and appointments, and acted as his hostess. As government buildings were considered male sanctuaries in those days, she must have created a stir as she moved through the Capitol corridors and offices. Small and slim, she dressed fashionably and wore her hair in the flattering Gibson Girl style. Her capabilities, enthusiasm, and ease in handling politicians and adjusting to their way of life quickly became apparent to her associates. She soon had friends among the legislators, their wives, and other state officials.

During Jennings's frequent visits to Tallahassee on business and to see May, there were many places the two could go. With a population of only 2,000, the city was particularly exciting when the legislature was in session. There were parties, dinners, dances, picnics at Hall Lake, and concerts by the Tallahassee Silver Cornet Band. One local newspaper noted that "the young folk of Tallahassee enjoy [the] lovely moonlight nights. Long [buggy] drives over the hard clay roads [on] cool, clear, nights arouse all the poetry in one's being." [33]

In one of Tallahassee's most elegant weddings Sherman Jennings and May Mann were married on 12 May 1891. She was eighteen, he was twenty-nine. The ceremony took place in the Methodist church (the Baptist church had recently burned down). Mann gave his daughter away and the members of the Legislature stood as a body to escort the newlyweds down the aisle. [34] The local newspaper reported that the young couple left the following day for a honeymoon in St. Augustine. [35] A message from May's former schoolmates at St. Joseph's read: "We extend our sincerest wishes to the newlyweds, and hope that as they glide over the silvery ocean of time, the tide of a just life may bear them to a heavenly felicity." [36]

May and Sherman Jennings were well suited to each other, a partnership sealed, figuratively and literally, in the halls of government. Similar in background, education, and aspirations, they were to work side by side for the next thirty years.

CHAPTER 3

Sherman

WILLIAM Sherman Jennings was destined for a distinguished career. Eventually he would be elected governor of Florida, his ascent within the Democratic party one of the most rapid in the state's history. Born 24 March 1863 at Walnut Hill, Marion County, Illinois, Sherman was one of nine children.[1] His parents, Josephus Waters and Amanda Couch Jennings, longtime residents of the area, were both descended from colonial ancestors. Josephus Jennings was an attorney and for many years justice of the Marion County court.

Sherman Jennings attended the local public school and, in 1882 and 1883, Southern Illinois Normal University at Carbondale, serving there as a first sergeant in the Douglas Corps of Cadets.[2] Afterward he went to Salem, Illinois, where he read law with his brother, Charles, and his uncle, Silas Bryan, father of William Jennings Bryan, the "Great Commoner." Jennings's mother and Silas were sister and brother. Although Sherman, three years younger than Bryan, neither resembled his famous cousin nor possessed his oratorical skills, family members noticed their similarity in physical build and in personal philosophy, political ideology, and religious beliefs. Bryan's wife, Mary, would later write May, "Our husbands are so alike in body and in mind." [3] The cousins' lifelong friendship would prove an asset to Sherman's career; on serveral occasions Bryan came to Florida to give Sherman a political boost, including three times in the 1890s. [4]

In 1885 Sherman attended Union Law School, where his brother and Bryan had received their legal training. It was located in downtown Chicago "in a single building and consisted of a solitary lecture room, an office shared by the dean and his faculty . . . [and] a roof garden [which] had been transformed into a library." [5]

Jennings moved to Brooksville, Florida, in late 1885. At twenty-two, of medium height and stocky build, with brown hair and eyes and a prominent mustache, he was a careful dresser, of dignified appearance and reserved in manner. Jennings had paid for his trip south by working as a drummer, or salesman, for a patent medicine company. Years later, in the heat of a political campaign, he would be charged with having arrived in the state on a medicine wagon "hawking snake oil." Far from denying the accusation, Jennings turned it to his advantage, saying that he was proud to have been a workingman from modest circumstances, who, ambitious and hardworking, could improve his position and become a leader.

Jennings's intelligence and industriousness gained him admission to the Florida Bar in May 1886, just a few months after his arrival in Brooksville. Eventually he practiced before the Florida Supreme Court. [6] In 1887 Jennings was appointed court commissioner of the Sixth Judicial Circuit and the following year county judge of Hernando County. A few months later he was elected to the same office for a full four-year term. As his involvement in local politics increased, so did his influence and prestige within the Democratic party.

Active in Brooksville and Hernando County civic affairs, Jennings served for several years as a county commissioner and for a decade as a city councilman; eight of those years he was president of the council. [7] He was also president of the Brooksville High School board of trustees and held a commission as colonel in the Fifth Florida Regiment. Jennings's first wife was Corinne Jordan, the daughter of a Brooksville merchant, who died only a few months after their March 1890 wedding. [8] He married May Mann the following year.

After their honeymoon, May and Sherman returned to Brooksville. In 1891 it was a bustling community of about five hundred inhabitants. It had twenty stores, a newspaper, a printing office, a courthouse, a Florida Southern Railway depot, but not a single paved street or sidewalk.

Brooksville lay among gently rolling hills whose numerous hammocks harbored magnificent stands of hardwood trees. One visitor described the area as "the most un-Florida appearing place imaginable."[9] The area especially appealed to midwesterners for it reminded them of home, although one traveler thought it resembled western New York state.[10] A land sales booklet published in Chicago said that land near Brooksville was "as good as Illinois soil."[11] It also claimed that the area had "no snakes," a false but apparently comforting idea to urban northerners. Agricultural enterprises formed the largest industry. Before the two great freezes of 1894–96 extensive orange, lemon, and grapefruit groves covered the hillsides. From Brooksville alone "100,000 boxes [of citrus] were shipped annually."[12] Phosphate mines and timber added to the area's economy.

May and Sherman's large house in Brooksville became a center of social activity for the community's young married set. A few months after their marriage an item in the local paper announced that "the frame of Judge Jennings' new residence looms upon Howell's Hill. It will be the handsomest residence in town."[13] A large, white, two-story wood structure, the house had porches, lead glass doors, and balconies. One contemporary who commented upon its attractiveness and its spacious grounds also noted that "Mrs. Jennings, as well as her husband, takes great pride in keeping [the] home in the most excellent and inviting condition. She carefully superintends in person every detail of home management."[14] May enjoyed the outdoors and worked energetically in her yard, surrounding her home with flowers and trees and vegetable gardens. She also kept chickens and a cow. One observer described her domestic proclivities: "While [Mrs. Jennings's] many graces of mind and person eminently qualify her to preside over the social functions incident to her exalted position, she is at the same time more domestic than many a farmer's wife, and loves her poultry, her garden and her flowers."[15]

Fashion conscious, May made dress patterns, often employing a seamstress. Small of stature and dignified in appearance, she impressed her contemporaries with her bearing, perhaps the result of her training in "refined deportment" at St. Joseph's Academy. She never appeared in public without gloves and a hat, even years later when styles were less formal—her hats, usually large and decorated with bright bows and flowers, would become her trademark. Although self-confident and not afraid to speak her own mind, May was neither overbearing nor arrogant and was well liked by her many friends.

For ten years May and Sherman, Brooksville's most active couple, busied themselves with the political, civic, business, and social activities of the community. They shared common aspirations and goals and were motivated by a sense of noblesse oblige. They viewed community service as the duty of all good citizens.

In November 1893, their only child, Sherman Bryan Jennings, was born. As he grew up his parents took him into their confidence, excluding him from very few of their activities, treating him more "like a dear chum" than a son, according to one observer.[16] As her father had treated her, so did May treat her son, who was to become one of her closest allies and friends.

The Jenningses were active members of Brooksville's First Baptist Church, where Sherman was a deacon and a Sunday school teacher. In 1889 he had attended the eighth annual convention of the Florida Sunday School Association, pledging $25.00 to its support.[17] For many years thereafter he held church offices, including the vice-presidency of the Florida Baptist Convention and membership on the Baptist State Board of Missions and on the board of trustees of Stetson University.[18] When the Brooksville church burned in 1899, Sherman and May led the drive to raise building funds.[19] Because of their Baptist beliefs neither smoked tobacco nor drank alcohol; both were sympathetic to the temperance movement.

Jennings was elected to the state legislature in 1892 and again in 1894. In the 1893 House of Representatives he served on the finance and taxation, judiciary, and constitutional amendments committees and as chairman of public health and rules. Well liked by his colleagues, he was viewed as one of the ablest young men in the state. During the 1895 legislative session, Jennings garnered many friends and admirers as Speaker of the House. The following year, he was a presidential elector on the Bryan-Sewall ticket, and by 1898, when he served as chairman of the Democratic state convention at Ocala, Jennings's name was recognized throughout the state.

During this same decade, Jennings also built a lucrative law practice. His professional card read "W. S. Jennings, Atty, at Law. Solicitor in Chancery. Office in the Bank Building."[20] In addition to his political and legal interests, Jennings owned and managed several citrus groves, including a sizable operation near Leesburg, organized and managed the Brooksville Orange Company, was vice-president of the Brooksville State Bank, and invested extensively in real estate. By 1900 Jennings could be regarded as a man of substantial wealth.

While her husband's political and fiscal fortunes were rising, May had become one of Brooksville's most active clubwomen. Although she worked to enhance her husband's career, her involvement in club and community work increased over the years. It is likely that May helped organize Brooksville's first woman's club, the Whittier Club (later the Ladies Improvement Association), for she was its recognized leader, intelligent, articulate, and too interested in political and civic matters to remain uninvolved. Notices such as "The Ladies' Improvement Association will meet at Mrs. W. S. Jennings' Thursday the 31st" began to appear with regularity.

One irritating public problem of concern to Brooksville clubwomen was the nuisance created by the town's lack of a fence law. Livestock roamed everywhere; animals slept in streets and doorways and on private lawns. On several occasions emergency action was taken and men were employed to "chase down and capture the animals." [21] The ladies pressured city officials (in many cases their own husbands) to do something about the matter, which was fast becoming a health menace. One letter to the editor asked, "Can you tell me why we have to run the risk of breaking our necks over a lot of sleeping cows everytime we go out?" [22] The problem created by free-roaming livestock, common to all Florida towns, was of such magnitude and so pervasive that when the Florida Federation of Women's Clubs was formally organized in 1896, it was the first major issue addressed. [23] May Jennings was one of the leaders in this controversy, which was to last more than fifty years.

In 1899 May turned her attention from clubwork to helping her husband win the race for governor of Florida, as she had earlier supported her father in his political ambitions. She had attended the previous three Democratic state conventions as well as the 1891, 1893, and 1895 legislative sessions and would prove to be one of Jennings's best political assets. One newspaper wrote, "There is little doubt that the rise of young Jennings was promoted by his marriage to May Mann, a lady of great charm [who] inherited much of her father's political ability. She was just such a person who would impress all those who came in contact with her, just such a one as would prove a most fitting helpmeet to a husband who had both ability and political ambitions." [24] Another contemporary noted that May had acquired "from her gifted and confiding father a keen interest in public affairs [and was] from girlhood equipped for the brilliant social career which is offered to the wife of an ambitious, able and influential public man. . . . Jennings owes much of his subsequent success at the bar and in the field of politics to the keen intelligence and winning tact of his wife [who] takes a very intelligent interest in political affairs. The advancement of her husband . . . is very near and dear to her heart. Her modest and unassuming manner stops her from claiming any credit . . . but it is certain that he owes much to her excellent judgment and untiring efforts in his behalf." [25]

From the time Jennings joined the Democratic party he had been identified with its liberal, anti-Bourbon wing, regarded by many as a middle-of-the-road moderate, far from the radical "wool hatter" image of his controversial father-in-law. ("Wool hats" were farmers and small businessmen; "silk hats" were bankers, lawyers, and developers.) Nevertheless, he was a progressive, as defined in early twentieth-century American political history. Other liberals of Jennings's generation included Stephen Mallory, Frank Pope, Duncan Fletcher, Wilkinson Call, B. H. Palmer, and the Jacksonville "straightouts," John N. C. Stockton, J. M. Barrs, and Napoleon Bonaparte Broward.

The liberals opposed the party conservatives and the "silk hat" railroad and corporate kingpins who, since the end of Reconstruction, had orchestrated and benefited from Florida's version of "the great American barbecue" in which the resources and rewards of the state were controlled by a small business elite known as the Bourbons.[26] This conservative faction included William D. Chipley, James Taliaferro, Ziba King, William D. Bloxham, Henry B. Plant, F. A. Hendry, and Henry M. Flagler. For more than twenty years these two party factions were to fight for control of the state, clashing over land policy, railroad regulation, state financing and taxation, political patronage, and nomination and election reforms. The tumultuous nineties that witnessed the rise and demise of the Populists and the bitter battles over Senator Call's elections was a decade filled with skirmishes over railroad regulation and election reforms. These confrontations finally resulted in such diffusion and dilution of power within the Florida Democratic party that, as one historian noted, "no single interest [could] control Florida politics," and it was every man for himself as the party developed into a formless union of "warring, amorphous personal factions." [27] The Democratic party's nominating convention in 1900 would be the last to select nominees for state office. Thereafter Florida parties would shift to nomination by the primary system. But in 1900 the Democratic nomination would still go to the man who could corral the most convention delegates. And, in a one-party state like Florida, nomination was tantamount to election. The time seemed right for an ambitious and relatively fresh newcomer. Sherman Jennings decided to enter the race.

Although Florida Democrats had no pervasive state political machine, as existed in other southern states. Jennings felt that he had as good a chance as any other political hopeful. His quiet inquiries to friends around the state asking for an assessment of his chances had brought encouraging replies. In the spring of 1899 he and May journeyed to Tallahassee and there dined with Governor and Mrs. Bloxham. Whether Jennings discussed his intentions with the governor, Sherman and May began preparing for the preconvention campaign when they returned to Brooksville. Aware of the disadvantages of his northern birth and his lack of Confederate service (though that was less important by 1900), Jennings in June purchased a copy of George R. Fairbanks's newly published *History of Florida* and began to learn as much as he could about his adopted state.[28] He subscribed to the *Jacksonville Florida Times-Union,* the state's most influential newspaper. He composed a biographical sketch of himself, sat for a formal photograph, and gave an interview to a reporter representing the *Atlanta Constitution.*

Until Sherman appointed George C. Martin, a Brooksville attorney and a prominent party official, as his campaign manager, May continued to help devise strategy and organized letter and mailing operations. A circular letter was sent to every county asking for precinct information and for the names of local delegates. According to one writer Jennings was the last Florida "gubernatorial hopeful to sit on his front porch and conduct his preconvention canvass by mail."[29] Despite the restrained tone of his campaign compared to later ones in Florida, Jennings did some politicking but combined it with legitimate business travels. His appointment to the Democratic state executive committee late in 1899 was a boon to his candidacy, for it gave him greater exposure and allowed him to keep tabs on the other gubernatorial hopefuls.

Jennings had support from delegates throughout Florida, but most of his strength came from the central and southwestern portions of the state. His supporters represented all segments of the population. His earliest backers included Asa Roberts, De Soto County editor; J. F. Dorman, Suwannee County tax collector; Herbert Drane, Lakeland insurance agent and party official; and Frank M. Simonton, a powerful Tampa politician.

While her husband traveled around the state May remained in Brooksville and ran the law office, which also served as campaign headquarters. One contemporary wrote that she organized and executed "the hardest and most fatiguing, yet quite the most important work of the struggle [and] the masterly manner in which she handled the mass of correspondence and routine work of the campaign [could] be attested to by hundreds of prominent Floridians."[30]

Many campaign issues seemed to be generated by the newspapers. Numerous front-page cartoons in the *Florida Times-Union* poked fun at the plethora of gubernatorial candidates.[31] One paper lamented the "scarcity of state political news," while another declared that "the people [were] tired of politics."[32] Only Jennings's campaign managed to create any excitement, when his famous cousin, William Jennings Bryan, came to the state. In February 1900, Bryan spent four days in Brooksville, where he gave one speech from the balcony of the Jennings home. His visit, which received statewide press coverage, proved a publicity bonanza for Sherman's candidacy.

The real campaign, however, took place not in the newspapers but in the county conventions, where delegates who would attend the state convention were chosen. The local caucuses were generally volatile affairs as the candidates finagled and maneuvered to secure delegates. By the time the state convention met in Jacksonville on 19 June 1900, the gubernatorial slate had been reduced to five recognized candidates, although the counties had selected only 115 instructed delegates out of a possible 282. The *DeLand Record* declared that "so many of the counties are sending uninstructed delegates that what will be the convention's will is simply guesswork."[33] Another paper ran a banner headline telling the public to "Pay your money—Take your choice."[34]

In addition to Jennings, the candidates were Fred T. Myers, Leon County state senator; James D. Beggs, Orange County judge; William H. Milton, Jr., Jackson County committeeman and son of Florida's Civil War governor; and Danette H. Mays, Jefferson County legislator. All were more politically conservative than Sherman, who was considered to have a slight advantage over the others. The *Tampa Tribune* endorsed him: "The political signs of the times point almost invariably to Jennings [whose] strength has proved a revelation to his opponents and a little surprising even to his friends."[35]

The 1900 convention, one of "the most remarkable political conventions ever held in Florida," was certainly one of the rowdiest and most tumultuous.[36] Though there were fewer than 300 delegate votes, more than 2,000 people crowded into the session at Jacksonville's new Emory Auditorium, which had been specially outfitted with electric lights and grandstands and decorated with potted ferns and palms, 1,500 yards of red, white, and blue bunting, and large pictures of past Democratic party greats. "A giant portrait of William Jennings Bryan gazed benignly from the back wall of the rostrum."[37] A band was hired to entertain the spectators and delegates during lulls in the proceedings. With "no tickets . . . required to admit ladies to the hall at anytime," May attended every session, sometimes accompanied by Hernando delegates' wives or by Mrs.

Napoleon Bonaparte Broward, wife of the prominent Duval politician who was a close friend of Sherman's.[38]

Flooded with politicians and curiosity seekers, Jacksonville was almost overwhelmed by the convention. The local press was provided with plenty of colorful copy. When the Tampa delegation arrived, a reporter covering the event noted that "one of the features of the trip [had been] Colonel F. A. Salmonson, and his famous fighting gamecock 'Fred' . . . one-eyed and generally disreputable looking as any bird that ever came to the city . . . [who the] colonel insisted on having crow at every station on the way up." Delegates were provided with free streetcar passes and free excursions on the St. Johns River and to Pablo Beach. Dances were held every evening in the city's hotels, and there were many dinner parties, receptions, and soirees in private homes. The Jennings party stayed at the Windsor Hotel, reported to be the convention's "storm center. . . its lobbies and piazzas crowded until late hours."[39]

Although Sherman Jennings was conceded to be the favorite—he had the largest number of committed votes and the support of the most important newspapers—his victory was by no means guaranteed. With 188 votes required for nomination, Jennings had 29 committed votes when the convention opened; Begs, Mays, Myers, and Milton had 28, 27, 20, and 11 votes, respectively. Winning would mean some compromising and "horse trading."

Liberals and conservatives, businessmen and farmers, citizens from all over Florida vied for control of the convention. The Hernando County delegates, strong endorsers of Jennings, had only one-sixteenth of a vote each, compared to one-fifth, one-fourth, one-half, or one vote per man in the other delegations. It was reported that "Jennings' fractionalization plan was a puzzle to the politicians, a source of deep regret, and established a new and ingenious method of preventing losses except in immaterial fractions."[40] It also created a stable base on which to build convention support. "Jennings' opponents tried to sabotage his candidacy by drawing attention to his Northern origins and alleging he was named for the hated Yankee general William Tecumseh Sherman. Jennings was also accused of engaging in 'South-hating antics.' The 'Bloody Shirt' of the Civil War and Reconstruction was still being waved."[41] The charges failed to sway many of Jennings's supporters.

The business of choosing a gubernatorial nominee began on the convention's third day, after two days taken up with choosing a chairman, drawing up a platform, endorsing the 1896 national Democratic platform, and nominating minor candidates. Jennings was nominated by C. M.

Brown of Marion County and seconded by J. H. Curry and General Allen Thomas of Hillsborough County. After eight votes, his total had climbed to 81, leading Myers, who had 76½ votes. The secretaries, "taxed in calling and announcing the votes [and] in the constant work of listening for the faintly heard answers . . . from the far ends of the hall and in footing the long columns of scores, [were] all heartily glad of the relief that came with adjournment." [42]

As balloting continued on the fourth and, as it turned out, final day of the convention, only once did Jennings trail. By late afternoon, the hall was filled to capacity, every seat occupied, with people standing in the rear and thronging the corridors. It was hot, the delegates were tired, and the roll calls seemed endless. Several times during the day rumors had swept the hall, causing "the convention [to] become wild with excitement and confusion." [43] By the thirtieth ballot there was so much noise and confusion that the band was called upon to play so as to restore order. At 6 P.M., when the chair declared a suppertime recess, Jennings had 130 votes, Mays 122½.

Shortly after the convention reconvened, the deadlock was broken when Mays arose and solemnly announced his withdrawal. After a few seconds of silence, there was a mad scramble to switch votes. On the forty-third ballot Beggs withdrew, removing the final obstacle to Jennings's nomination. On the next ballot, cast at 10 P.M., the Leon County delegation threw its support to Jennings, putting him over the top with 192 votes.

The delegates and spectators broke into cheers. May and the ladies with her applauded. "Delegates left their places and crowded around the nominee's chair. . . . He was lifted to the shoulders of a dozen stalwarts and carried the length of the hall." [44] Not everyone was happy; seated in the gallery, Mrs. Mays remarked, "Anybody can be governor of Florida these days, even a jack rabbit. All you have to do is wag your ears and you are chosen." [45]

In a brief acceptance speech Jennings pledged his commitment to the party's platform and said he viewed his nomination as "an honor and sacred responsibility." [46] When the final gavel of the convention sounded at 4 A.M., only a few delegates remained in the hall. "The band, worn out with the labors of the day and night, were stretched on chairs sound asleep or lolling around waiting with hardly concealed impatience for the last tune." [47]

Almost before the convention formally ended, the questions began. How did Jennings win the nomination? Why did Mays withdraw from the race? Why did the Leon County delegation switch its vote? Did Henry Flagler and the railroads buy the convention? It was speculated that Jennings and Mays, a corporate man, had made some kind of deal during the 6 P.M. recess. It seems unlikely that Mays would have withdrawn without expecting to benefit from that action. Yet no evidence of a deal has ever been uncovered, and the questions remain unanswered.

The 1900 convention earned mixed reviews. J. D. Beggs, in a letter congratulating Jennings, conceded that he had been "fairly and honorably nominated." [48] Similarly, J. M. Barrs felt that "for the first time in many years [the convention] was truly democratic and thoroughly representative of the people . . . [and] many of those who had hereto dominated the party [did] not enter the convention hall during any of its sessions." [49] But Herbert Drane saw the convention as "the hardest most vindictive fight ever." [50] And two modern students of Florida politics find the 1900 convention "significant because it pointed out how difficult it had been to keep factionalism within the bounds of the convention system [with] party leaders badly divided over Jennings' candidacy, [some] clearly feeling that he was too progressive and too much a Yankee to be their gubernatorial candidate. The forty-four ballots had established a record." [51] Perhaps Jennings was nominated for no more complex reason than having been the only middle-of-the-road candidate both sides could accept.

Jennings's nomination was celebrated by liberals and progressives throughout Florida. For the moment, the silk hats had been defeated, and a new era was beginning. One supporter wrote the new nominee, "I thank God the old fossil [Bourbonism] in Florida is dead. Now we trust to have new blood, new ideas." [52]

When the news of Jennings's nomination reached Brooksville it touched off a wild celebration. Most of the town's population met the Jennings party at the train station, accompanied by the firing of "Roman candles, firecrackers, and even .38 calibre guns. . . . The skies [were] aglow with happiness and hilarity." A carriage drawn by two horses and carrying onlookers to the festivities "ran away" and dumped all its occupants out on the street.[53] The celebrating continued for several days.

In August, Sherman, May, and their son, Bryan, now six years old, traveled to Illinois to rest and to visit relatives. Jennings attended the national Democratic convention in Indianapolis and was present when his cousin William Jennings Bryan won his second presidential nomination. When the Jennings family returned to Florida, they began preparations for the fall campaign. Austin Mann, now fifty-three, had offered to "bring up [his] Alliance Forces" if Sherman needed them. The offer was tactfully declined.[54]

Although the Democratic nomination was tantamount to election, it was deemed important to the ticket for the gubernatorial candidate to campaign. In addition to Jennings, the party's nominees included John L. Crawford for secretary of state; William B. Lamar, attorney general; James B. Whitfield, treasurer; William N. Sheats, superintendent of public instruction; Benjamin McLin, commissioner of agriculture; William H. Reynolds, comptroller; J. D. Morgan, railroad commissioner; and Stephen M. Sparkman and Robert W. Davis for Congress. Jennings's two opponents were Republican Matthew B. MacFarlane and Populist A. M. Morton. Neither was considered a threat.

The Florida platform called for the adoption of a state primary law, municipal ownership of utilities, improvement of public roads, reorganization of the state supreme court, reform of the convict lease system, and support of the railroad commission.[55] Jennings wanted the state to increase the responsibilities of the State Board of Health, adopt free school textbooks, and equalize assessments and taxes. Two issues dominated the campaign: a referendum on removal of the capital from Tallahassee and a proposal for teacher examinations. Tallahassee, Jacksonville, St. Augustine, and Ocala vied for the capital site, each lobbying vigorously and making promises in an attempt to win the selection. Jennings had approved the teachers' examination, but he was noncommittal concerning the capital site.

The campaign was launched in Miami in September, the first stop in an exhausting itinerary. It was Jennings's first visit to the city, and he was favorably impressed. For over a month and a half he and the other Democratic candidates toured the state giving speeches, attending receptions, eating barbecue, and meeting with voters. They traveled by boat, buggy, and train, in 53 days visiting 53 towns and every Florida county. Although the travel and speaking were fatiguing, Jennings enjoyed the campaign. At Crystal River he sang with a quartet, and it was reported that he had a "fine tenor voice."[56] At Ocala he toured Silver Springs. In Defuniak Springs his host told the crowd that "Florida had had the ugliest Governor in the Union, she was now to have one of the handsomest."[57] During each speech Sherman made it a point to recognize the ladies in the audience, remarking at Pensacola, for example, that "women were more interested in good government than [was] any other class of citizens."[58] Reporters noted that on more than one occasion "nearly every lady in the audience" shook Jennings's hand.[59]

The campaign created little real news. As expected, Jennings stuck to the issues, rarely mentioning his opponents. MacFarlane, however, called Jennings a Yankee, a carpetbagger, and a "snake oil salesman." It was also claimed that the only reason he had received the nomination was because he was William Jennings Bryan's cousin.

On election day, November 6, Sherman, May, and their friends waited for the returns in Brooksville with little doubt about the outcome. As expected, all of the Democratic candidates won. In one of the largest Democratic victories in Florida's political history, Jennings received 81 percent of the total, 29,251 votes; MacFarlane had 6,248 votes and Morton 631. The national democratic party was less fortunate. William Jennings Bryan and his running mate, Adlai Stevenson, were defeated by McKinley and Roosevelt. Once again the "Great Commoner" was denied the presidency. Sherman received a kind congratulatory note from his defeated cousin urging him to be "a Jeffersonian and an equal rightist" and ending, "Well at least I can be known as the cousin of a governor." [60]

May had never been happier or prouder of her husband as she began to make plans for the move to Tallahassee, which had been reaffirmed as the state capital. Four years of political duty and personal satisfaction lay ahead.

CHAPTER 4

The Governor's Lady

A s THE 1901 Florida gubernatorial inauguration approached, an air of optimism and excitement permeated the state. The people arriving in the capital city for the event seemed happier and more enthusiastic than past inaugural crowds. The state was installing a man of youth, vitality, and new ideas, and Floridians, at least those concerned with political matters, were satisfied. In the new century, the state was recovering from the calamitous freezes of 1894, 1895, and 1898, yellow fever was coming under control, tourism was booming, personal income was up, and the state's population was growing. Floridians believed that their state was approaching a new era of development and progress. William Sherman Jennings, at thirty-seven the youngest governor to date, seemed to personify a confident future for Florida.

The years between 1900 and 1905, when Sherman and May served as governor and first lady, were a time of both political and technological change. The Boer War in South Africa and the Philippine campaign would be concluded; Queen Victoria would die and, with her, stability in Europe

33

and the Western world; President McKinley would be assassinated, and his successor, Theodore Roosevelt, would stamp his own personality on the country's political thought. Marie Curie would win the Nobel Prize, and the automobile and the Wright brothers' "flying machine" would begin to revolutionize transportation. The equations of Albert Einstein and Max Planck would turn topsy-turvy the very laws of the universe.

These first years of the twentieth century would also see America begin to discover and develop a new social conscience. "Public weal" would become political watchwords, with reform and redress issuing from every hall of government. In reaction to the social and economic abuses of the Gilded Age, the new social ideology would accord to government a bigger role in citizens' lives. Political reformers would call for the establishment of primary elections; direct election of U.S. senators; adoption of the Australian ballot; the right to initiative, referendum, and recall; public ownership of utilities; more vigorous regulation and curtailment of monopolies and trusts; laws regulating the drug and food industries and female and child labor; reform of public education; abolition of the poll tax and the convict-lease system; improvement of roads and highways; and adoption of a national income tax and the commissioner-manager type of city government. Later generations would label this period the Progressive Era.

Progressivism would coincide with Jim Crowism, a movement to deny many American citizens their civil rights. The southern establishment viewed blacks as intellectual and moral inferiors and would work to keep them impoverished and uneducated, inadequately paid and housed, and with a shockingly high mortality rate. As one historian wrote, "[Progressives] did not envision racial tolerance or political equality for the Negro. The gifts of Jeffersonian democracy were to be accorded only to the white population."[1] But these years were also a time of economic oppression and hardship for poor whites, illiterate and uncultured, their children plagued with hookworm and rickets, the adults kept from the ballot box by the poll tax. Though it embraced the conservative viewpoint on racial questions, the Jennings administration would provide Florida with four years of generally progressive government.

A week before Jennings's inauguration on 8 January 1901, visitors began to arrive in Tallahassee, some to participate in the festivities, others to observe an exciting state event. Each incoming train was filled to capacity. Reporters noted that three times Tallahassee's population of less than 3,000 had crowded into the capital during inauguration week. Dances, dinner parties, and public entertainments kept the visitors busy, and they visited the Capitol and other public buildings and took carriage rides into the nearby countryside. Several days before the ceremony, the Jennings family arrived: Sherman, May, eight-year-old Bryan, Sherman's mother, Amanda, and the Manns, Austin, Alsina, Grace, and Austin, Jr. They stayed at the elegant Leon Hotel, where ten rooms had been reserved for them. In addition to family members, many friends and political acquaintances took rooms at the Leon, the St. James, and at other city hostelries. By inauguration eve a carnival atmosphere pervaded, and "the streets [were] thronged with handsome soldiers in bright uniforms accompanied by lovely women," all laughing and talking animatedly.[2]

Inauguration day proved "delightful, fair and balmy, fitting for the first great event of the new century."[3] An impressive military parade led off the procession, which formed behind the Capitol building, stepping off at 10 A.M., and proceeding slowly through the downtown district and back up to the east side of the Capitol. Marching were the Pensacola Brass Band, the Governor's Guard and military staff, fifteen colorful military units from around the state, and Florida's small but impressive naval militia. These units were followed by the official party and other dignitaries riding in open carriages, including Governor Bloxham and Jennings, Mrs. Bloxham and May, cabinet officers and their wives, city officials, and a detachment of Confederate veterans, who were enthusiastically applauded when they drove by in their gray uniforms. The local newspaper hailed the inaugural as "a red-letter day in the capital city's history" and described the parade as "a spectacle not soon forgotten."[4]

Sherman Jennings took the oath of office on the east portico of the Capitol at high noon.[5] May sat on the dais dressed in a fashionable black crepe dress and a large colorful hat. She did not participate in the formal ceremony, but her presence was acknowledged by all the speakers. Chief Justice Fenwick Taylor administered the oath of office to Jennings, who was dressed in a new black broadcloth suit that May had ordered from New York City. After presentation of the state seal and remarks by Bloxham, Jennings delivered his inaugural address in a strong, forceful voice. Though written in ponderous prose and over 7,000 words long, the speech went beyond mere rhetoric to outline specific problems in the state and to offer concrete solutions.[6] The new governor called for reform of the state's overcrowded and stalemated judicial system, establishment of uniform statewide property tax assessments, liberal support of public education, and rigorous enforcement of the state's health laws.

At the conclusion of the formal ceremonies, the Jenningses were greeted in the governor's chambers by the cabinet and other prominent state officials. At midafternoon May returned to the Leon Hotel to rest and to prepare for the evening's events. Sherman, accompanied by a retinue of politicians and state dignitaries, walked over to Wayne Square for a barbecue and a review of the state troops. That evening a splendid reception and ball at the Leon Hotel saw ordinary folk—"crackers," farmers, and small-town businessmen—rubbing elbows with high-ranking state officials. The new governor was applauded by the state's newspapers for insisting upon a "people's inaugural."[7] Hundreds of people jammed the Leon for vocal and piano entertainment, a dance orchestra from Jacksonville, and a lavish buffet. May and Sherman received well-wishers in the hotel's east parlor until 10 P.M., then were escorted into the ballroom, where they led off the grand march. They were a handsome couple, Sherman in a new tuxedo and May, twenty-eight and at the peak of her beauty, in a ballgown that elicited much comment. The white satin gown featured chrysanthemums and lace which May had embroidered and tatted herself. The dance lasted until 2:00 A.M. and was reported to have been "one of the most magnificent balls Tallahassee had ever witnessed."

The Jenningses settled into a busy political and social routine in the state capital. Since they had lived in the city before, they were quickly accepted by the local residents. They visited in the homes of many and were frequently entertained by friends and political acquaintances. May was a hostess with extraordinary flair and verve, and whenever she entertained it usually elicited newspaper comment. They hosted such distinguished national persons as Thomas A. Edison and Ransom E. Olds, the founder of the town of Oldsmar. For the first two years of their stay in Tallahassee, the Jenningses lived at the Leon Hotel, moving in late 1902 to the elegant Cohen mansion on McCarthy Street, described as one of Tallahassee's "handsomest and most commodious residences."[8] It was a practical choice, for Grace still lived with the family and the Manns were frequent visitors. Bryan Jennings was reluctant to leave the Leon, however, and years later he remembered the old hotel with fondness, especially its great central mahogany staircase with its "smooth-as-silk" banisters, tempting to an active and imaginative youngster.[9]

May spent most of her time working with her husband, continuing to serve as his confidante and frequently participating in informal political and policy discussions. She was deeply interested in the daily workings of her husband's administration, and Sherman in turn respected her opinions.

One contemporary called May the governor's "right hand man." [10] Another referred to her as Sherman's "trusted counselor." [11] May kept abreast of both state and national political events and, when required, could expound confidently upon most current issues. She was a good debater who knew her topics, reading extensively and talking to people. In a city that had known few such politically astute females, May quickly acquired a reputation for her keen mind and political knowledge.

When the legislature was in session, May worked in the governor's office, greeting visitors, helping keep tabs on critical legislation, and sharing with the staff the many tasks required to keep the office running smoothly. The governor's personal secretary was Charles H. Dickinson of Madison County, who had been clerk of the 1895 House and who had held his county delegation firmly in the Jennings camp at the 1900 state convention. [12] Jennings's chief stenographer was his sister-in-law, Grace Mann, who had worked earlier in his Brooksville law office, Her secretarial skills and knowledge of legal matters were so extensive that at one time Sherman attempted to get her admitted to the Florida Bar, but the hue and cry raised by this all-male organization reached such a crescendo that even the state's chief executive had to abandon the idea. According to Grace's daughter she carried the disappointment with her for many years. [13]

Jennings proved to be one of Florida's ablest chief executives. He is described by historians as an activist governor, although his personal style of leadership was quiet, dignified, and unassuming. [14] The first governor to challenge the Bourbons, the railroad and big business interests that controlled the state, he is credited with launching the progressive trend that characterized Florida's gubernatorial politics for the first two decades of this century.

Jennings's administration established an impressive record. It increased state appropriations to higher education, provided aid to certain classes of high schools and rural grade schools, and endorsed free textbooks. It was responsible for the passage of the state's first bird protection and timber protection laws, the first pure food and drug law, the first law preventing cruelty to children, and a law raising the age of female consent from sixteen to eighteen. It reorganized the state militia, enlarged and renovated the Capitol building in 1902, established a state auditing department, and reorganized the state court system, which resulted in the appointment of three new Supreme Court justices and additional circuit court judges. When Jennings took office, the state's finances and land policies were in a tangle. The state was in deep debt, having deeded away or granted more public land to railroads and corporations than it owned. It was essential for the state to reestablish its authority over the public domain, and Jennings had the skills to do it: he was a pragmatic fiscal conservative with an unblemished record and superior administrative skills. In four years Jennings reduced the state's bonded debt by $1,032,000. By settling Florida's Indian war claims against the national government, the state was able to pay off $132,000 in bonds, saving $40,000 per year in interest and receiving a large cash settlement from Washington. Reforming the state convict-lease system brought an additional $500,000 into the treasury. During his tenure Jennings increased the amount of revenue from the sale of swamp and overflow lands by 100 percent, as well as revenues from licenses, stamps, and minor taxes. He also vetoed numerous unnecessary appropriation bills. By 1905 the treasury balance had grown from $32,805 to almost $500,000, the bonded debt had been reduced 40 percent, and, most important, the general tax rate had dropped from three mills to just one-half mill. All this occurred alongside increased funds for education, state institutions, internal improvements, and pensions. It was a truly remarkable fiscal record, one enthusiastically endorsed by Florida's citizens.

By far the greatest accomplishment and legacy of the Jennings administration was its land policy. For over twenty-five years public lands designated for drainage and reclamation purposes had been routinely granted to railroads and corporations as subsidies, although less than half of the 564 railroads chartered ever laid track. By 1901 this misguided giveaway policy had not only depleted the public domain but also had left railroads and corporations holding grants to more land than the state could supply. Outraged by the scandalous practice, Jennings and other progressives argued that the lands belonged to the people. The state's most prized resource had been squandered. The governor felt strongly that such a policy could be legally reversed for it was subverting the intent of the Internal Improvement Act of 1855, which had reserved the lands for the people and for reclamation and drainage.[15]

For two years Jennings and his staff investigated, researched, studied, and prepared legal briefs on the status of the public lands. The work was painstaking and tedious; few reports and records were extant. But Jennings persevered for he saw the administration of the state's lands as "one of the greatest trusts" with which he had been vested.[16] He ordered a thorough search of all state offices and archives and directed that pertinent minutes, records, and laws be published and put into the public record. In the course of these investigations he found that a vast tract of the Everglades had never been patented. With the help of Florida's congressional delegation and by personally pursuing the matter in Washington, Jennings won for the state a patent to 3,863,080 acres of South Florida land. The railroads, citing earlier state grants to them, immediately laid claim to this acreage, but the governor had other ideas.

In his 1903 message to the legislature Jennings unveiled an elaborate drainage and reclamation plan for the Everglades. The idea was not original, but Jennings was the first political leader to act on it. The newly patented lands were surveyed and engineering studies were begun. To prove such an ambitious undertaking workable, Jennings produced tables, charts, graphs, expert opinions, and what he later called "the famous map." This document, he wrote, "served a great purpose [for] it brought to the attention of the public the whole situation of the lands and incited keen interest." [17] The legislature approved Jennings's plan, but the actual work of draining and reclaiming the Everglades would not begin until the year after he left office. Few projects before or since have captured the imagination of Floridians as did the Everglades drainage and reclamation program. During the Jennings administration not one acre of public lands was deeded to any corporation. As a result, and because of opposition to drainage, the railroads and corporations instituted numerous suits against the state, and for years these legal battles threatened to slow down and even halt the reclamation work. Jennings acted as counsel for the state in many of these suits. Eventually Florida's ownership of the lands and its right to drain, reclaim, and tax them was upheld in the courts.

Most people viewed the reclamation of the Everglades as a wise undertaking which would conserve and make productive a hitherto useless area. With a few canals here and a dike or two there, the Everglades could be made lush and fertile. The long-term detrimental consequences of the project on the land, the animals, and the Indians were never fully contemplated. Few questioned the wisdom of the project. Floridians still live with both the positive and the negative results of the great dream of William Sherman Jennings and his successor, Napoleon Bonaparte Broward.

May supported her husband's plans for the Everglades, visualizing a land of milk and honey rising out of the swampy vastness of South Florida. As early as 1885, her father had toured South Florida in search of a route for a cross-state canal, and for years May had heard him describe the paradise that lay south of Kissimmee. Her natural affinity for nature and for tropical Florida turned May's interest in the Everglades into a lifelong commitment.

Despite its many accomplishments the Jennings administration was not progressive on every front. One of Jennings's first acts as governor was to investigate and renegotiate the state's convict-lease contracts, part of a deplorable system which many progressives sought to abolish. But after thorough study, Jennings became convinced that convict lease was the most practical way for the state to avoid supporting a large and costly penal system and that any financial profits from the system belonged to the state. Although the assertion of his supervisor of convicts that the prisoners were in the main "healthy and cheerful" met with some contradiction, Jennings felt the system's cruel abuses could be eliminated.[18]

Under his leadership, the cabinet renegotiated a more lucrative contract through a series of ploys and deft political maneuvers. It brought to the treasury $148,000 per year for 975 convicts, a more than sevenfold increase over the previous amount received. Many hailed the new contract as a great victory and the governor as one who had outfoxed the state's omnipotent phosphate and naval stores companies. Progressives, however, were disappointed that an entirely new penal system had not been established. The inhumane practices of the system continued, despite the good intentions of the Jennings administration. Jennings had "achieved economy at the expense of the convicts."[19]

In another action early in his tenure, Jennings signed into law a bill establishing a "white only" political primary system in Florida. The new law would be hailed by progressives as necessary and forward-looking even though it closed the door in Florida to black involvement in the political process. In 1901, when Booker T. Washington dined with President Roosevelt at the White House, Governor Jennings remarked to the newspapers that the event only encouraged "the Negro to demand a social equality that [could] not be granted him" and that he "personally regretted the [White House] matter exceedingly."[20] To Jennings and other southern liberals, physical freedom for blacks would be tolerated, equality and full civil rights would not.

Probably the most controversial event of Jennings's term was the passage of the "Flagler Divorce Bill." Henry Flagler's second wife was confined to a New York insane asylum, a situation Flagler tolerated for some years until in 1900 he determined to marry Mary Kenan, a young and vivacious North Carolina belle. After transferring his legal residence from New York to Florida, Flagler got supporters in the 1901 legislature to introduce a bill making incurable insanity grounds for divorce. The bill caused an immediate sensation across the state. Politicians, clergymen, and newpapers exchanged charges and countercharges. There were rumors that Flagler had paid off the legislature, that he had Jennings in his pocket. The state's Baptists were enraged and issued a call to arms. The governor, a trustee of Stetson University and Florida's most prominent Baptist, was bitterly criticized by preachers and press for supporting and signing the bill. It was charged that Flagler had used his great wealth in the 1900 state convention to secure the nomination for Jennings in return for Sherman's support of the bill. That Jennings was acquainted with Flagler was well known, but there is no evidence to substantiate the charges.[21] There is no answer, however, to the question of why the governor, a staunch Baptist churchman, supported such an unpopular and morally controversial law. Flagler got his divorce, although the bill was later repealed. And the governor's Baptist brethren would remember his involvement the next time he ran for public office.

On 3 May 1901, the greatest conflagration ever to strike a Florida city occurred when a large section of Jacksonville, the state's largest city, burned to the ground. When the news reached Tallahassee, the governor and his staff responded quickly. Martial law was declared, and a train with state troops, newsmen, officials, and Jacksonville's legislative delegation aboard was dispatched to the still-burning city. More than 100 blocks of the city's business and residential area were gutted; 2,368 buildings had been destroyed, and thousands of citizens were homeless. The governor visited Jacksonville to inspect the damage and review the troops. His quick response to the emergency was noted, but some criticized the amount of financial aid he had sent to the city. Damage had exceeded $15 million, but state aid totaled only $20,000. Hundreds of thousands of dollars were donated by people throughout the country.

On 17 December 1902, the governor, while working quietly in his office, narrowly escaped assassination. An escaped inmate from a Georgia asylum had gotten as far as Tallahassee and entered the Capitol building undetected. Suddenly he appeared in the governor's suite screaming that he needed protection from pursuing persecutors. Wild with rage he made a dash for the governor, but Dickinson, Jennings's secretary, was able to close the door to the inner office, wrestling the convict to the floor while others summoned help. Jennings was unharmed.[22]

When the legislature was not in session, activity in the capital city slowed down considerably. Secretary Dickinson wrote at one of those times that "everything is as dull as can be here."[23] With his gubernatorial duties cyclical and limited, Jennings concentrated on noncritical state business and on his own law practice between sessions. However quiet life in Tallahassee became, there was much to demand May's attention, particularly Bryan, who was attending Miss Ames's private academy. May chaired a committee to raise money for a new sanctuary for the Baptist Church, attended to her personal and official correspondence and activities connected with her duties as first lady, saw to the upkeep of the rented Tallahassee mansion and the Brooksville homestead, and kept up her stylish wardrobe.

An accomplished hostess, May handled the governor's official entertaining. She was responsible for several soirees that received statewide publicity. An elaborate dinner party which the Jenningses gave in 1901 in honor of the cabinet established her reputation in Tallahassee. The *Daily Capitol* reported that the dinner, given at the Leon and attended by seventeen people, was the "first time in the history of the capital that the cabinet had been so feted." At "one of the most enjoyable social functions ever given in Tallahassee," according to the paper, "a notable feature [was] the absence of formality, and the atmosphere of cordiality and geniality which the accomplished hostess so successfully imparted to the occasion." [24] A reception at the Jenningses in honor of the legislature in 1903, coinciding with their twelfth wedding anniversary, made headlines: "Governor's Reception a Brilliant Function—Elite of Tallahassee in Attendance." [25] Over 500 guests caused "a jam of carriages" in front of the Jennings residence several times during the evening. Again a news reporter commented that "there was absolutely no formality about the function, and all guests spent a most delightful time." [26]

Not all of the Jenningses' entertainments were elaborate. The family enjoyed picnics, ping-pong, and card games. They often read aloud to one another and joined in parlor "sing-alongs." Music played an important role in the Jennings household: May enjoyed it and was proud of her singing ability. Once a week May and Bryan went buggy riding, often with Sarah Lamar, wife of the attorney general, or with Colonel C. W. Walker, a family friend. When riding alone they toured the city and countryside in a "victoria and span" drawn by white horses, May modishly dressed and sporting a parasol.

Although the records do not show that May participated in formal clubwork while living in Tallahassee, she may have helped organize the local woman's club, for the Tallahassee Improvement Association was established shortly after the Jenningses arrived in the city in 1901. Supported by local women, the organization's first goal was to beautify the community by cleaning up the parks, sidewalks, and streets. By 1903, its successor, the Tallahassee Woman's Club, had become involved in more serious civic matters. It wanted the state to build or purchase a home for the governor and his family, and it became an outspoken opponent of the local educational establishment. The club endorsed the creation of a graded high school with a modern and comprehensive curriculum to replace Leon Academy, which had served the town for over a generation. The local paper wryly noted that "there is a woman's club in Tallahassee, and judging by the way in which they haul the local school board over the coals the club doesn't exist merely for the purpose of discussing social events and fashions." [27] It later stated that "the ladies are aroused [but] the school board ignores them." [28] Their persistence eventually won out, and Tallahassee's school system was reformed.

Apparently May considered it impolitic to belong to such an outspoken organization while her husband governed. She took no public stand on issues, although judging from her later battles she probably supported the women's goals behind the scenes. She did oversee one beautification project of her own, the landscaping of the Capitol grounds. After renovation of the Capitol was completed late in 1902, from January until April the following year she supervised the marking out of paths, the planting of flowering shrubs and trees, and the sowing of rye grass in time for the legislative session. Some of the local women aided in the work. She also helped decorate both the Capitol, for the dedication in December, and the governor's new office, whose appointments included nine brass cuspidors.

The Jenningses traveled extensively during Sherman's term of office. In February 1901 they made an official trip to Pensacola to participate in Mardi Gras festivities, which coincided with a visit by the U.S. Navy's North Atlantic Squadron. There were dinners, a parade, and a ball held in honor of the visitors. While the governor conferred with Admiral N. H. Farquahar and Secretary of the Navy John D. Long about Florida's naval defenses, May was feted at the home of Mrs. William D. Chipley. Whether traveling alone or with her husband, May usually received special attention from the local women, a practice that over four years enabled her to meet most of the prominent women in Florida and to build up a network of statewide friendships that would prove helpful to her future work.

The invitations the Jenningses accepted out of the many they received reveal their wide range of interests: the launching of the U.S.S. *Florida* at Elizabeth, New Jersey, in 1901; the 1901 Tammany Society's July 4 lecture series in New York City; Florida Bar Association conventions; Florida

Press Association conventions; Florida State Horticultural Society meetings; the annual Florida Baptist convention; the 1902 California State Fair in San Francisco; the Southern Turpentine Association convention; the Florida Education Association convention; the Florida State Fair (May served on its women's board); the St. Louis World's Fair; and the National Good Roads Association convention in New York. In 1904 Jennings and his father-in-law attended the second official automobile races on the beach at Daytona, where the governor spoke at the Good Roads Convention held in conjunction with the races.[29] In addition to these travels, the Jenningses attended scores of Democratic party functions, political rallies, high school and college commencement exercises, and minor civic events. The state legislature met only once every two years, and the governor's duties were such that he could travel, conduct private business, lead an active social life, and still have time to carry on his responsibilities as chief executive. May enjoyed traveling, and later in her statewide club work she would travel thousands of miles in the performance of official duties. Living out of a suitcase never seemed to bother her.

Two trips the Jenningses took were especially important. In September 1901 they traveled by train with a number of Floridians to the Pan-American Exhibition in Buffalo, New York, a fair which featured exhibits from all the states and countries in the Western hemisphere.[30] The Jenningses had come to participate in "Florida day" activities and to open the Florida exhibit, which was housed in a booth built to resemble a palmetto hut, its beams and girders draped with Spanish moss.[31]

The gaiety of the event was dampened, however, because in a house near the fairgrounds President McKinley lay dying from an assassin's bullet received while he was touring the fair only a few days before the Jenningses arrived. They paid their respects at the president's residence, then were accorded the honor of being shown the fairgrounds in a "horseless carriage," a privilege reserved for only the most distinguished guests.[32]

The second unique trip came in the spring of 1902, when the Jenningses were among the official party at ceremonies in Havana for formal recognition of Cuban independence from the United States. Mainly because Florida was nearest to Cuba and claimed centuries-old ties with the island, Florida's chief executive was chosen to represent the United States at the ceremonies. The official party included Sherman, May, their son, Bryan, Grace, a number of Washington dignitaries, and William Jennings Bryan, who traveled as a correspondent for the news magazine *Collier's Weekly*. The visitors were treated to a tour of the city, an elaborate banquet, a fancy dress ball, a jai alai game, a fireworks display, and a yacht club breakfast. On 20 May, at an impressive ceremony at Moro Castle, with guns saluting, soldiers standing at attention, and a band playing anthems, the 35-star American flag was lowered and the new flag of Cuba was raised.[33] The American flag was presented to May, who cherished it for many years.[34]

Among the Jenningses' invitations was one from Professor E. Warren Clark, who lived outside Tallahassee on the old Croom plantation, Casa de Laga, 1,000 acres on the shore of Lake Jackson. Clark was a kind-hearted man dedicated to the advancement of blacks. Periodically he held day-long entertainment for Leon County's ex-slaves on 20 May to celebrate Florida Emancipation Day, a gesture not endearing to Leon County whites but tolerated by them.[35] Clark viewed the former slaves as children who needed whites to protect them, educate them, and save their souls, an attitude that in 1901 represented the most enlightened that white liberals could bring to the race question.

In 1901 Clark invited Governor and Mrs. Jennings to his celebration, but it is not recorded whether they accepted. "Next Monday is Emancipation Day," he wrote. "Sixteen years or more ago I gave a grand entertainment here at Lake Jackson for the Colored People, nearly a thousand of them came, and I invited Governor Perry out here to spend the night and address the Colored People, which he did. Could you drive out? After a five minute address to your 'colored constituents' we could show you immense stereopticon views. This time our subject is 'Types of Colored Races of the World.' The illustrations will include the native Hawaiians, Filipinos, Chinese, Japanese, Singalese, Hindoos, Brahmins, Mohammedans, ancient Egyptians, and Ethiopians. . . . a dense Black Crowd would listen to you and such a little visit would do a great deal of good."[36] The professor concluded his plea with the information that he was at the very minute writing a new book entitled "Uncle Tom's Cabin Up to Date."[37]

By 1903 Sherman was assessing his chances as candidate for a higher office. There were rumors that he would become a "dark horse" candidate for vice-president on the national Democratic ticket, along with speculation that he would run for Congress. Finally, in August, he declared his intentions: he would enter the 1904 primary and seek a seat in the U.S. Senate. To his supporters his gubernatorial record made him an unbeatable candidate. More astute observers, however, were less optimistic. He had waited too long to announce his candidacy, they believed, and he would be running against a popular and powerful incumbent, James P. Taliaferro, a conservative Democrat from a wealthy Jacksonville family. In addition John N. C. Stockton, also from Duval County and a protégé of Napoleon Broward, was a candidate.

By waiting so long to declare his intentions, Jennings had lost momentum before the campaign began, and from the beginning of the race he was the underdog. Although his record as governor was impressive and he was well liked by most Floridians, Jennings had angered many in the party by some of his actions as governor. There was some feeling that he lacked the force and personal magnetism required to win a wide-open primary race. In addition he was faced with the burden of having to justify his candidacy to his fellow Democrats. Why, they asked, did he dilute the liberal challenge to Taliaferro by making the primary a three-way race? Wasn't Stockton as much a liberal as he? Indeed, one historian has stated that even "the voters were inclined to regard Stockton as a more sincere liberal than Jennings." [38]

The three candidates attended the state Democratic convention at Punta Gorda. At a large rally held to kick off the campaign, each was called upon to speak. Jennings's supporters must have realized their candidate was in trouble when it was reported that "the Governor has not yet forsaken free silver, and his bold declaration of continued affiliation with a dead issue was not unnoticed by his hearers [who] regard [him] as a third party." [39] From that time onward Jennings's campaign went downhill in a primary full of charges, countercharges, and mud-slinging. While at times Jennings seemed overwhelmed by the bitter attacks, he tried to bypass personalities and campaign on the issues.

May worked hard to reverse the trend. Again in charge of the campaign paperwork, she supervised a statewide mailing and publicity operation, and she organized the governor's speaking tour. Her formal title was "Chairman of the Jennings Campaign Committee on Publicity and Promotion." [40] She was also president of the Tallahassee Jennings Club. Despite her efforts and a valiant speaking tour in which Sherman tried to present himself as a forceful, dynamic leader, the primary election returns showed Sherman trailing both other candidates and eliminated him from the race. He was philosophical about his defeat and seemed almost relieved to have the ordeal behind him. He threw his support to Broward, who was running for governor, and then set about making plans for the future.

The Jenningses had several options. They could return to Brooksville, where Sherman would resume his law practice. He could try for another public office, or he could accept one of the offers of employment being tendered. In November 1904 the governor made his decision. He would become vice-president and legal counsel for a new financial institution in Jacksonville, purported to be the state's largest. For May the move was to prove fortunate for it would place her in the state's largest city, the best location for her to pursue her avocations of club and civic work. May would make her mark in Jacksonville.

CHAPTER 5

Jacksonville, the
Federation,
and Other Matters

THE MOVE to Jacksonville proved the right decision for the Jennings family. In 1905, the city's population was nearly 40,000. As the state's industrial and financial capital it had an active civic and social life and a good school system. Bryan Jennings would graduate from Duval High School, then leave home to attend Stetson University, where he would acquire a law degree. Grace Mann attended Wesleyan College in Macon, Georgia, continuing to live with the Jenningses until 1910, when she married John M. Bell, a Jacksonville businessman.

During their first years in Jacksonville, Sherman solidified the family's finances. He became a vice-president of the Florida Bank and Trust, bought stock in the Barnes-Jessup Naval Stores Company, and acquired extensive real estate holdings.[1] He developed a law practice which became so large that eventually he took on Bryan, his son, and Benjamin F. Brass as junior partners. The Jennings firm was located in the Dyal-Upchurch building on Bay Street.

After two years of living in rented homes including the Meunart House at 129 East 7th Street, in 1907 the family moved into their own house, on the corner of Main and Seventh streets in Springfield, a rural suburb north of Hogan's Creek, which contained some of the city's most elegant residences. The house was at the end of the trolley line, which ran through the city in the center of a landscaped esplanade on Main Street.

One of the largest houses in north Jacksonville, the Jenningses' two-story frame house cost an impressive $6,000 to build.[2] Its twelve rooms included eight upstairs rooms and on the first floor a large entrance hall, parlor, dining room, and kitchen. Among the house's fine points were its grain-edged pine flooring, curley pine doors, chandeliers, leaded glass windows, and a mahogany staircase. Heavy, dark furniture of oak, ebony, and mahogany included a piano in the parlor and the governor's magnificent rolltop desk of burl and mahogany, which were prominently displayed. A parting gift from Sherman's cabinet, the desk carried a silver plaque with their names and the dates of Jennings's administration.[3] All linens used in the house were hand embroidered by May and carried the family monogram. Outside were "broad airy porches" and a stable at the rear of the property, later converted into a garage.[4]

Austin Mann wrote his daughter when she moved into her new home, "God has sure been good to you."[5] Mann too built a new home, even larger than his daughter's, which he named "Olivewood." It was located on the northwest corner of Silver and Eleventh streets only a few blocks from the Jenningses' home.[6]

Soon after moving into her new home May planted trees, flowers, and gardens. The grounds, while not spacious, were tastefully landscaped. Gardening was one of May Jennings's favorite activities, and her appreciation of the outdoors and the beauties of nature continued throughout her life. She was especially fond of aromatic flowers such as roses, hollyhocks, snapdragons, larkspurs, and sweetpeas. Her garden also contained a bed of prize-winning lilies. Over the years May was to become a skilled amateur horticulturist, spending much time ordering seeds and plants and writing friends and experts to exchange information about gardening and farming. When the house was demolished decades later, several of the palm tress that she had planted in 1907 were transplanted to the grounds of Jacksonville's city hall.[7] In its early years the Jenningses' house also had a small chicken yard on the premises. At one time May ordered an incubator, a novel device which friends and neighbors made special visits to view. Occasionally, May raised pigeons and doves for their eggs, which she considered a delicacy. The Jenningses also kept a cow for its milk.

Sometimes May's attachment to her beloved state of Florida manifested itself in curious and humorous ways. Shortly before the family moved into their new home, she chose as the house's number 1845, a sentimental choice based on the date of Florida's entry into the Union. The number worked out fine as long as the Jenningses' home was out in the country, but the Springfield area grew rapidly, and eventually the house address caused a monumental headache for the U.S. Postal Service. May was determined to keep her house number. Threats and cajolings gave way to negotiations. Finally, despite the consternation of the postal service and the inconvenience the illogical number caused her neighbors, May won the right to retain the address of 1845 Main Street, and so it remained for many years.[8]

Because of the family's social position and the size of the house, the Jenningses always had servants: a laundress, who had moved from Tallahassee to Jacksonville with the family; a black kitchen maid, Lizzie Logan; and a black houseman, Benny, who served as handyman, gardener, and chauffeur, all employed by the family for many years. May was kind to her servants, but she always "expected from them a full day's work for a full day's wages."[9]

The Jenningses quickly immersed themselves in Jacksonville's civic life. Because they preferred philanthropic, civic, or political activities over social affairs, they never belonged to exclusive social organizations like the country club or the Seminole and Yacht clubs. Neither did they indulge in that faddish social activity, whist playing. Their circle of friends included prominent local, state, and national business and political leaders. As in Tallahassee, May gained a reputation as a hostess with exceptional abilities. The local paper predicted before one of her parties that "all the guests will be talented, and an artists' evening will be enjoyed. That the evening will be a success, and every moment will be full of pleasure, goes without saying since Mrs. Jennings is the hostess."[10] In addition to hospitality with her husband, she frequently entertained her own friends, and for many years she played host to eminent clubwomen from Florida and other states who were passing through the city. It was not uncommon for the Jenningses to have a dozen or more overnight houseguests in the course of a month.

Although Sherman Jennings was never again to hold elective office, he remained active in politics and continued to speak out on major issues. In 1908 he and Austin Mann, at that time a high official in the state and national Good Roads Association, were delegates to the national Democratic convention in Denver. That same year Jennings served as his cousin's southern campaign manager in William Jennings Bryan's third try for the presidency. In 1911 Jennings served on a special commission to study

Florida's outmoded tax system. He supported the Democratic candidates—Albert W. Gilchrist and Park Trammel—in the 1908 and 1912 gubernatorial races, and in 1916 he backed William V. Knott in his contest against Sidney J. Catts for that office.

Jennings's primary interest until his death was the great Everglades drainage project. In 1905 Governor Broward appointed him counsel to the trustees of the Internal Improvement Fund, a position he held for five years. If Broward was the driving force and the spokesperson of the vast reclamation project, Jennings was its architect and "brains," untangling legal ambiguities and threats to the project. Almost singlehandedly Jennings would see that all challenges were met and successfully resolved in the courts.[11] He drafted both important enabling legislation and bills to finance the undertaking.

His work on the Everglades project embroiled Jennings in several controversies. In 1906 he won a libel suit against the *Jasper News* for its editorials concerning his efforts on behalf of the drainage project.[12] In 1907 Jennings allegedly struck Congressman Frank Clark over the head with a hickory cane in a flap caused by Clark's remarks about the so-called profits Jennings had received from his work for the state. The reclamation program was much misunderstood; Jennings and Broward were frequent targets of ambitious politicians and newspapers which printed sensational but often incorrect stories.

In 1909 Jennings resigned his post as counsel to the trustees but shortly thereafter became attorney for the State Board of Drainage Commissioners. Again he defended the state's actions in the courts. Through the years the Jenningses' faith in the reclamation project never diminished. Sherman became a nationally recognized authority on the dual subjects of canals and drainage and gave numerous speeches around the country. May also promoted the drainage project whenever she could. Several times they journeyed to the work sites to observe the progress of the mammoth dredges as they plowed their way across the glades. The family combined one such trip up the Caloosahatchee River with some "unexcelled duck shooting and fishing."[13] In 1911 the Jenningses traveled to Europe on behalf of the National Drainage Association to observe firsthand the great European canal projects, returning to the United States aboard the British liner *Lusitania*.

In 1912 Governor Jennnings organized and hosted on behalf of the state a trip from Fort Myers to Fort Lauderdale by way of the newly cut drainage canals. A free excursion for northern newsmen and prominent Floridians, the journey marked the official opening of a cross-state waterway and successfully blunted criticism of the costly Everglades project. The participants returned to their homes with glowing reports about what they had seen in South Florida. Apparently, however, they did more than just observe the canals and scenery, for in Jennings's expense logbooks of the expedition one finds outlays for items such as playing cards, poker chips, tumblers, cigars, straw hats, and bathing suits.[14] Among the guests was Austin Mann, who had been promoting a cross-Florida canal for decades. The trip was one of the highlights of his life.

Entranced with South Florida, the Jenningses began spending more and more of their time in the area. In 1912 they purchased two waterfront lots in Miami and in 1916 built a large vacation home, "House-in-the Woods," at 3633 Brickell Avenue, between the James Deering estate, "Vizcaya," and the Williams Jennings Bryan home, "Villa Serena."[15] "House-in-the Woods" was the scene of several important meetings and parties that the Jenningses held to promote Everglades drainage, conservation, political candidates, and women's rights.

In 1910 Jennings became attorney for Richard J. Bolles, one of the largest landowners in the Everglades. Jennings, Mann, and Broward had met Bolles at the Democratic convention in Colorado in 1908. A land speculator, Bolles eventually purchased more than half a million acres of Florida's swamp and reclaimed lands. He was a controversial figure, accused by some of using questionable land promotion tactics, and eventually he was investigated by the U.S. Senate. Despite his reputation, Bolles's purchase of swampland aided the state by rescuing Broward and his associates from accusations of "draining the treasury" as well as the Everglades.[16] For Jennings and other officials, Bolles was the one who saved the beleaguered project during its most serious financial crisis.

Because of friendship and legal services performed for Bolles, the Jenningses became large landowners. They acquired two large tracts of land from Bolles: nearly 60,000 acres of timber and farmland in Clay County that had been owned jointly by Bolles and Austin Mann and thousands more acres in Dade County near Homestead. The Jennings family formed several companies. One, the Dade Muck Land Company, operated a truck farm and citrus grove on 300 acres, but it proved only marginally successful. Eventually most of the South Florida land was sold or lost to the banks during the economic depression of the 1930s. On the Clay County land the Jenningses built a large farmhouse, later named "San Lebrydo," and organized the Artesian Farm Company of Middleburg, which farmed vegetables and sold acreage to out-of-state buyers.[17]

By 1915 the Jenningses owned homes in Brooksville, Jacksonville,

Miami, and Middleburg. Because of Sherman's busy law practice it was May's responsibility to oversee these properties and also much of the operation of the lands, tasks she performed with her usual efficiency and aplomb. Through the years she had acquired a good knowledge of agricultural affairs from her father and husband, and she followed her father's lead in conducting most of the day-to-day operations through the mail. At one time she supervised work on a tangerine grove, a pecan orchard, a large potato patch, and a strawberry farm, each in a different location. Both May and her father were able to handle simultaneously a variety of family, business, and political obligations.

May Jennings appeared to outside observers as a woman who was "all business"; but while she had little outward sympathy for moral weakness or indolence, for many years she privately loaned money to relatives and friends who needed help. She financed the college education of her husband's niece, Marie Kells; she helped support her brother's family because of his alcoholism; and she loaned money to her dressmaker and her servants when they needed help. Her manuscript collection is full of letters from strangers, as well as friends, requesting help. Over the years she gave money to such organizations as the Children's Home Society, the Daniel Memorial Orphanage, St. Luke's Hospital, the Audubon Society, and the Jacksonville YWCA. Her own talents as a fund raiser were often sought, for she was not hesitant to ask her many friends for a donation to what she considered a worthy cause.

Within a short time of moving to Jacksonville, May had joined the Jacksonville Woman's Club, Ladies' Friday Musicale, Daughters of the American Revolution, and the Springfield Improvement Association. She was then thirty-three years old, and photographs of her at that time show a slim, elegantly dressed woman with strikingly attractive features. Her hats, always large and colorful, were already her trademark. During those early years in Jacksonville, May particularly enjoyed her membership in the musicale and was a member of its chorus, which rehearsed weekly. At one musicale gathering she sang a solo entitled "Absent," which, according to a newspaper report, was performed in a "manner which called forth repeated applause." [18] In 1907 the musicale's chorus performed at the Dixieland Theatre as part of a Saengerfest sponsored by the local German society. A few weeks prior to the performance May read before her fellow chorus members a paper she had written about Wagner's *Tannhauser*. [19] Eventually she resigned from the chorus because of other obligations, but she retained membership in the musicale and continued to attend its many functions.

From 1905 until 1914, May's ablest efforts were expended on behalf of the Jacksonville Woman's Club (JWC), because it more than any other organization seemed to meet her earnest need to be actively involved in community affairs. Through it she felt she could participate in the progressive political movement under way in Florida, a movement which her husband's administration had helped to launch. Through her club work May Jennings was to become one of the first women in Florida to enter the state's political arena. She became one of the first women to take advantage of the social and political changes that were beginning to allow American women an involved role. Those changes would make her one of the best known personalities in the state.

One way in which women gained entry into the new worlds of political and civic responsibility was through the local woman's club. These clubs were part of the national progressive movement of the 1890s but had their roots in the abolition societies of the 1850s and 1860s, the women's missionary societies of the 1870s, and the women's temperance unions of the 1880s.[20] Many clubwomen in the 1890s had belonged to each of these earlier organizations.

After the Civil War more and more women, North and South, had found employment outside their homes and had begun to handle their own property. The 1890s marked an important point in this evolution. With changing public attitudes toward women came technological advances that helped to free them from household drudgery. Both changes offered women a degree of liberation from a male-dominated society and allowed them to devote themselves to interests beyond the family. Even in the conservative South, women approached the twentieth century enthusiastically, a few daring to believe in the possibility of moving from "pedestal to politics," to enter the mundane and hitherto forbidden areas of public and political life.[21]

Woman's clubs became a major forum for participation in social and political matters. In the early period of the woman's club movement, 1890–1920, membership was confined almost entirely to those from affluent, upper-middle-class families. Organizations formed throughout Florida during the 1890s, following the establishment of the Green Cove Springs club in 1883.[22] During the 1890s no Florida town seemed to be too small for a female reading society or village improvement association. Ladies met in their homes to study history, literature, music, art, and political science. As their participation in charity work led them to discuss community problems, many women began to see that they had a responsibility to help resolve problems relating to education, housing, health, libraries, parks, crime, and sanitation. They met with local officials to coax or coerce them into taking action. While their political involvement was tempered at first by timidity and circumspection, their goals and tactics grew bolder as they gained confidence.[23] Successes in the early days of the movement were few. Confrontations with male public officials became routine, leaving each club with its own disaster stories to insert into its minutes.

Florida's early clubs sometimes chose names that were purposely obscure in order to avoid publicity: Fortnightly Club of Palatka, Housekeepers of Coconut Grove, Progressive Culture Club of Titusville, Caxtons of Pensacola, Entre Nous of West Palm Beach, Current Topic Club of Lake City, Twentieth Century Club of Gainesville, Avila of Rockledge, and Literary and Debating Club of Melrose. Most clubs eventually took more mundane names; for example, the Brooksville women who first organized as the Whittier Club became the Ladies' Improvement Society and finally the Brooksville Woman's Club. Whatever the designation, the organization furnished the camaraderie, intellectual stimulation, and leadership training that the women sought. Usually the first goal of each club was to build a clubhouse on a prominent site in town. In smaller towns these buildings also served as community centers, and many were still standing in 1985.

In 1894 the General Federation of Women's Clubs (GFWC), a national association of state federations, had been organized in New York City.[24] Through the years the GFWC would work for municipal and national governmental reforms, child welfare legislation, penal reform, equitable taxation, improved public education, health laws, and national conservation laws. The strength of the General Federation was to lie in its numbers: By 1914 every state federation had joined it, and it represented more than two million American women.

The General Federation offered up to twenty topics for local committees and state departments to study, from political science, music, and art to conservation and public health. Subjects were dropped and others added as the times and political interests of American women changed. At the General Federation's biennial convention, programs were presented on selected subjects, after which the women voted on issues that they wanted to support. In 1985 the General Federation of Women's Clubs was still a viable organization.

By 1895, Florida's clubs were ready to discuss a state federation. On 21 February eight women representing five village associations met in the library of the Green Cove Springs Village Improvement Association.[25] Attending from Green Cove Springs were Mrs. E. N. Burrows, Mrs. E. V. Low, Mrs. E. G. Munsell, and Mrs. E. A. Graves; Mrs. S. B. Safford from Tarpon Springs; Mrs. Emma C. Tebbetts from Crescent City; Mrs. S. L. Morse from Orange City; and Mrs. L. E. Wamboldt from Fairfield.[26] That same day the women voted to federate, establishing the Florida Federation of Women's Clubs (FFWC). The constitution and bylaws set forth the objective: "To bring the women's clubs [of Florida] into acquaintance and mutual helpfulness."[27] Clubs applying for membership were expected to be "free from sectarian or political bias and [to express] the spirit of progress on broad and humane lines."[28] The federation was governed by a state president, other officers, and a board of directors to be composed of veteran clubwomen, all officers serving two-year terms.

Some Florida clubs at first refused to join the state federation, particularly clubs in the conservative Panhandle area; they accused the organization of "radicalism." Yet the federation grew, by 1910 representing 1,600 women in 36 clubs and by 1914 some 6,000 women.[29]

The Florida Federation's organizational framework was patterned after the General Federation's, which it joined the following year. By 1920 there were twelve state sections of contiguous counties, each headed by a vice-president who worked under the state president.[30] Each section held an annual meeting, and once a year the whole federation met in convention. The first statewide convention was held in 1896 at Green Cove Springs.[31] In the early years delegates sometimes had to overcome formidable odds just to attend the conventions: long distances between cities, poor traveling facilities, and opposition from skeptical and hostile family members. Only eleven women attended the fourth annual state convention in Jacksonville in 1899.

The Florida Federation's departments duplicated the General Federation's, with additional departments added or deleted as local interests dictated. These included departments that promoted bird protection, forestry, waterways, good roads, and Seminole welfare. Florida women reflected a more than ordinary interest in the development and conservation of the state's natural resources.

From its inception in 1895 the Florida Federation was a politically minded organization. The first official action taken by the women at the 1895 historic Green Cove Springs organizational meeting was to direct each of the five member clubs to "hold a meeting for the purpose of drawing up a petition to the legislature of Florida, praying it to rescind the act [which] allowed cattle to run at large in towns of less than twelve hundred inhabitants."[32] Thus was the federation's first legislative program launched.

The animal problem was a familiar one to Floridians. May Jennings and her sister clubwomen had tackled the problem in Brooksville as early as 1891. Amazingly the fledgling federation almost made good on its stated objective for "on May 6, 1895, Mr. Fleming introduced in the Senate, Bill Number 284, amending the act defining what cities shall impound live cattle." The bill passed the Senate on May 17 but failed in the House.[33]

The battle over free-roaming and tick-laden Florida livestock had been joined, one of the longest and toughest the federation was ever to face. May Jennings would lead much of the fight against the Florida range industry, among the state's most powerful and entrenched interests. Lucy Blackman, historian of the Florida Federation, writing in the 1930s, described the consequences of that 1895 call to legislative action: "Thus has it been for more than thirty years that between the Federation of Women's Clubs and the Legislature of Florida, the sacred Florida cow has been an ever present bone of contention—skin and bone literally. It looks as though there might be thirty more years of contention ahead of us before this ticky and emaciated beast shall have been sufficiently immersed and groomed, and made fit for good society. I can promise the legislators of those coming days that the Federation women will still be on hand with their resolutions and persuasions."[34] Mrs. Blackman's prediction was true: the livestock problem was not completely resolved until the 1960s.

From 1895 the federation was never without a legislative program. At each annual convention the clubwomen discussed the major issues pertinent to the organization's departments and then by motion and vote produced a political action program that would become the following year's goal. This statewide solidarity on issues was a key to the federation's success. Since the federation objectives became the goals of each club, then each member was a fighter for the cause. A word from the leadership was enough to flood the legislature or specific officials' offices with hundreds of letters and telegrams. Some federation-backed programs took many years to accomplish: the fight for compulsory school attendance laws, for example, lasted fourteen years; the struggle to preserve part of tropical South Florida, more than forty years; the battle over unfenced and undipped livestock, seventy years. Beginning in 1908, the federation's legislative committee was responsible for seeing that the organization's political program was publicized and presented to the state's representatives at each session of the legislature. The women who chaired this committee had to be articulate and politically knowledgeable, and few would equal May Jennings in political astuteness. She served as a member of this important committee longer than any other woman in the federation's history.

Through the years the FFWC supported a myriad of political objectives, moving gradually from an early progressive position toward a conservative political point of view by the 1920s. During its first decades several themes tended to repeat themselves in the federation's political programs. Two of these themes were "social purity" (i.e., morality) and women's economic and legal rights. In 1897 federation members petitioned the legislature to raise the age of moral and legal consent for females from ten to twenty-one; in 1901 the age was finally set at eighteen. In 1911 the organization issued a booklet entitled *Some Laws of Importance to Women in Florida,* the first of several pamphlets on female rights published in the state.

Public education was another issue that the federation consistently promoted. As early as 1901 the women were urging the establishment of tax-funded kindergartens, modernized school curricula, improved teacher training, compulsory attendance laws, adequate public funding, and the appointment of females to school boards. For twenty years the federation sponsored a free traveling library which was open to the public and used by the public schools.

Conservation and beautification issues were particularly championed by a small but vocal group of South Florida women. At the federation's 1905 convention several of these ladies introduced a motion that would have far-reaching consequences for Florida and the nation. As adopted it called for the creation of "a Federal forest reservation on Paradise Key in the Everglades, in order to preserve the unique groups of Royal palms, this being the only spot in the United States where these palms are found growing naturally." [35] When May became president of the federation years later she used this motion, which was still on the federation's books, to help bring its promises to fruition. The federation also worked for the establishment of a state forestry commission.

From the beginning the federation was concerned with public health and child care. The clubwomen sold Christmas seals, with proceeds going into antituberculosis work, sponsored "health days" in the public schools, organized a speaking tour in 1910 by Dr. Ellen Lowell Stevens, female doctor and clubwoman, and in 1911 were responsible for establishment of a State Conference of Charities. The federation was also a major pressure group in the successful move to create the state's first tuberculosis sanitarium and school for the retarded and feebleminded.

The federation's impact was first felt at the local level as each club became a vehicle for social and civic change in its own community. In 1899, for instance, the Green Cove Springs Village Improvement Association launched a city beautification program, organized a forestry and bird club, and provided funding and staffing for a free public library. The St. Petersburg Women's Town Improvement Association worked to get an ordinance to prevent loose chickens and other fowl from polluting public sidewalks and roadways. Other clubs were protecting birds, planting trees, cleaning streets, and establishing libraries; "sidewalks, bicycle paths, fences, and even school houses were built by these intrepid women." [36] They raised money for their projects by sponsoring exhibitions, banquets, and candy and bake sales.

The clubwomen's activities were not always applauded. City and county officials were often startled and usually perplexed when groups of local women marched into their offices, demanding that they clean up the communities and provide better services. Official consternation and anger were often confounded when the women confronting them were their own wives, daughters, sisters, and mothers. Lucy Blackman refers to these path-breaking clubwomen as "heroines" and "captains courageous" who were consistently faced with "the old Adam war-cry 'Woman's Place Is In The Home,' which reverberated through the pines and over the rivers and lakes and oceans from Pensacola to Key West." One of these women, a member of a prominent Jacksonville family, remembered that in those early days she was often reviled for associating with such an "iniquitous movement" as a woman's club. Others recalled "that the men of the towns were bitter in their denunciations of Women's Clubs [but] that there were always enough women with spinal cords starched stiff, who raised eyebrows and went forth anyway to do as they saw fit." [37]

If local officials resented the women, the members of Florida's all-male legislature were especially indignant. The politicians' ridicule, sarcasm, and mockery were routinely reported in the state's newspapers. It seems that the women had an "annoying habit of talking back to the legislators after they had been told politely to go home and tend to their babies." [38] With the exception of two early allies among the Jacksonville papers, the *Florida Times-Union* and the *Metropolis,* most of the state press was skeptical of what the women were trying to do. In an editorial entitled "No Women in Politics Please," the *Jacksonville Sun* pleaded for some way to "save us from this catastrophe." [39]

A writer in *Florida Magazine* wondered, "What will the twentieth century woman be?" after observing that changes in manners and habits of thought had brought about radical "new conditions" in the domestic sphere.[40] And the *Ladies Home Journal* wishfully noted that "the tide of women rushing pell-mell into all kinds of business has been stemmed." [41]

On the contrary, of course, the tide was on the rise. Women in Florida and elsewhere began to play significant roles in public life.

May Jennings, more than any other female in Florida, was to personify the new civic-minded twentieth-century woman. Her rise to prominence would begin in the Jacksonville Woman's Club.

CHAPTER 6

"An Enthusiastic Clubwoman"

T HE JACKSONVILLE Woman's Club had its beginnings on 20 January 1897, when forty women met at the Windsor Hotel across from Hemming Park to organize a club for the "mutual improvement [and] entertainment of its members, [and] for the cultivation of the amenities of social life, and to give aid to all worthy objects."[1] Thus its purpose was threefold: self-improvement, entertainment, and good works. The women represented the city's most affluent and prominent families and included Lula Paine Fletcher (Mrs. Duncan U.), Julia Furchgott (Mrs. Leonard), Katherine Livingston Egan (Mrs. Dennis), Cordelia Durkee (Mrs. J. H.), Lucy Colby Wamboldt (Mrs. N. C.), and Lizzie Marsh Yerkees (Mrs. J. B.). Other members came from the Cummer, L'Engle, Barnett, Meigs, Broward, and Young families.

Soon after its establishment the Jacksonville club began offering a full slate of activities. Reading and study classes were organized; a nurse was hired to visit the city's poor and sick; and art and flower shows were held to raise money for the public schools and St. Luke's Hospital. When the great fire of 1901 nearly destroyed Jacksonville, the club supplied most of the workers for the Women's Relief Corps. By 1904, with a clubhouse at 18 East Duval Street, the club had become an influential part of the city's social and civic establishment. (In 1927 a more spacious club home was built on Riverside Avenue.)[2]

During the club's first decade the women studied such disparate topics as forestry, opera, flower arranging, conservation, municipal reform, Milton's *Paradise Lost,* child care, legends of Florida, bacteria, Shakespeare's plays, birds, Greek architecture, the legal status of women, and the nebula hypothesis. Two other subjects on the agenda were ship canals, perhaps suggested by May Jennings, and the question "Are We Healthier and Happier than Our Grandmothers?" To the latter the women answered in the affirmative, but the real importance of the question lay in their showing how far they had come by asking it at all.

May became one of the Jacksonville club's most active members. She was popular with most of the women, but her energy, her deep commitment to social progress, and her political bravura were sources of alarm to the club's more staid and conservative members. Some felt that she was too interested in politics and might involve the club in controversy. Although the woman's clubs claimed to be "the most democratic organizations in the world," requiring no "ancient lineage, adherence to a particular political creed, or specific religious belief,"[3] they tended to be exclusionary. New members had to be sponsored, and only a few lower-middle-class or Jewish women were ever invited to join. Victorian morality and social conservatism made some of the clubwomen frown on anyone who was not of an accepted class or who had talents or ideas that might be different. In spite of May's impeccable credentials, she differed from most of her associates in that she was not afraid of controversy and confrontation. A few of the Jacksonville members never truly accepted her, and later some women accused her of "playing politics" and of "grandstanding" for personal attention. Many seemed not to understand the importance of the work that she and other Florida clubwomen were undertaking, resenting anything that interfered with their own socializing or family responsibilities. May viewed her efforts to achieve the federation's political objectives not only as serious business but as social and intellectual entertainment. Her sense of citizenship gave club work a higher meaning than many of her contemporaries were able to accept. She was committed to a lifelong avocation of civic and public service.

May's rivals and harshest critics were women much like her: highly motivated, intelligent, and strong willed. Mrs. Minerva Jennings (Mrs. Frank E., no relation) and Margaret Young (Mrs. William B.) fell into this category. Like May both were married to prominent men, and they were much involved in civic work in Jacksonville. May was to clash with them often over club policy and tactics in a rivalry that occasionally threatened to erupt into open hostility. Although May's quick tongue and self-assurance sometimes intimidated people, most women she worked with over the years supported her and her ideas. One admirer later wrote, "Mrs. Jennings shows a marked degree of disregard of cliques. [She] has risen superior to them. In fact fairness is one of the attributes that has been most salient in all that she has done. She is approachable at all times." [4]

In 1906 the Jacksonville club supported a pure food and drug exposition by arranging a parade of decorated baby coaches and "goat carriages" on Bay Street. A women's lounge was opened in the club building for downtown shoppers and female employees to use as a "haven of rest," and the clubwomen protested to city hall about the "cows roaming free" throughout Springfield. They also petitioned the Board of Public Works to provide playgrounds in the parks. The club became so successful at getting things done that Claude L'Engle editorialized in the *Jacksonville Dixie* that "Women's Clubs with the wonderfully feminine energies underlying them, have the levers in their possession like Old Atlas to move Mother Earth off of its pegs." [5]

May Jennings was interested and active in many things during her lifetime, and through careful organization of her time she was able to involve herself in many types of civic, club, and political projects at the same time. While involved in the many activities of the Friday Musicale she could also solicit funds for an orphanage, lead a petition drive, organize political tactics for a lobbying effort on the legislature, and maintain a full entertainment and travel schedule. Her interests and her ability to work assiduously for disparate movements reveal a woman with an active mind and a high level of physical energy. She retained this energetic and peripatetic life-style all of her life. Occasionally she would narrow her vision to concentrate on one project, but it was usually just for long enough to get a favorite project started or terminated. The pace she set for herself was astonishing. Few women were able to match the number of projects she promoted, the number of clubs she belonged to, the many people that she knew on a first-name basis, or the intensity of effort which she brought to her work. Her name appeared frequently in the newspapers and on the rosters of scores of clubs and organizations. By 1910 she was well known to the general public, and four years later when she became president of the Florida Federation of Women's Clubs she was easily identified as the most prominent woman in the state.

May disliked inaction; she was a doer who saw inaction as weakness.

When named to head a committee or assigned a responsibility, she immediately began making plans and organizing the workers necessary to accomplish the objective, a somewhat unusual course among associates who lacked either confidence in their own abilities or the experience to take on difficult tasks. The Jacksonville club's yearbooks for 1906 and 1907 list May as a member of the social purity committee and as chairperson of the civics committee. For several years she also chaired the club's legislation committee. The earliest record of her leading a civic crusade concerned a railroad depot project that the Jacksonville club undertook in the summer of 1906. Characteristically, May turned it into a statewide movement.

In 1906, the Jacksonville Woman's Club members decided that the city's old railroad station needed renovating. Jacksonville was known as the "gateway to Florida," through which hundreds of thousands of tourists passed each year, most of them traveling by train. The local depot was a decrepit and uncomfortable building, an unsightly introduction to both Jacksonville and Florida. As chairman of a committee formed to look into the situation, May argued that the women should not limit their efforts to Jacksonville. The problem was statewide; most of Florida's depots were antiquated and uncomfortable. The women passed a resolution, the first of many such documents bearing May's signature, calling for a statewide campaign to repair, clean, and beautify every depot in the state.[6] Local citizens in each community were called upon to lead the effort. May mailed a copy of the resolution to every town government, village improvement association, woman's club, newspaper, and railroad official in the state. The Jacksonville officials who received copies also received a personal lecture on the problem from her and her committee members.

Publication of the resolution in newspapers throughout Florida helped rally public opinion. Although the campaign's results were mixed, May and her cohorts had put state and local authorities on notice that Florida clubwomen were a force to be reckoned with. In spite of the many stationmasters who refused to cooperate in cleaning up their depots, enough interest was created that R. Hudson Burr, state railroad commissioner, who had received a personal note from May, made an inspection tour of the railroads' public facilities. Newsmen noted that Burr was unfavorably impressed with what he found and was particularly appalled by conditions at the Brooksville station.[7]

Despite railroad resistance and lethargy among town officials, May was pleased that the resolution had stirred up public interest and had forced state officials to take some action. The campaign showed that if women acted together they could affect the quality of public life. In November

1907 May attended the thirteenth annual FFWC convention, in Gainesville, her first recorded attendance at such a convention. While there she reported that the railroad campaign, while not an overwhelming success, had resulted in significant improvements to the depots in Tampa, Jacksonville, and Tallahassee. On her return to Jacksonville, the *Metropolis* described her as "a very important member of the Florida circle of club women." [8]

By 1907, the Jacksonville club had 215 members. As chairperson of the civics committee, May had begun working on behalf of child welfare, a cause that was to consume much of her energy over the next decade. On her agenda was the State Reform School at Marianna, in which clubwomen had shown an interest since its establishment in 1897. Facilities were inadequate, and the inmates were often mistreated. The majority of children were black boys; only three were girls. Medical attention was lacking, the mortality rate was high, and the inmates received little formal education and no religious or moral teaching. Boys as young as ten years were observed working the school's farm with their feet shackled by chains. [9]

The clubwomen's publicizing of conditions at Marianna paid off for both the child welfare movement in general and the Marianna children in particular. In 1907 Governor Broward called for doubling the appropriation to the school to $10,000 per annum. May supported this action and made the improvement of the Marianna school the major objective of her committee. She read a paper to the Jacksonville club that she had written about the conditions there and called for a memorial to the legislature endorsing Broward's request. The women stated that they "heartily agreed that the institution should be made a real reformatory school [with industrial training] and not be a Juvenile Prison." [10] Signed by May and 173 Jacksonville clubwomen, the memorial was sent to the governor, the cabinet, and each legislator. Telegrams and letters poured in from the women, and the 1907 legislature, one of the state's most progressive, not only heeded the governor's request concerning the reform school but also passed Florida's first comprehensive child labor law. [11] Mrs. C. H. Raynor, FFWC president, was presented the pen with which Broward signed this bill. May was pleased for she had written and talked to every official that she knew urging support of the bills.

There was still much to be done at the state level to secure better conditions and rights for children. Efforts to establish a juvenile court system, improve the juvenile penal system and public education, and regulate child labor were grouped in what was termed the child welfare movement.[12] When the 1909 legislature convened, several other organizations united with the clubwomen. They included the Florida State Federation of Labor and a loose confederation of private child welfare agencies led by Marcus Fagg, superintendent of the Children's Home Society of Jacksonville, Florida's largest orphanage. Led by May, Jacksonville clubwomen again submitted a resolution to the legislature, this time calling for a $15,000 yearly appropriation to the Marianna insitution.[13] May visited Governor Albert W. Gilchrist, presenting him with a copy of the new resolution and one of her famous face-to-face lectures.[14] She also delivered a memorial from the Jacksonville club supporting another more comprehensive child labor bill that was ready for the legislature.[15] Unfortunately, she was unable to remain in Tallahassee to lobby fulltime. Despite a letter-writing campaign by clubwomen and lobbying by Marcus Fagg, the 1909 legislature refused to increase the reform school's appropriation or to enact the improved child labor bill. It did, however, appoint a committee to inspect the facility at Marianna.

Undaunted, the federation's legislative committee devoted 1910 and 1911 to an extensive study of the reformatory. The committee was now headed by Susan B. Wight (Mrs. Henry) of Sanford, an aggressive leader. The school was underfunded, and the women believed that the special legislative committee of 1909 had "whitewashed" its report on conditions there. One morning soon after the lawmakers had issued this report, Mrs. Wight and Mrs. William B. Young "put on their hats, and, uninvited and unannounced and unexpected and evidently unwanted, arrived at the Reformatory for a spend-the-day visit."[16] The report these women issued created a sensation in Florida, and it gave progressives the ammunition they thought they needed to convince the legislature that the school was a disgrace. May, now chairman of the Jacksonville club's legislation committee, again submitted a resolution on behalf of the school to the 1911 legislature. She felt that the combined forces of labor, Marcus Fagg, and Mrs. Wight's committee could push the needed bill through. To help the cause the federation published a small pamphlet entitled *Plea for the Marianna Reform School,* which was mailed to all legislators, woman's clubs, and newspapers. Speakers traveled throughout the state, among them Mrs. Wight, Mrs. Young, Mrs. Frank Jennings, Marcus Fagg, and May Jennings, to lobby among citizens' groups on behalf of the bill.

The women's 1911 resolution to the legislature urged the lawmakers to fund the Marianna school adequately, but it also called for enactment of other progressive laws, including compulsory education, a child labor law, and the prohibition of horse racing and all kinds of bookmaking and betting in the state. The women worked hard to get the legislation enacted. Unfortunately, neither May nor Mrs. Wight was able to spend time lobbying in Tallahassee. The women had pinned their hopes on J. C. Privett of the state labor organization and Mr. Fagg, but halfway through the session labor withdrew its support of the compulsory education bill and later abandoned the child labor bill in favor of a substitute measure which would create a bureau of labor and statistics. As a consequence, the child labor bill was allowed to die in committee. Mr. Fagg notified May, urging her to ask the women to contact their representatives. May immediately sent telegrams to clubwomen around the state. Florence Cay, wife of a Tallahassee businessman and former legislator, was telegraphed to "do everything possible to get [the] child labor bill reconsidered. The legislation is the only protection of the helpless children's best interests against corporate wealth, and for humanity's sake passage of [the] bill should be urged. Conservation of the child is our first duty." [17] The women's effort was for naught; the bill failed to pass.

The 1911 legislative session proved to be a mixed blessing. The legislature increased the reform school's annual appropriation to $17,500 and passed a juvenile court measure that revolutionized juvenile justice in Florida. However, it refused to enact either the child labor bill or the compulsory education bill. May had learned a valuable lesson; if lobbying was needed it had to be done personally, not through letters, telegrams, or third parties. She looked on Privett and his organization as self-serving and opportunistic and was thereafter reluctant to work with them, although she continued her association with Fagg.

Concurrent with her statewide activity on behalf of child welfare, May was involved in other causes. In 1907 she became connected with a movement that kept the city of Jacksonville in turmoil for many weeks. The temperance and prohibition movements were on the ascendancy throughout the nation, particularly in the South. Prohibitionists in Duval County had tried unsuccessfully to use the local option clause in the Florida constitution to make Duval "dry." Several events occurred in 1907 that encouraged local temperance advocates to try again. First, many counties in South Carolina and Georgia voted to adopt prohibition, leading to an influx of breweries and liquor establishments into North Florida. Second, a neighborhood protective association was organized when whiskey interests attempted to expand into the pleasant, tree-lined suburb of Springfield. Finally, several other counties in Florida voted to go "dry" in 1906 and 1907.

Disturbed by the encroachment of liquor interests and cheered by successes elsewhere, local businessmen, including former Governor Jennings, formed the Duval County Prohibition League to collect signatures for a petition to be presented to the city council, calling for a "wet-dry" referendum. Opposing this effort was the Business Men's Association. Midway into the campaign for signatures, women favoring the petition met at the First Baptist Church and organized the Women's Prohibition League. May Jennings was elected president and Mrs. Duncan U. Fletcher vice-president.[18] Within a month the organization had over 250 members. May quickly began assigning women to canvass every block in the city's wards, and late in November the women sponsored a public rally in a large tent on West Adams Street.

As the campaign heated up, so did the rhetoric. The "drys" were accused of selling their "birthrights for a mess of prohibition pottage."[19] Those favoring the free sale of liquor were said to be in cahoots with the devil. Evangelists and clergymen of every persuasion descended upon the city to preach at impromptu rallies and harangue citizens on the city's downtown streets, while local ministers used their own pulpits to exhort their congregations to vote the "right way."

In early 1908 May wrote Governor Broward an indignant letter concerning the many "blind tigers" (illicit liquor establishments) she claimed state and local officials were allowing to operate in northeast Florida. She received a rather cool reply from the governor and denials from sheriffs in the accused counties.

In February, Carrie Nation, the famous "Kansas Saloon Smasher," visited Jacksonville as part of a statewide tour. May scored a triumph when she persuaded Mrs. Nation to address the local Women's Prohibition League. Mrs. Nation, who said she "used her tongue now" instead of an axe to smash barrooms, delivered a rousing antiliquor talk. Mrs. Nation's addresses always "contained a liberal sprinkling of quotations from scripture on the evils of alcohol mixed with harsh words for local politicians and saloon keepers and their patrons."[20] At the reception following her speech, Mrs. Nation passed out her famous red hatchet-shaped lapel pins. For the duration of the campaign May prominently displayed her pin on the collar of her dresses.

Despite their hard work, the prohibitionists' campaign failed. The city council pointed out technical irregularities in the petition, and the anti-prohibitionists on the council refused to vote to call a special election. May continued to support the prohibition movement, particularly the Florida Anti-Saloon League, although there is no record of her joining the Women's Christian Temperance Union. Her involvement reflected more than an intellectual or moral stance. May's brother was an alcoholic, a fact that had caused her much grief. She had found it necessary on several occasions to provide financially for his wife and children. Her prohibition sentiments remained with her all her life.

In January 1909, Katherine Eagan spoke to a group of women about the deplorable conditions existing at the city jail, a facility nicknamed "Raspberry Park." The *Jacksonville Metropolis* had condemned the jail in articles and editorials, calling it a disgrace and no more than a "hole in the wall." [21] As the leader of a committee of clubwomen responsible for looking into the situation, May within the week addressed the city council, inviting its members to accompany her committee on a tour of the facility. On 1 February 1909, May, Mrs. Waldo Cummer, Mrs. Guy Pride, and councilmen St. Elmo Acosta, Maurice Slager, and Whitfield Walker visited the jail. The group was appalled; the situation was even worse than they had been told.

The jail accommodations consisted of two rooms; one (40' x 5') housed sixty-seven black men, and the other (20' x 5') housed seventeen white men. Neither cell had cots, windows, or plumbing. Inmates slept on the stone floor, winter and summer, surviving on bread and water once a day and corned beef on Sundays. The city's health officer had never visited the place. May was outraged by what she saw. The *Metropolis* reported that the "club ladies will not rest until conditions are bettered at Raspberry Park." [22]

At the next council meeting officials voted to implement May's plans for improving the facility; $967 was appropriated to add plumbing, enlarge the cells, and cut windows in the walls of the building. Still not satisfied, the clubwomen continued their surveillance of the facility. The following summer May went before the council again, securing an additional $300 to improve the building further. [23] Eventually the building was demolished, and a county penal farm was constructed past the city limits near north Main Street.

May continued her work on behalf of other organizations. In February 1910, she became an organizer and charter member of the Katherine Livingston Chapter of the Daughters of the American Revolution, one of two chapters in Jacksonville. In 1911 the chapter helped secure funds to buy a silver service for the newly launched battleship *Florida*. Years later, when the ship was decommissioned DAR members arranged for the service to be placed in the Florida governor's mansion. May served as a vice regent and later as state chairman of the organization's old trails and roads committee and as head of its state library committee. For many years the

Livingston Chapter helped sponsor "Flag Day" and "Americanism" programs in Duval County schools. During World War I it raised money for
the Red Cross and for entertainment of soldiers stationed in the area. In
the 1920s it paid for a scholarship for a veteran to attend the University of
Florida. The Jacksonville DAR chapters were also responsible for the
monument at Mayport to commemorate the landing of Jean Ribault and
the French in the sixteenth century. Through the years May worked on behalf of the DAR chapter's goals and hosted many of its meetings in her
home.[24]

May Jennings also worked on behalf of St. Luke's Hospital. Through the
Jacksonville Woman's Club health committee, she solicited funds for the
hospital and lobbied and wrote letters to secure a contagious disease ward
for the institution. She became upset with hospital officials, however,
when in 1914 the institution moved to what May felt was an undesirable
site in Springfield close to the homes, a school, and other public buildings. It was also believed the hospital would lower area property values.

In 1911, May, Mrs. Bion H. Barnett, Mrs. W. B. Young, and other interested ladies met to discuss establishing a Young Women's Christian Association in the city. The men had organized a YMCA several years earlier.
May was charged with drawing up the bylaws and securing a charter for
the new women's association.[25] She was also appointed to raise money for
the new enterprise. During the fund drive she wrote to her husband, "I
canvassed for the YWCA yesterday and got $212 without counting yours.
We go again tomorrow, then we are going to strike."[26]

The "Californian," a boardinghouse on Newnan Street, was leased as
the association's first home. Later, a large four-story building at 130 West
Monroe Street was purchased.[27] Elected to the association's first board of
directors, May served until 1915. During her years on the board she headed
the Y's physical department, which was supposed to provide girls with the
"right habits of life, healthful environment, and development of good
physique."[28]

May never seemed too busy to take on additional tasks. In 1912 she
became president of the Springfield Improvement Association, later known
as the Springfield Woman's Club. While serving as president in 1912–14,
May continued as chairman of the Jacksonville Woman's Club legislation
committee and as an officer in the state federation. Since the Springfield
and Jacksonville clubs were friendly rivals, May eventually resigned from
the Jacksonville club and retained her Springfield membership.

The Springfield club concerned itself mainly with Springfield matters.
During May's first tenure as president of the club (she was reelected in

1920), the organization worked to preserve the suburban integrity of the area by sponsoring beautification programs, maintaining Springfield Park, and organizing band concerts during the summer. As the self-appointed watchdog for the area, the club gained a reputation as an activist organization. During the 1920s, May was among the leaders in the club's unsuccessful fight against the removal of the Main Street esplanade and the destruction of many of the area's large oak trees.

By 1912, May Jennings had become perhaps the best-known woman in Florida. She had confronted almost every Jacksonville and Duval County official and many on the state level. Generally acknowledged to be very effective, she was in demand to sponsor organizations or speak on behalf of special causes. Her popularity was enhanced by her unfailing gentility and decorum. The public perceived her as an honest, intelligent, but determined gentlewoman who had the best interests of all citizens at heart.

In 1912 May spoke before several religious groups. At the annual Baptist State Missionary Union at Lakeland she described to an audience of women what true public service meant to her, citing the many organizations that needed workers—YWCA, Mothers' Clubs, Woman's Clubs. She urged women to work to purify and reform American life, warning that if they did not, America's institutions might be destroyed by the foreign-speaking immigrants who were flowing into the country in great numbers. Such views were not unusual during the Progressive Era, when many middle-class citizens resented and feared the newcomers because their strange customs, languages, and religious practices threatened to dilute America's traditional white Anglo-Saxon Protestant values. Educated women particularly resented male immigrants who became citizens because they could participate in national and state elections, while native-born women could not. May ended her speech with the exhortation "Let us be more practical with our religion, and apply it to our own life work. There are comparatively few enlisted in public service. We need more recruits to lighten the burden of the few in this fast growing and much needed work."[29] In reporting her speech the *Jacksonville Times-Union* noted that "Mrs. Jennings is an enthusiastic clubwoman who sees herself and others as social workers."[30]

At the annual FFWC convention at West Palm Beach in 1912, Elizabeth Hocker of Ocala was elected president of the organization. May became vice-president and chairperson of the federation's department of education and thus a member of the board of directors and part of the organization's inner circle. Mrs. Hocker and May wrote letters of encouragement and spoke before many unaffiliated clubs urging them to join the federation.

The results were impressive. Susan Wight wrote May: "Good for you Lady, I am proud of you and our prospects for advances. Things are beginning to move. Our Federation is finally going to realize some dreams I've dared to entertain for it."[31] By 1913 the federation had grown to include 72 clubs with a combined membership of 3,600 women.

Led by some of the ablest women in Florida, the federation and local clubs had an impact on public opinion and legislation on every level—local, county, and state. The federation was no longer a joke, even to the legislature.[32] During the Hocker administration women in clubs began to feel a real sense of statewide camaraderie and of belonging to an important movement. The officers convened regularly for board meetings and through correspondence and visiting each other's homes developed into a sisterhood with special meaning for each member. Their letters to one another evolved from formal businesslike communications to include references to insiders' jokes and to personal family matters. Some of the women even took to using nicknames. One club friend referred to May as "Lady Bug," while another addressed her as "My Dear Heavenly Twin," perhaps a reference to the fact that May was a Gemini on the astrological chart.[33] This spirit of fun, of family, and of camaraderie coincided with the period of the federation's greatest growth and most spectacular successes.

In 1912, May was the right person to head the federation's department of education. Apart from the many years when she supported her husband's involvement in public education, May had her own credentials. In Jacksonville she was an active member of the Springfield Mothers' Club and had been instrumental in organizing the Duval County Federation of Mothers' Clubs.[34] She served on the committee that had entertained delegates to the Florida Education Association's convention. In 1910 State Superintendent William Holloway had appointed her to the executive committee of the Florida Women's School Improvement Association, on which she served for three years.[35] Also on the committee was Lucy Blackman, May's close friend and wife of William F. Blackman. The association's objectives were to make "schools the center of gravity of community life and arouse in parents a greater sense of obligation and responsibility" to education. It oversaw the establishment of local chapters, which in turn were supposed to work for the establishment of school libraries and improved school grounds. There were 150 of these groups in the state by 1911. In addition, the Jenningses were personal friends of many of the state's most prominent educators; William N. Sheats, William H. Holloway, Edward Conradi, Lincoln Hulley, A. A. Murphree, and William F. Blackman had all been entertained in the Jenningses' Jacksonville home.

Thus by the time May became head of the federation's education department, she was well informed about the problems and needs of Florida's
schools. Organizing a program of action for the upcoming 1913 legislative
session included choosing a committee to work with her: Mrs. Park Trammell of Tallahassee, Mrs. J. C. Huber of Tampa, Rachel Gaines of Leesburg, Mariam Pasteur of Palatka, Mrs. Lee Spear of Fort Lauderdale, and
Mrs. Charles Boneaker of Pensacola. One of the committee's responsibilities was to raise funds for the federation's scholarship, established in 1906,
to train kindergarten teachers at the Florida State College for Women at
Tallahassee.

As chairperson of the education department May recommended that the
federation support the work of Agnes Ellen Harris of the Home Economics Department of the women's college. The U.S. Department of Agriculture was promoting rural extension work in conjunction with the land-
grant colleges, and Agnes Harris was the agent in charge of girls' clubs
related to this promotion effort.[36] One aspect of the work was to urge
counties to promote boys' and girls' corn and tomato clubs. There were
also potato, cotton, poultry, and hog clubs organized to teach children
ages ten to eighteen the rudiments of sowing, harvesting, canning, and
marketing produce. Each child was to till a tenth of an acre and then market the harvest.[37] Thirteen Florida counties had enrolled in the project by
1912, and 622 girls had put up 18,000 cans of tomatoes which sold for
thirteen cents each.[38]

May was impressed with Agnes Harris's work and was aware that she
was getting little help from state officials. With Mrs. Hocker's approval,
May set up federation prizes of $50.00 toward the winners' education for
the girl and boy who achieved the best annual production records. May
persuaded officials of Cohen Brothers Department Store in Jacksonville to
donate the sum for the boy's prize and urged each federation club to donate
to the girl's prize fund. She also asked each club to sponsor a tomato club
in its county, helping establish a club in Middleburg near the Jenningses'
Clay County farm herself. The scheme was a success, and the awards were
continued for some years. In the 1920s these groups became known as 4-H
clubs.

In February 1913 May sent a letter to each federation club outlining her
goals. She stated that her committee would direct every effort toward establishing vocational education throughout the state. As a first step each
woman's club should make the school building in its own locality a social
center, with fairs, exhibits, and "story hours" for small children. They
should assist in establishing tomato clubs and help fund the prizes, as well

as contribute to the kindergarten teachers' scholarship at the women's college. May pledged that her committee would work with the legislation committee to secure an increased appropriation for the state reform school at Marianna and that it would work to get women appointed to school boards. She urged each club to work for better school buildings and playgrounds and to endorse medical inspection and school hygiene programs.[39] May's vigorous approach to the committee's work surprised many of the clubwomen; they were used to more conservative leadership. Elizabeth Hocker wrote her, "You certainly have revolutionized our Education Department."[40] May's enthusiasm often inspired her colleagues to action. One woman informed May that by herself she had inspected her local school and had found "many faults." The writer also told May she was so interested in the education work that she was unable to "control her tongue" whenever she saw something that needed improvement.[41] Another clubwoman wondered if the education department was also planning to work for women's suffrage, for she thought it would be a "super subject" for the committee to tackle.[42]

On 28 May 1912, May was in Gainesville to address the State Conference of Superintendents, Members of School Boards, and High School Principals. Of the eighty-four speakers at the three-day conference, she was the only woman and the last on the agenda.[43] She told the educators what the federation was doing to aid education and called for better teacher training, higher salaries, longer school terms, smaller classes, uniform textbooks, school libraries and playgrounds, compulsory education, and allowing women to serve on school boards. She described the tomato and corn clubs and urged cooperation. She also urged the men to back improvements at the Marianna reform school. She was given a standing ovation, presented with a bouquet of flowers, and escorted from the dais by Superintendent of Public Instruction William Sheats.

When the 1913 legislative session convened, May and other clubwomen were ready. The memorial they submitted was no timid document; it included a list of fifteen demands that the women wanted the legislators to act upon. The women called for amendments to strengthen the 1911 juvenile court law; an annual $25,000 appropriation for the reform school; creation of a state board of charities; enactment of a comprehensive child labor bill; a prohibition against newspapers printing gory details of murders, executions, and suicides; establishment of a hospital for the feebleminded; a law prohibiting placement of advertising signs on trees, telephone poles, fences, and other structures along public highways; a bill allowing women to be elected to school boards; a law giving women the right to enter into contracts relating to their own property; a law making wife and child desertion a felony; and a law that would establish certification of nurses.[44]

May and her colleagues worked closely with the Florida Child Labor Committee, a new organization to promote child labor legislation, headed by John W. Stagg of Orlando, Marcus Fagg of Jacksonville, and Mary E. Randall of Lawtey, a federation member and close friend of May's. This committee and the clubwomen organized "parlor meetings" to promote their legislation.[45] They sponsored exhibits and lantern slide shows to educate the public about the issues. And while the legislature was in session they mounted an active letter-writing campaign. In addition, Julia Lathrop of the U.S. Children's Bureau in Washington was brought to Florida for a series of lectures. Ion Farris and St. Elmo Acosta of the Duval delegation introduced the child labor bill and guided it through the legislature. May knew both men well. Acosta had been one of the councilmen who had accompanied her on the publicized inspection tour of the Jacksonville jail in 1909, and Ion Farris's wife was an active clubwoman. Mrs. Frank E. Jennings, head of the federation's legislation committee, led the women's lobbying effort in Tallahassee. May also spent time there. She sent copies of the federation's memorial to the state's five major newspapers, and upon publication she personally distributed copies of the papers to each member of the legislature. Fagg and his associates also worked at the Capitol.

The results of their efforts were gratifying. The 1913 legislature voted a sizable two-year appropriation of $65,000 for the reform school and reorganized the facility, fired the management, and renamed the place the Florida Industrial School for Boys. It passed the most comprehensive child labor laws that had ever been enacted in the state, a wife and child desertion bill, and a measure authorizing women to serve as county probation officers. It enacted laws regulating the certification of nurses, strengthened the state's pure food and drug law, created the office of rural school inspector, raised the standards leading to teacher certification, and authorized special taxing districts to issue bonds for public education. In addition to these progressive measures it enacted conservation laws that established a game and fish commission and protected wild birds and animals. To May's personal satisfaction the lawmakers appropriated $3,000 to aid the tomato clubs. It was a very impressive record, but it left women without full property or legal rights and without the right to hold elective office, and it left Florida without a compulsory education law.[46]

After the session May returned to her club and civic activities. With the help of Caroline Brevard of Tallahassee, she secured a United Daughters of the Confederacy scholarship for the Women's College, to be awarded to the girl who was the runner-up in the federation's kindergarten teachers' scholarship selection. In June, Governor Trammel appointed May as Florida's delegate to the seventeenth Child Welfare Conference of the Parents' and Teachers' Association to be held in Boston. Because of family obligations she could not go but gave her proxy to the secretary of the Florida Federation of Mothers' Clubs, Mrs. Mary P. Brownell, who reported back to May. Selected a delegate to the National Hygiene Congress in Buffalo a month later, May was again unable to go; this time she gave her proxy to the medical inspector of the Duval County Schools.

The year 1913 continued to be a busy one for May. On October 10 she spoke before the Duval County School Board at a public meeting called to discuss the creation of a taxing district and the issuance of school bonds. She cited figures, statistics, and laws to show that the money was direly needed and that the proposed tax district was the proper means by which to raise the funds.

On other fronts, May became a sponsor of Pi Beta Phi sorority at Stetson University, where her son was enrolled, and attended several of the sorority's functions. She joined a committee to promote the improvement of the Columbia College Library in Lake City, and she worked for the Jacksonville Infant Welfare Society. She accompanied Elizabeth Hocker to Washington, D.C., to attend a General Federation board meeting and the convention of the National Council for Social Centers. She wrote an article on education for a special women's issue of the *Miami Herald*.[47] She helped push a resolution through the Jacksonville City Council regulating midwifery in the city. With the help of the Jacksonville Equal Franchise League, she worked to get a Sunday "blue law" passed by the council; a modified version was adopted. She organized the Jacksonville Woman's Club "legislation day." At year's end she and her husband packed and sent crates of oranges from their private groves to President Woodrow Wilson and all the members of his cabinet. William Jennings Bryan was Wilson's secretary of state.

It was also a year of trials and sorrow for the family. The Brooksville property demanded much of May's time. A large pecan orchard and strawberry patch had to be managed. Her brother's alcoholism worsened during the year and precipitated several crises, and her brother-in-law, Charles Jennings, became ill and died at the Jenningses' home in November. Perhaps May yearned, like her friend Lena Shackleford, "for the good old Brooksville Days when they lived the simple life."[48] But she never had time to look back; she was too busy making plans for the new year.

The whole of 1914 was a whirlwind of activity, with May setting a terrific pace for herself. In January she secured the woman's club building for a lecture and slide show presented by Dr. Eugene Swope, field agent of the Florida Audubon Society. That same month she met with Mrs. Frank E. Jennings and her federation legislation committee to discuss the new year's objectives. The legislature would not be in session, but both agreed that there was much publicity work and friendly preparatory lobbying to be done. May Jennings and Minerva Jennings, while rivals, respected each other's opinions and abilities and cooperated with one another for the good of the federation.

In February, May attended the third annual Conference of Florida Charities and Corrections in Gainesville, of which Marcus Fagg was then secretary. That month she also attended the first annual meeting of the Jacksonville Infant Welfare Society and journeyed to Tallahassee for a federation board meeting and to confer with Miss Harris. Later she led a discussion at the Jacksonville Woman's Club on practical politics.[49] She traveled to DeLand for a Pi Beta Phi social function.

Along with her travels, conventions, and speaking engagements, May had become the de facto president of the federation because Mrs. Hocker did not like to travel and was not as good a public speaker. Scores of letters arrived almost daily, seeking advice on how to form a woman's club, how to become a member of the federation, how to set up an education committee, how to present a public meeting, and so on. May employed a stenographer to help with the correspondence, paying the woman's wages herself and using supplies and postage furnished by the federation. May had to reject most of the requests to speak and appear at club functions. While all correspondence was conscientiously answered, May selected her personal appearances carefully. She attended only the important functions, although she tried to visit as many clubs as possible as she traveled around the state.

In March 1914, May spoke for the second time before the convention of superintendents and leading Florida educators in Fort Myers. Mrs. Edna Fuller of Orlando, chairperson of the federation's civics department, also was on the program. May called for cooperation between the federation and state educators. She outlined the work of the federation's education department, described the women's hopes for the coming years, and put the men on notice that it was time to "agitate forcefully for a compulsory education law."[50] While in Fort Myers she was feted by the local woman's club and toured Thomas Edison's winter home.

Upon her return to Jacksonville, May helped Marcus Fagg conduct the

Children's Home Society's annual Re-Union Week and invited Marie Randall of Lawtey, chairperson of the federation's social conditions department, to speak before the Jacksonville clubwomen. Later in March she met with Jacksonville probation officials about local juvenile delinquency problems, and she successfully petitioned the school board to retain the city's school nurses. Finally, she wrote all federation clubs urging them to wire their congressmen in support of the Smith-Lever Agriculture Extension bill, which was mired down in Congress.

In June 1914, May attended her first General Federation convention, held in Chicago. She heard addresses by Jane Addams of Hull House fame and by feminist Carrie Chapman Catt.[51] May enjoyed it immensely, especially meeting intelligent, hard-working women like herself who were committed to progressive change. After the convention the Jenningses took a brief holiday in North Carolina. Upon returning to Jacksonville May received a telegram summoning her to Bar Harbor, Maine, where her father was gravely ill. He died shortly after her arrival. Hundreds of prominent people from around the state attended the funeral services at the Jenningses' home and the burial at Evergreen Cemetery.

May missed her father terribly, for the two had remained very close to the end. But by the middle of October she was again deep into clubwork. The twentieth annual state federation convention was only a month away, and she was busy preparing a canning demonstration and education exhibit for the delegates. By the time of the 1914 convention at Lakeland, the Florida Federation of Women's Clubs was a mature and energetic organization; few officials failed to recognize its political strength. Scores of woman's clubs around the state now belonged to the organization, though there were still a few maverick holdouts in the Panhandle.

The convention opened on Tuesday, November 19, in the Lakeland Civic Auditorium. The women filled the hotels and overflowed into private homes. Receptions were held in the Kibler Hotel. Many delegates displayed the green and gold ribbons of the federation but were reminded that no hats were to be worn in the auditorium so that everyone would have an unrestricted view of the proceedings. After the usual greetings by local officials, a club member played a piano concerto and Mrs. Hocker gave her farewell address. Official business began the following day. Reports from seventy-two clubs described achievements and successes all over Florida. May's report on the education department was fourteen typewritten pages long. There were also talks by William Sheats, Dr. J. Y. Porter, and Judge William H. Baker. Election of a new slate of officers occurred on the third and last day of the meeting. There was no doubt who would be named president: May Jennings was chosen unanimously.

A cheer rose from the auditorium when her victory was announced. May's short speech was followed by a discussion of the federation's legislative program. There were calls for a compulsory education law, a state forestry board, a state board of charities, and a state bureau of vital statistics. Also on the list were a girl's industrial training school, a state tuberculosis sanitorium, a school for the feebleminded, a law allowing women to serve on school boards, and passage of a prohibition amendment. At the banquet that night, May pledged to fulfill her duties faithfully and to uphold the objectives of the federation. At forty-two, May Jennings had become the most politically powerful woman in the state.

CHAPTER 7

Madam President and the Old-Girl Network

U NDER May Jennings's guidance the Florida Federation of Women's Clubs increased in numbers and in political strength. During her three-year tenure fifty-nine new clubs joined the federation, bringing its membership to 9,163. The federation became one of the state's largest organizations. During May's first month as president one goal was quietly added to those that had been determined at the Lakeland convention: on the federation's books since 1905, the conservation resolution called for the preservation of Royal Palm Hammock on Paradise Key, an Everglades islet twelve miles southwest of Homestead in Dade County. As soon as May's election as president was confirmed, delegates from South Florida approached her to urge her to revive the resolution and to join them in the effort to save the endangered hammock. These women were led by Mary Barr Munroe, wife of the distinguished author Kirk Munroe, and by Edith Gifford, wife of John Gifford, a forestry expert and a former Cornell University professor who was living in Coconut Grove.

The women spoke to May about the long-forgotten federation resolution to preserve the key. They described the magnificent stand of royal palms and the lush tropical vegetation that grew on the key, citing past preservation efforts by their husbands and other naturalists and scientists, including H. P. Rolfs, forestry professor at the University of Florida; N. L. Britton, director of the New York Botanical Garden; Charles Simpson, operator of a private botanical garden in Dade County; Edward Simmonds, chief botanist for the Agriculture Department in Dade County; David Fairchild, head of the U.S. Office of Foreign Seed and Plant Introduction in Coconut Grove; and James K. Small, curator of the New York Botanical Garden. Over the years each of these men had visited Paradise Key to admire and study its palms and vegetation, and since 1893 they had been trying to get the national government to preserve the hammock. Now in 1914 the hammock was in danger of being destroyed. Surveyors and road crews were at that very moment mapping the area for future development. Flagler's Key West railroad extension lay only a few miles east of the key, and a highway from Homestead to Flamingo was in the planning stages.

Captivated by what she heard from the women, May was moved by their pleas for help. She had never visited the key, but she had always liked South Florida and was drawing up building plans for a vacation home on the Jenningses' property in Miami. From her earlier travels with her husband to inspect the dredges and drainage canals, May realized that the construction of roads into the interior would probably destroy much of the wildness and serenity of the Everglades. Her decision only hours after her election as federation president to make the preservation of Paradise Key one of her administration's main goals was to have historic and far-reaching consequences for Florida, launching her upon a political, economic, and public relations struggle that would span thirty-three years.

During May's tenure as federation president, many of the organization's major goals would be achieved. Under her guidance the federation would wield effective political power by capitalizing on its unique old-girl network, a web of statewide friendships among the clubwomen, many of whom were related to the state's most powerful male business, political, and civic leaders. During May's presidency the federation would use its only real political weapon—these family and friendship connections—to gain access to the state's highest circles of power.

An aggressive and perceptive federation president had only to call upon the network to gain entry to the governor's mansion, the legislature, the courts, state boards and commissions, county commissions, and town and village councils in a roundabout but effective way. Many, though not all, men seemed to be more receptive to the urgings of female relatives—

mothers, wives, sisters, and daughters—than to demands of nameless clubwomen. These first contacts often smoothed the way for May and her lobbyists. Even the "cult of southern womanhood" occasionally worked in the federation's favor, disposing men to give the women respectful, if grudging, audiences. But it was the network—a device well known to men for so long—that May relied upon the most often to gain the ears of Florida officials and politicians.

During her years as federation president, May called upon the services of perhaps a hundred of the organization's most prominent members. Among the women's families were one sitting governor, three former governors, one U.S. senator, nineteen state legislators, six prominent journalists, two state supreme court justices, one state railroad commissioner, two members of the state Board of Control, three state judges, a private secretary to two governors, and three college presidents.[1] In addition to this core, there were hundreds of members who were related to prominent local businessmen, bankers, civic leaders, and city and county officials.

May's first use of the federation's network was on behalf of Paradise Key. The women from South Florida had notified her that Flagler's widow, Mary Kenan Flagler, had offered to donate 960 acres of the key and surrounding land to help preserve the hammock. News of this offer had been relayed by James Ingraham to Kirk Munroe, and hence to Mary Munroe, an avid conservationist and bird lover. May thought that in light of the Flagler gift, the state might be willing to donate the remaining land for a park, provided it would not have to assume maintenance of it. It was a bold idea to think that the federation could maintain and operate a public park.

In early December 1914, May wrote a letter to federation officers describing the hammock and setting forth her plan to develop it as a park. She wanted those who approved to accompany her to Tallahassee to speak to Governor Trammell and other state officials. Although many of the officers agreed that preservation of the hammock would be a fine civic gesture, several questioned the feasibility of the federation assuming such a financial burden.[2] Fortunately, the doubters were in a minority, and May proceeded with her plans, including a request for a $1,000 annual state appropriation for the park. No one volunteered to accompany her to Tallahassee, but the old-girl network smoothed her way. Florence Cay telephoned Virginia Trammell to (as Mrs. Cay described it) "touch upon the subject of the hammock."[3] Cautious but encouraging, Mrs. Trammell said she would speak to the governor.

During the second week in December, May took a train to Tallahassee, where she apparently stayed with the Trammells in the governor's residence. Few people knew the real purpose of her visit. A Tallahassee paper reported: "Mrs. William S. Jennings, the brilliant wife of former Governor Jennings . . . is making a brief visit to the Capitol city, and is being charmingly entertained at the Governor's Mansion by Mrs. Park Trammell." [4] While in the city May also met with Agnes Harris at the Women's College to discuss home economics and the extension work the federation was sponsoring. Florence Cay accompanied May when she met with the cabinet members, all trustees of the Internal Improvement Fund. Governor Trammell must have been won over, for he promised to present the federation's request at the next meeting of the trustees. On 23 December, the trustees approved a letter authorizing the Dade County Commission to take action to prevent trespassing on the hammock land owned by the state. Mrs. W. J. Tweedell, the wife of one of the commissioners, was a prominent clubwoman in Homestead and May's friend.

The next day, the state trustees voted to grant tentatively the federation park request, subject to legislative approval. The trustees planned to visit South Florida in January, and May, who was apprised of their action, was asked not to reveal the news to the public until after that trip. In fact, the trustees did not need legislative approval to grant and convey the land, but the unusual nature of the federation's request may have made them more cautious than usual. Endorsement by the governor or the trustees was no guarantee that the lawmakers would give their approval. Only intense lobbying efforts would ensure success.

The day after Christmas the Jennings family traveled to Miami for a round of official federation visits. Much time was taken up with routine club business, but on 28 December, accompanied by her husband and son and Mrs. T. V. Moore, Mrs. A. Leight Monroe, and Mary Barr Munroe, May journeyed to Paradise Key to see Royal Palm Hammock for herself. The trip must have been bone-jarring since the road out to the key was little more than a boggy cow path, barely passable by auto during the wet season. Pictures of the region during that period often show a stranded Model T hub-high in mud, the occupants digging and pushing to get it unstuck. In a letter to Elizabeth Hocker, May referred to the trip: "The Hammock is entirely surrounded by water, the palms tower much above the other growth. . . . The women down in that part of the country are very enthusiastic over the Park subject." [5]

When, after visiting the key, the trustees notified May that they approved of the property grant to the federation, the news was released to the public. This action marked a quiet but dramatic change in state government policy, no matter how grudging the approval or how reluctant the assumption of the care of the proposed park, or that, as some said, they concurred only because the land was unfit for anything else. The hammock would become Florida's first state park, albeit privately owned, and would be an important step toward establishing the Everglades National Park in the future.

After May received notification of the trustees' action she began to mobilize the federation. Her husband drafted a bill to be presented to the legislature, calling for the state to deed to the federation 960 acres to match the Flagler grant and to provide $1,000 annually for maintenance of the park. May and her friends knew that the public had to be rallied in support of the project; legislators had to be alerted; pamphlets and other material about the proposed park would have to be printed; speeches would have to be given and press releases written. And the legislature would convene in only a few weeks.

During this period May also supervised a statewide campaign to register births, a cause the federation had adopted to alert the public to the need for a bureau of vital statistics. The work was done under the auspices of Julia Lathrop, director of the Children's Bureau of the federal government. May also corresponded with William Sheats, state superintendent of public instruction, about education bills to be submitted to the upcoming legislature. Sheats favored a county-option compulsory education bill, while May wanted a stronger law to compel attendance. She was also working with a federation committee to present to the state officials plans for rebuilding the Industrial School for Boys at Marianna, which had just had a major fire. The women favored a new facility based on a family-style cottage plan. In addition, May was working with home economist Agnes Harris to prevent state officials from usurping all the funds that Florida was receiving from the new federal Smith-Lever Act. In one nearby state the local land-grant college had already announced that only 24 percent of the money would be allotted to female educational needs, despite the fact that half was designated by law for extension work among rural farm women. Florida women had received only $2,000 of a $10,000 federal grant.

As soon as news of the proposed Royal Palm Park was released to the public, May began to enlist support for the project. She tried to get Washington to declare the hammock a national bird and wildlife sanctuary but was unsuccessful in her effort. As the time for the legislative session approached, she and her officers worked diligently to complete the federation's 1915 legislative program. May wrote a friend, "I am very hopeful that we shall succeed in getting many things through the Legislature for there are a great many clubwomen who are wives of legislators, who will be on the ground in Tallahassee to keep in close touch with our bills."[6] Chairing the legislation committee was Jessie McGriff (Mrs. John Mc-Griff) of Jacksonville, who planned to spend the first weeks of the session in Tallahassee directing the federation's lobby efforts. May had a federation speaking tour planned and was to go to the capital only after Mrs. McGriff returned home. Hindsight would show that May's time would have been better spent if she had canceled the tour and gone directly to Tallahassee.

When the federation's legislative resolution was approved, copies were sent to the governor, the cabinet, and all members of the legislature, including Cary Hardee, speaker of the house, whose wife was a club-woman, and A. E. Davis, president of the senate. The federation resolution called for the land grant to establish the park; enactment of a compulsory education bill; creation of a girls' industrial school; rebuilding of the boys' school at Marianna; erection of a state tuberculosis hospital; establishment of a forestry board, a bureau of vital statistics, and a board of charities; land for the Seminoles; development of roads; and a law allowing women to serve on school boards. It was a formidable list.

Assured that all was proceeding without problems, May departed on her speaking tour and to attend a federation board of directors meeting at Dade City that included a visit to St. Leo Abbey and College hosted by Abbot Charles Mohr. Informed by correspondence preceding the meeting that only the abbot could get the women into the college's buildings, "Who," May asked in jest, "could get them out?" The reply came that "after the women saw the Abbot none would want out."[7] The handsome abbot proved to be a charming host; he served luncheon to the clubwomen, then conducted them "through the buildings where they had the privilege of viewing the beautiful vestments and symbols and received special prayers in the chapel."[8] May, who shared stories of her St. Joseph school days adventures with Abbot Mohr, corresponded with him for many years.

Unfortunately, all was not well in Tallahassee. Jessie McGriff, who was inexperienced at legislative work, personally edited the federation's resolution and deleted the request for a $1,000 annual park appropriation. The sum for the girls' industrial school was also reduced, and a new demand for free textbooks was inserted. In addition, Minnie Moore Willson, a longtime champion of the Seminoles, arrived at the Capitol to lobby for the Indian land grant. Outspoken and abrasive, she generated resentment among the legislators by threatening reprisals if the bill was not enacted, thereby doing much damage to the federation's cause. May was furious when she learned of these actions. Mrs. McGriff, who was lukewarm to the park project, seemed to be unaware of the trouble that had been created, but the lawmakers were already balking at granting either the park land or the Seminole grant. Many felt that the Paradise Key acreage was not good for anything, especially a park.

May wrote Mrs. McGriff, "If the park tract is so dense and useless, I do not see why the men are so anxious to keep it if we are anxious to have it." [9] A letter from Lena Shackleford about the woes of lobbying reached May at Dade City and added to her alarm. Mrs. Shackleford wrote, "I will be glad to see you back over here, perhaps you can do something. . . . [The Legislators] all look so kind and promising when we talk to them and then turn away and forget that we were ever there." [10] May had to go to Tallahassee to mend fences and to reestablish the federation's credibility.

May's trip to the capital at first appeared successful, for the $1,000 for the park was put back into the bill. She lobbied Senator Glen Terrell and others on behalf of the boys' and girls' schools, and she pushed the education, Indian, and vital statistics bills before the appropriate legislative committees. She left Tallahassee falsely assured that the measures would pass without further trouble. The park bill again met with resistance, and several of the other bills were killed outright in committee. During the last days of the session, when the outcome seemed dismal, Governor Jennings and Bryan, who had just graduated from Stetson University law school, traveled to Tallahassee to lobby for the bill. May had planned to be in the capital up to the last moment working for the bill, but illness, brought on by severe exhaustion, kept her at home. Time was crucial not only because the session was closing but also because publicity had incited vandals and road crews to dig up many of the palms and other exotic plants on the key. The legislature was scheduled to recess 4 June 1915; it would not meet again for two years. Finally on 2 June, May received a telegram from Bryan: "House passed Park Bill." The next day her husband wired: "Park Bill passed Senate midnight." [11] The bill had been enacted literally at the last minute.

May's joy was short lived. She soon learned that the appropriation had been cut out of the bill by its opponents. How was the federation to develop a state park for public purposes with no funding? Grateful yet frustrated, May sent letters of appreciation to Herbert Drane and Harry Goldstein, sponsors of the bill, and to all the others who had voted for the park as well as other federation legislation. Trying to boost everyone's morale, May notified her officers that the paths, lodge, and pavilions envisioned for the park could still be built and that the federation would secure the funds elsewhere, but, in truth, she had no idea where the money would come from.

Despite the disappointments, it had been a successful legislative session for the federation. The boys' industrial school had received adequate funding and a new cottage plan was adopted for its campus. A girls' industrial school had been created, though it was not well funded and there was talk of locating it at an old Marion County prison farm. A county-option compulsory education bill was passed. Several laws promoting good roads were enacted, including one that created the state's first road department. A state bureau of vital statistics was established, and retention homes for delinquent children were mandated for each county. However, there were failures: There was still no forestry board, state tuberculosis hospital, land for the Seminoles, or law allowing females to serve on school boards. But, in general, May was satisfied with the outcome of the session.

Beyond the group's legislative program, May had many other federation business matters to attend to during her first year as president. The volume of her correspondence continued to grow; she was the leader of an organization with twenty departments, ninety-one clubs, and 6,000 members. She employed a second part-time stenographer to help not only with her federation correspondence but also that relating to her duties as president of the Springfield Improvement Association, and of the DAR and the YWCA. She had also been appointed state chairperson of the Belgian Relief Committee with the responsibility of raising money and goods for war-stricken European refugees, and she was laboring tirelessly to promote the club movement and to bring even more women into civic work. She wanted the women of Florida to become better educated in practical politics and civic service. She wrote a paper about the federation and its work and her views and feelings about woman's clubs and mailed a copy to each unaffiliated club in the state.[12]

May was often asked to solve domestic problems stemming from family opposition to her colleagues' club work. When one woman wrote May that her husband was demanding that she stop her club work, May wrote back, "I do not think a man has any right to ask a woman to stay home and do everything for him. It takes a good deal of conceit to imagine he is so complete that he can satisfy anybody all in himself. . . . I am not going to give you up without a struggle, husband or no. . . . I am very belligerent just now."[13]

With the adjournment of the legislature, work on the federation's other objectives continued. South Florida women managed to get the Dade

County commissioners to name the new highway to Flamingo in honor of J. E. Ingraham, who had helped to secure the park land from the legislature and the Flagler estate. The federation's civics department sponsored a statewide cleanup campaign, urging cities to beautify their parks, public facilities, and roadways. Beautification programs had a long and popular history with the federation, and it was a logical step for the women to take an interest in highway beautification, especially since the state was at the beginning of a "good roads" boom. A special federation committee began making plans to beautify the Dixie Highway being built from Chicago to Miami. It ran from Thomasville, Georgia, to Tallahassee, then to Jacksonville and down the east coast to Miami. The federation took on the responsibility for the last seventy-eight miles of the road that ran through Miami to the newly acquired park. Governor Jennings, a member of the Dixie Highway Commission, and Carl Fisher, whose wife, Jane, was a federation member, were the highway's chief promoters. The federation later sponsored statewide antilitter and antibillboard campaigns. Its other projects during 1915 included funding a bed for an indigent patient at Dr. Hiram Byrd's private tuberculosis sanatorium in South Florida and funding the travels and lectures of a home economics demonstration agent from Stetson University.

Most of May's time was occupied with the park project. Besides money, she needed public support. To secure funds she wrote every newspaper, organization, and individual that might be interested in helping the federation, including such philanthropists as John D. Rockefeller, Andrew Carnegie, and Charles Deering. Thomas A. Edison, a winter resident of Fort Myers, whom May had met, sent $50. The small amounts of money that began to trickle in to the park fund were never enough. Mrs. Flagler's endowment was secured, and renting some of the land to area farmers brought in several hundred dollars.

During 1915 May took no vacation. In July she spoke before the State Board of Control on behalf of the Smith-Lever funds and the girls' industrial school. In August she held a federation board meeting at Fort Lauderdale. By September she was back on the club circuit. One friend wrote her, "Your energy is colossal, surpassed only by your ability." [14] To lighten her burdens Governor Jennings suprised her in September with a new Welch automobile that he purchased while on a business trip to New York City. Thrilled, May wrote to a friend, "The president is going to ride in style from now on, if she has sense enough to run the machine." [15] But even though her son offered to give her lessons, it was many years before May Jennings learned to drive. Her immediate transportation dilemma was solved when Benny, the Jenningses' houseman and gardener, became May's chauffeur. On long trips she continued to travel by train.

By 1915 the move for equal suffrage for women was beginning to develop in Florida, although the state was never to play a major role in the national suffragist movement. There were several women's rights organizations operating in the state. The first, organized in Jacksonville in 1912 by friends of May's, many of whom were federation members, was the Florida Equal Franchise League, affiliated with the National American Woman Suffrage Association.[16]

Prior to 1918, membership in Florida's suffrage leagues read like a Who's Who of the FFWC rolls. Dr. Mary Jewett, Mary Bryan (Mrs. William Jennings Bryan), Annie Broward, and Ivy Stranahan took turns guiding the Florida Equal Suffrage Association. In many cases the membership rosters of the various town and city suffrage leagues were identical to those of the federation. On more than one occasion the federation and the Florida Equal Suffrage Association shared the place and date of their yearly conventions, so that the state's clubwomen could conveniently attend both meetings without economic hardship.

May was especially sympathetic to the goals of the suffragists, although as president of the federation she felt she could make no public endorsement without the membership's official approval. On several occasions, she was urged to support the movement publicly. Edith Stoner, officer of the Southern States' Woman's Suffrage Conference, wrote, "You are the one woman in Florida who can carry your state for suffrage."[17] Mary Jewett, federation member from Orlando and friend of Dr. Anna Shaw, national leader of the National American Woman Suffrage Association, also urged May to take a stand. When Dr. Shaw arrived in Jacksonville for a public lecture, May did escort her around the city, but she felt tied by the views of the rank and file of the federation, who were opposed to becoming involved in as controversial a subject as equal suffrage. But she had determined that it was time to change those views; she believed that the federation should endorse suffrage, and she began to work to that end.

The twenty-first annual federation convention was held at DeLand in November 1915, marking May's first year as president of the organization. Over a hundred clubwomen attended. Among those on the program were J. L. Boone, superintendent of the Boys' Industrial School, Dr. H. W. Cox, professor of psychology at the University of Florida who spoke about industrial education, and L. C. Spencer, U.S. Indian Agent to the Seminoles. May's address to the convention, tracing the history of women's struggles, was sprinkled with phrases like "Divine Plan," "great scheme of life," and "Eternal Ideal."[18] It was not one of her better speeches, but she received a standing ovation from an appreciative audience. Her official report noted that during the year she had visited each of the state's five club sections, held five board of directors meetings, talked before 101 clubs, written 1,869 letters, and traveled 5,164 miles on club business.

During the meeting a motion supporting equal suffrage for women and making it an official subject for federation study was brought before the convention. After a brief discussion, at which only token opposition emerged, the motion was passed. The federation also voted into membership the Orlando Suffrage League, the state's most active suffrage organization. Other leagues would soon join, making the federation Florida's largest organization supporting suffrage. Freed to speak upon the subject, May would urge all clubs within the federation to study the subject of equal suffrage, believing that education would weaken the arguments of those women who opposed the movement.

During 1916 May continued to promote suffrage, the park, land for the Seminoles, and public health. The financial situation of the park remained desperate. She tried to get a U.S. weather station assigned to the key, but there was one nearby in Miami. A statewide "mile-of-dimes" campaign was launched, in which foot-long cardboard folders with slots for twelve dimes were distributed, but the campaign brought in less than $1,000 toward a $6,000 goal. Nevertheless, the federation hired a park caretaker, Charles Mosier. He had worked at "Vizcaya," James Deering's Miami estate, and was knowledgeable about the hammock region, having explored it with Dr. Small and Dr. Fairchild. In March the Mosier family moved to the park, setting up housekeeping in a tent. Mosier's letters to May were full of accounts of bouts with mosquitoes, poisonous snakes, torrential rains, scorching heat, and grass fires. He cut paths, constructed picnic tables, and guided sightseers. And, despite the lack of money, work on a lodge at the park was begun.

Referring to the park as her "great hobby," May continued her search for money.[19] She wrote to E. A. McIlhenny, tabasco sauce tycoon from Avery, Louisiana, about raising and selling tropical birds. She even explored the possibility of President Woodrow Wilson making the park a national monument, but to no avail. Some women thought that amusement rides at the park would bring in visitors and money, but May quickly vetoed this idea. She wrote, "If they want a merry-go-round and shoot-the-shoot let them go to the [Miami] beach."[20] When funds were critically low, the old-girl network was pressed into service. Several local clubwomen, wives of Dade County commissioners, succeeded in securing a one-year $1,200 appropriation from the commission. With this $1,200 and money borrowed from federation funds designated for other purposes, the lodge and other improvements were eventually completed.

May also spent much time supervising the federation's public health committee, headed by Dr. Grace Whitford of Ozona. During the year the committee sponsored the sale of Red Cross seals, a statewide "Baby Week," the medical inspection of schools, the dissemination of information on communicable diseases, and health exhibits which toured on a train. It also aided in the hiring of nurses in fifteen of the state's health districts. Two members of the committee served on a state commission that investigated the need for a state institution for the feebleminded and the retarded.

Another matter that consumed much of May's time in 1916 was developing plans to help the Seminole Indians. Ivy Stranahan of Fort Lauderdale was chairman of the federation's Indian committee. She and May worked to further congressional passage of the Sears bill, to provide for a government grant of nearly 100,000 acres to the Indians, which Senator Fletcher and Congressman Sears were backing. Factions developed over what lands to award and how they should be used. Minnie Moore Willson and others felt that only unspoiled Everglades acreage, good for hunting, should be granted to the Seminoles. May and Mrs. Stranahan, as well as the Bureau of Indian Affairs, argued that the Indians should receive drained lands that could be used for farming and cattle grazing. They also favored building an industrial training school for the Indians on the land. Mrs. Willson's contentiousness and threats finally alienated many people, and May broke off federation cooperation with her.

During 1916 May continued her tours of Florida. While speaking before clubs and other groups she always talked about her favorite project, the park. As she once told Mosier, the park was special; she "was more fond of plants and plant growth than anything in the world."[21] She began to make plans for a grand celebration at the park during the federation convention scheduled for the following fall in Miami.

May's hectic pace continued for the rest of 1916. She urged the presidents of Stetson University and the two state universities to make Spanish a requirement for graduation. She sponsored Charlotte Dye of Birmingham, Alabama, as matron of the new girls' industrial school. She authored a paper entitled "Beautification of Florida Highways," which was read at the annual Florida Good Roads Association convention in St. Augustine. She secured the federation's endorsement of the Keating-Owens child labor bill pending in Congress. And she attended the General Federation's biennial convention in New York City in June 1916, where she saw her resolution calling for beautification of the Dixie Highway passed by the group. Always an ardent gardener, she was pleased when Dr. Henry Nehrling, a South Florida horticulturist, honored her by naming a beautiful new hybrid amaryllis after her.

The major event of the federation's twenty-second annual convention in Miami in 1916 was the formal dedication of Royal Palm Park. On 23 November a motorcade of 168 cars, "Fords, Cadillacs, Maxwells, Overlands, and every other kind," left Miami's Halcyon Hotel for the park. More than 1,000 persons attended the ceremony, with May Jennings presiding. After introductions, a dedication prayer, and the federation park committee's official report came a speech by James Ingraham, guest of honor. The *Miami Herald* reported that he made "a most delightful speech, telling in intimate conversational terms first of his early discovery of Paradise Key, of his talk with both Mr. and Mrs. Flagler on the subject, of the title claim made by the railroad and then most whimsically of Mrs. Jennings's attempts to have a bill put through the legislature. . . . The difficulties in this line were depicted, the promises of legislators, the consultation with the wise old lawyer [Governor Jennings] and the last indefatigable efforts which resulted in the land being given, but not the money." [22]

Following the keynote address by the General Federation's conservation chairperson, Mrs. John D. Sherman of Chicago, Dr. Charles T. Simpson, who had identified and tagged the park's trees, described the botanical characteristics of the park. Then May rose and dedicated the park with simple words, "With the power vested in me as president of the Florida Federation of Women's Clubs I hereby dedicate this Royal Palm Park to the people of Florida and their children forever." [23]

Even though the lodge was not yet completed, a picnic lunch was served on the grounds. No prominent state official attended, but among the crowd were loyalists who had supported the park from the beginning: Mary and Kirk Munroe, Mr. and Mrs. W. J. Tweedell, Mr. and Mrs. Bion H. Barnett, Ivy Stranahan, Lucy Blackman, Annie Broward, Dr. P. H. Rolfs, Florence Cay, Sudie B. Wright, Dollie Hendley, Iva Sproule-Baker, Mary B. Jewett, Grace Whitford, Mrs. Harry Minium, Minerva Jennings, Mrs. E. C. Loveland, and Governor Jennings and Bryan.

Returning to the Miami convention, the women took up the matter of suffrage. After Mary Bryan's address on the subject, an equal suffrage plank was endorsed and added to the legislative program. Other speakers at the meeting were Dr. E. M. Nighbert, who talked on wiping out the cattle fever tick, and state agriculture agent Bradford Knapp, who talked about rural extension work. An endowment fund was established for the federation, and Stephen Foster's "Suwanee River" was recommended as the state song. In the president's report, May noted that since the last convention she had delivered forty-eight speeches, handled 5,364 pieces of mail, and traveled over 10,000 miles on club business.

The 1917 legislation resolution that the women adopted contained some twenty-five items. It called for an annual state appropriation of $5,000 for the park, land for the Seminole Indians, creation of the position of state forester and of special forest fire tax districts, endorsement of state amendments on prohibition and equal suffrage, an act allowing women to serve on school boards, a special appropriation to the home economics department at the Florida State College for Women in Tallahassee, equal division of the state's Smith-Lever funds, health examinations for teachers, free textbooks for all school children, appropriations for the boys' and girls' industrial schools and women members on their boards of managers, stronger child labor laws, a minimum wage and hours bill for female employees, a state tuberculosis sanatorium, regulation of medical advertisements, and endorsement of bills outlawing public executions, prohibiting signs and billboards on public highways, and setting aside Alligator Bay rookery as a bird reservation. Many of these demands supported measures that were already advocated by the General Federation or that were pending before Congress. Florida women and the federation had come a long way since 1895 when one modest proposal of less than forty words had been submitted to the legislature. Now, even though the women could still not vote or hold office, they were a constituency to be reckoned with, and the legislature was aware of their political influence.

The Jennings family celebrated Christmas 1916 at their home in Miami, where May and Sherman began to spend more and more time. Their cousins William and Mary Bryan had a home, "Villa Serena," next to their own Brickell Avenue house, and the two couples often entertained together. The Bryans were outspoken supporters of prohibition and equal suffrage and stumped the state on behalf of these issues. Mrs. Bryan was chairman of the Florida Equal Suffrage Association's legislation committee and a member of the federation. The Bryans sometimes held open houses and teas at their villa to raise money for their causes. At one such event on behalf of women's suffrage, "a plate was discreetly left by the door into which the thoughtful made contributions. . . . Sixty-six dollars was raised and when the amount was announced, Governor Jennings promptly announced he would double [it]." [24]

The 1917 inauguration of Sidney J. Catts as governor signaled a move to the right in Florida. While progressives did not completely relinquish their hold on state government, conservatives were gaining the initiative. While progressive reforms that had been under way for some time retained their momentum, many were instituted only after strong resistance from conservative legislators. Catts's racial, moral, and religious views cast a pall over the state, creating situations that tended to polarize the people. Governor Jennings had supported James V. Knott, Catts's opponent, and both he and May were alarmed when Catts was elected. To quell her uneasiness about the outcome of the 1917 legislative session after Catts assumed office, May struck up a friendship with the new governor and tried to maintain an open mind about his administration. In turn, Catts was impressed with May when they met, and he wrote, "We all like you very much indeed and I am also charmed with your son whom I met." [25]

Just as supporters of equal suffrage were to be found in large numbers in the federation, many women were members of both the federation and the Women's Christian Temperance Union. Prohibition sentiment mounted in Florida, in part as a result of Catts's tirades against "blind tigers" and sinners. Although May favored prohibition, she never joined the WCTU. At the 1914 federation convention, clubwomen had gone on record in favor of prohibition. Two years later, they had endorsed a stronger prohibition plank. Those who opposed prohibition objected when its supporters sang a popular WCTU rally song:

> Florida, Florida
> Dry! Dry! Dry!
> Hear us tell it.
> Everybody yell it.
> 1917 is the day.
> You help, I help.
> That's the way.
> We will do it.
> See us try.
> Line up, Florida.
> Dry! Dry! Dry! [26]

The state prohibitionists' organization was the only organized group that from the beginning of the suffrage movement supported the women in their call for the franchise.

Before the 1917 legislative session, May made several trips. After organizing the Duval County Federation of Woman's Clubs in January, she traveled to Macon, Georgia, to address the Conference on Industry and Education of Southern Women. In New Orleans she addressed a General Federation council meeting on the subject of cooperation, which she saw as a necessity if Americans were to do their part in the war effort against Germany, declared in April. May then spent four weeks in Tallahassee tending the federation's legislative program.

The lawmakers of the 1917 session seemed more intransigent and opposed to the women than ever. Despite strong pressure from the old-girl network and telegrams and letters from the federation's rank and file, the legislators refused to fund the park, create a state forester position, or enact a law allowing women to serve on school boards. They did, however, set aside nearly 100,000 acres of Monroe County for the Seminoles, only about 5 percent of which was arable. They also created a State School Book Commission, permitted the building of county-option tuberculosis hospitals, and created a livestock sanitary board. Debates on prohibition resulted in a resolution endorsing national prohibition.

May spent much time talking to legislators and appearing before committees. On weekends she traveled to Jacksonville to attend to her voluminous correspondence, writing to a friend, "You cannot realize what an exacting task master legislative work is. . . . I am worn completely out, have been before two committees on appropriation and before the Forestry committee. I am simply snowed under with work." [27]

The fight for equal suffrage was the most heated and prolonged battle of the session. May worked tirelessly with Mary Bryan, Ivy Stranahan, and Annie Broward, all officers of the Florida Equal Suffrage Association. When Mrs. Bryan addressed a joint session of the legislature on behalf of suffrage, May, Ivy Stranahan, Florence Cay, Mary Jewett, Lena Shackleford, Marjory Stoneman Douglas, and scores of enthusiastic supporters filled the gallery. Mrs. Bryan was introduced by Cary Hardee, speaker of the house and no friend of suffrage. Although she spoke for over an hour and received a standing ovation, it was unlikely that she changed the minds of many lawmakers, despite the fact that suffrage had won the support of several of the legislature's most respected members, including Ion Farris and Doyle Carlton, other prominent Floridians, and many of the state's largest newspapers. "The suffragists brought two bills to Tallahassee with them. One was an equal suffrage primary bill which if adopted would permit women to vote in all primary elections and hold certain offices. The second was a resolution providing for a constitutional amendment granting equal suffrage to be submitted to the voters for ratification. Governor Jennings wrote both measures. . . . In the House, W. H. Marshall of Broward introduced the two measures. . . . Companion bills were introduced in the Senate by W. L. Hughlett of Cocoa."[28]

The legislature balked at the primary suffrage bill, but the state constitutional amendment resolution was reported out of committee. On 20 April, a long and sometimes heated debate on the bill began in the senate. Senators Hughlett, W. A. McWilliams of St. Augustine, James E. Alexander of DeLand, Doyle Carlton of Tampa, Ion Farris of Jacksonville, A. S. Wells of Tallahassee, John L. Moore of DeFuniak Springs, and H. L. Oliver of Apalachicola supported the resolution. John B. Johnson, president of the senate, led the opposition, which argued that if women had the right to vote, blacks would also want to vote in the Democratic primaries. There was some fear that equal suffrage would destroy "home and American motherhood." Adopting both prohibition and equal suffrage in one year was too much for some legislators. The bill was defeated by a vote of eighteen to eight. Three days later, however, the resolution was brought up for reconsideration at a time when some of the measure's opponents were absent, and it passed by a vote of twenty-three to seven.[29] Supporters were jubilant, and women in the gallery who had kept a round-the-clock vigil cheered wildly when the results were announced.

The battle then shifted to the house, where debate was likewise vigorous, with a very vocal minority led by Hardee. After two days of debate, the measure was defeated by a margin of five votes. The following day when the resolution was reconsidered, it again lost. The primary suffrage bill failed even to clear committee, and May asked to have it withdrawn. A bill favoring presidential suffrage was not even introduced. While these battles were going on, the legislature was passing a series of acts that gave women in some designated communities the right to vote in local elections.

May saw victory in defeat: Against great odds, women had come within five votes of securing approval of a state constitutional amendment granting them the franchise. She felt that the effort had provided a political education for Florida women, but many suffragists, especially those in South Florida, were not satisfied with the legislature's actions or with May Jennings's leadership. Several clubs threatened to withdraw from the federation, blaming May for poor judgment and for buckling under to the men by allowing the primary suffrage bill to be withdrawn. May was also attacked by the *Miami Metropolis*. Always the pragmatist, she explained that she had withdrawn the bill to cut her losses, to avoid a long, no-win confrontation between the legislators and the federation.

She wrote a friend, "I am rather disgusted that all my efforts put forth in behalf of suffrage should have been so misinterpreted. . . . I have worked very hard for the bills but felt it would be better to have all than only halfway measures. . . . It would give the men a loop hole to say they had given us something. It would make it harder for us to secure full suffrage in time to come. . . . It is much better to push and work for a better campaign for the next two years, and stir up interest in the constitutional amendment. I am frank to say there will have to be a great deal of work done among the women of Florida, and be sure there will be no representatives returned to the legislature who will not support the suffrage amendment. This means a great deal of work, if we thoroughly organize the state, and begin at once, there is no reason why we should not succeed." [30]

During the legislative struggle over suffrage, Alice Paul, radical feminist and president of the controversial National Woman's Party, had visited Jacksonville to promote her organization and establish a local affiliate. May rejected her invitation to join forces, writing a friend, "Alice Paul was here a few weeks ago [and] nearly pestered me to death. . . . I made it plain to her as possible, that I did not approve of a new organization being formed, and that I understood this was the republican party, and whenever there were two parties in the state, it would probably defeat any legislation. . . . She insisted she would do no state work, only concentrate on the Susan B. Anthony amendment." [31]

Considering the atmosphere surrounding the 1917 legislative session—the country at war, a controversial new governor, and two major emotional issues—the outcome was probably as good as could have been expected. May was nevertheless disappointed, especially over the failure to get the park appropriation: "I am brokenhearted, after all our work and the promises made us . . . the House refused to let the park bill come up. I know now more than ever that women *must* have the vote if they are to accomplish anything. The legislature gave away thousands to themselves but the only thing asked by the women they never intended from the first to grant. . . . I am worn out with our so called wonderful lawmakers and I am beginning to think that women are fools to work as they do for the good of the world . . . the men make promises one minute and vote the other way the next." [32] In spite of the failure, May planned to resubmit her park bill to the 1919 legislature. She informed one club officer that the park committee was also thinking of submitting a bill to create still another state park on the Suwannee River, "which would of course include a great deal of the river bank." [33] At the conclusion of the legislative session May made plans for another state tour. Besides her responsibilities for the federation, she had accepted new duties connected with the war. She was

serving on the General Federation's war emergency committee. Herbert
Hoover, head of the U.S. Food Administration, had appointed her to Florida's State Food Commission, an agency charged with publicizing the need
to produce and conserve food. Governor Catts had appointed her to the
Florida chapter of the National Defense Council, to the state commission
on the sanitation of army and navy camps, and to the state's War Library
Council, which was supposed to raise part of a national goal of $1 million.
May was also in charge of organizing Red Cross volunteers from among
the state's woman's clubs, and she was appointed to chair the women's division of the state's Liberty Loan Drive.

Florida women engaged in all types of war work. Thousands signed
pledge cards to conserve food, volunteered for Red Cross work, saved
books and magazines for the armed forces camps, staffed canteens and
hospitality houses for the soldiers, and knitted sweaters, mufflers, and
caps for the troops. They collected hundreds of pounds of string and tin
foil, a practice which caused Governor Jennings much consternation and
inconvenience as the material was stored in the Jenningses' home until it
could be bundled and shipped to Washington. Some patriotic Florida clubwomen objected to any German music being played at federation functions. At the 1917 convention so many protested over the music committee's plans to play selections from Beethoven, Mendelssohn, and Wagner
that President Wilson himself was wired and asked for an opinion. He replied that "he did not regard the use of good music as unpatriotic." [34] One
clubwoman informed May that she "went out and pulled up all of the German iris plants in her garden after war had been declared." [35]

May's war work soon overwhelmed her federation duties, and by
autumn she had four stenographers and six volunteers helping with her
paperwork. Her regular federation responsibilities continued; she just
worked longer and harder than before. Planning for the new girls' industrial school in Marion County consumed a lot of her time. The federation
had submitted plans to the governor and to the state board of control regarding the establishment of a family-style cottage system of housing like
the one adopted for the boys' school. The officials ignored this concept,
even though the legislature had recommended the cottage plan. May wrote
to Florence Cay: "We are in a stew about the Girls' School because the
board is planning a large building with a flat roof for the school instead of
the cottage plan which had been adopted. The Ocala women are up in
arms. We have to see what we can do about it right away. I shall write the
governor at once." [36] After an exchange of telegrams and letters with Catts
and the board members, May was informed that plans would go forward

for construction of the barracks-style dormitory. Angry and frustrated, May wrote Elizabeth Hocker, an Ocala resident, "I never saw anything like this board. They seem to think they know it all, and that the fact that they are officially elected gives them unusual ability and knowledge without ever having to study the question."[37] So it was that the boys got cottages and the girls barracks.

During the summer of 1917, May outfitted Royal Palm Park's new lodge. She purchased linens, kitchen appliances, and furniture for the living quarters and twelve large hickory rockers for the screened porch. The Homestead clubwomen made braided rugs for the floors, and other clubs sent bedspreads and curtains. The federation had small handbills distributed throughout the state extolling the virtues of the park, as the facility was now receiving visitors on a regular basis. Supervising the landscaping around the lodge, May instructed Mosier to plant roses and brilliant red bougainvillea near the front door. Both he and May worried about the grass fires that continually threatened the park and about a fungus that was attacking South Florida's royal palms and eventually destroyed many of them. In September, May held a federation board of directors meeting at the park, at which time the women decorated the lodge and had their picture taken.

Suffrage continued to be a subject of concern for many of the federation's officers. May stayed in touch with Mary Jewett, and together they developed plans to make the suffrage issue a subject of formal study within every club of the federation. May also corresponded with Ivy Stranahan, the new president of the Florida Equal Suffrage Association, and helped her make arrangements for its convention to be held the same week in Tampa as the upcoming federation convention.

The Florida Federation of Women's Clubs convened its twenty-third annual meeting in November 1917. Convention business primarily concerned mobilizing the women for the war effort, electing new officers, and promoting suffrage, good roads, and public health. Rose Lewis (Mrs. Edgar Lewis) of Fort Pierce was elected president to succeed May, whose name was submitted to the General Federation as a Florida director. May was also appointed to chair the state federation's conservation committee, a position she accepted because of her attachment to the park.

In her final address as president of the Florida Federation, May thanked the members for their help during her three-year administration, listing all that had been achieved during that period. She was particularly proud of the creation of Royal Palm Park and the construction of its facilities. She was also pleased with the endorsement of equal suffrage at two federation conventions and its near acceptance by the 1917 legislature, passage of a prohibition resolution, establishment of the federation's endowment fund, creation of the girls' industrial school near Ocala, the antituberculosis work that had begun in every Florida community, adoption of Red Cross work within the federation, promotion of rural extension work, and the growth in federation membership, now numbering more than 9,000 women. She reported that in three years she had handled 15,132 pieces of mail, had made innumerable speeches, and had traveled 26,543 miles on club business.[38] One of the federation's most popular presidents ever, May was given the federation's large wooden gavel as a permanent token of esteem and appreciation. But her services to the federation and the state had only begun. New challenges lay ahead.

CHAPTER 8

A Dedicated Life

THE YEARS following her tenure as president of the federation were May Jennings's busiest and most successful. Among the state mobilization boards and committees she served on during the war were the State Food Commission, National Defense Council, War Library Council, War Savings Council, Belgian Relief Committee, and Armenian-Syrian Relief Committee. Around the state, scores of mobilization committees urged citizens to buy war bonds, grow victory gardens, join the Red Cross, volunteer in hospitals and hospitality houses, save food, cloth, paper, and other commodities, and join the armed forces. The public was exhorted to "Give Until It Hurts" and to "Beat Back the Hun." Housewives were urged to "can vegetables, fruit, and the Kaiser, too" and to make "Every Garden a Munitions Plant." [1]

Anti-German feeling ran high and included the boycotting of German music and food. Dachshunds were renamed "liberty pups," frankfurters became "liberty sausages," and sauerkraut "liberty cabbage." The populace endured "wheatless," "meatless," "heatless," and "lightless" days. [2] Families with members serving in the armed forces hung in their windows a red and white service flag with a blue star for each person in uniform. If a serviceman died in the war, a gold star was sewn over the blue. One thousand forty-six Floridians perished in the conflict. Part of the Jennings family's contribution to the war effort was doubling the production of vegetables, beef, and poultry on their Middleburg farm. Bryan Jennings, a recent law school graduate, joined the navy and became an intelligence officer. He was stationed first in Washington, D.C., then at Key West. During the conflict he married his childhood friend, Dorothy Isabel Brown.

A shipbuilding center of some importance, Jacksonville was especially affected by the war, as were other port cities such as Pensacola, Tampa, Miami, and Key West. The development of Camp Johnston near Orange Park brought thousands of soldiers and their families into the area. Housing shortages, economic inflation, and increases in crime troubled the Jacksonville community, which became known as the "booze oasis" of North Florida. May and other prominent prohibitionists worked hard to quarantine the military facility and place it in a dry zone. After a bitter struggle May wrote a friend, "We had an awful fight here for the wet and dry election, but we won out." [3] The "moral sanitation" around Camp Johnston was attacked, too, and clubwomen under May's leadership sent President Wilson and other government officials a resolution regarding the moral climate near the camp. During the effort to establish a zone of moral purity, May obtained for distribution pamphlets from the American Social Hygiene Association, one of which was entitled "Prostitution in its Relation to the Army on the Mexican Border." [4]

Hundreds of Jacksonville women participated in the war effort, volunteering to sell bonds and stamps and joining the Red Cross's first aid, nursing, relief, and hospitality committees. Leaders of the local Red Cross branch included Louise Meigs, Annie Broward, Minerva Jennings, Ninah Cummer, Lina Barnett, and May, who was responsible for the acquisition and distribution of supplies, food, and clothing to area families adversely affected by the war. During the conflict Red Cross volunteers in Duval County made, packaged, and shipped over one million surgical items. [5] In addition to her Red Cross duties, May served on the Jacksonville Commission on Training Camp Activities, which coordinated invitations to convalescing soldiers for meals and social entertainment in private homes.

May Jennings was ideally suited to head Florida's Women's Liberty Loan Committee for she knew how to organize the state's women. She wrote at that time, "I probably know more women in the state than any other woman." [6] Of the women whose support May and her staff solicited throughout Florida, clubwomen furnished the bulk of the workers. The first need was to secure fifty-four county chairpersons, who in turn needed assistants and scores of general volunteers. Hundreds of letters and printed pamphlets were mailed before enough chairpersons could be found.[7] Most women agreed to help, but few were willing to assume supervisory tasks or to take on the responsibilities of chairing a county organization. The old-girl network came to the rescue, however, and many of the federation's state and local officers became county leaders.

Occasionally, when May had difficulty organizing a county, her characteristic patience would run out. To one recalcitrant group of women she wrote, "I must confess that it is quite a suprise to me that none of you Fernandina women seem to realize the great importance of financing the war. . . . When women are giving their sons to the trenches, it does not seem possible to me that anyone should feel they have a right to refuse a request from their government as long as they have strength to hold out. Will you kindly say to the women whom you have consulted about this work that I more often than not work until two o'clock at night. . . . The soldiers have in a way sacrificed their lives uselessly, while some women have stood idly by, unwilling to assist."[8] When the chairwomen wrote May of their difficulties in enlisting volunteers, May advised, "You must not get discouraged. . . . If you had 54 counties to furnish with chairmen, you'd have something to complain of, so be thankful you have only one county to look after."[9] Since the loan campaigns were administered from Washington through regional headquarters, May attended frequent meetings in the nation's capital and in Atlanta. During this period, she wrote a friend, "This war business has just about put me in bed."[10]

May also had the responsibility of arranging tours and schedules for nationally known persons who came to Florida to speak on behalf of bond sales and food conservation. During the war she accompanied several speakers on tours, including Jane Addams of Chicago, who was a Jennings houseguest. At another time she joined Mrs. Antoinette Funk, national vice-president of the Liberty Loan Committee, on a swing down the Florida east coast through more than twenty towns. At Daytona they spoke to some 800 people, and in Miami they addressed a crowd estimated at over 3,000. Everywhere they exhorted their listeners, mostly women, to buy bonds and to volunteer as salespersons. On another drive May accompanied Sergeant-Major Edward Lowery, a decorated English solidier, on a tour of the state. At other times she alone was the featured speaker at community rallies.

Selling bonds was not without its hazards. The women, who wore identifying armbands and buttons, canvassed every community in the state. It was tiring work; a nationwide influenza epidemic nearly canceled the fourth loan drive, and May often had to travel to many out-of-the-way places. Soliciting in some parts of Florida offered its own unique perils. One county chairwoman wrote May, "I have just returned from Crystal River and the insects nearly ate me up. A whole regiment of German mosquitoes attacked me. Casualty list: 5 seriously wounded. The enemy were driven back with heavy losses, but I lost some mighty good American blood." [11]

Liberty Loan and food conservation work put May in contact with many black women throughout the state and encouraged interracial cooperation among clubwomen. Having previously corresponded on public health matters with Mary McLeod Bethune, president of the Florida Colored Women's Federation, May wrote her during the war, "I am exceedingly interested in the war work among the negro women of Florida, and I have a great deal of pleasure in cooperating with Eartha M. M. White, president of the City Federation of Jacksonville. She is an exceedingly bright and energetic woman, and seems never to be weary in well doing. The colored people of Jacksonville owe her a great deal more than they realize. . . . The production and conservation of food and the elimination of waste is being pushed thoroughly and successfully among the colored women." [12] Although the South's pervasive racism defeated attempts by national leaders to bring black women into the liberty loan program, cooperation between the women of the two races existed elsewhere in the nation, and May continued to correspond and work with Mrs. Bethune and Miss White to help them organize war work among Florida's blacks. She later publicly acknowledged that the black women in Florida had done much to promote food conservation and bond and stamp buying.

Each liberty loan drive was accompanied by public rallies, parades, bonfires, band concerts, military demonstrations, or other activities which the loan people referred to as "stunts," all designed to arouse patriotic spirit. During the fifth and last loan drive in April 1919, May and other city leaders arranged to have the Carlstrom Flying Circus perform over Jacksonville. The aerial team "dived, looped, rolled, and roared to simulate aerial combat as crowds took to their rooftops to get a better view, and watch open mouthed with awe." [13] In addition to the air circus, an army tank on tour was engaged to demolish an abandoned building located downtown. These two events brought out one of the largest Florida crowds to assemble during the war. At the end of the war, May's final loan report to Washington showed that Florida women had sold over $17 million in saving bonds, certificates, and stamps, in addition to the amount sold by Florida men.

During the war May's interest in other activities continued unabated. On 26 January 1917, she organized the Duval County Federation of Women's Clubs, an amalgamation of twenty-four organizations which would support a number of important social and civic issues. May served as an officer of this organization for many years.[14] As director of the Florida Anti-Tuberculosis Association from 1917 to 1919, she made numerous speeches throughout the state. The association sought not only to reduce the spread of the disease by improving public sanitation but also to see a state sanatorium established.

In December 1917, May was called upon to help female telephone operators in Jacksonville who had gone on strike. She urged Mrs. Raymond Robbins of the National Woman's Trade Union League in Chicago to come to Jacksonville to guide the women in their demands. She wrote J. C. Privett, state labor inspector, for a list of industries in Florida that employed women, statistics she used in a campaign to publicize the operators' plight.[15] Unsuccessful in getting a more liberal hours and wages bill through the Florida legislature, May did bring the operators' working conditions to the attention of the appropriate Jacksonville officials. Though short lived, the telephone strike eased conditions under which the women worked.

May's work on behalf of woman suffrage continued during 1918 and 1919 as she and others kept pressure on Florida's Congressional delegations to vote for the Anthony amendment, the suffrage bill pending in Congress. Both Florida senators, Park Trammell and Duncan Fletcher, adamantly refused to change their antagonistic views about women's rights despite the fact that May and her colleagues launched a campaign to swamp them with what the women called "hot stuff" letters. When Fletcher coolly replied to one of May's "hot stuff" letters, in which she had enclosed a list of the Florida newspapers supporting equal suffrage, she wrote Dr. Mary Jewett, an ardent suffragist, "The stubbornness of these men makes me sick. I do not care if either is defeated. I am going to support the man who supports suffrage."[16] Dr. Jewett replied, "It will be a great day when we no longer have to have suffrage societies and political equality committees and when we are recognized as 'real folks.'"[17]

When Dr. Anna Shaw, the nationally prominent suffragist, visited Florida on a speaking tour, May introduced her to a Jacksonville audience. She later received from Dr. Shaw a card picturing Susan B. Anthony and quoting an Anthony phrase which May repeated whenever she gave a speech:

"To desire liberty for one's self is a natural instinct . . . but to be willing to accord liberty to another is the result of education, of self discipline, and the practice of the golden rule." [18] During the Florida primary in June 1918, the suffragists worked openly for candidates who had supported suffrage or who promised to do so. May wrote of one of the candidates, "He opposed everything women asked for during the last legislature and I am anxious to see him left at home this time." [19] This candidate, George Wilder, was not only reelected but also chosen speaker of the 1919 house.

As the controversy over the Anthony amendment became more intense, both May and Governor Jennings stepped up their efforts on its behalf. During the summer of 1918 they wrote an open letter, which was reprinted by the Florida Equal Suffrage Association and given prominent play by many of the state's major newspapers. In November, May addressed both the FESA and the FFWC conventions on the importance of each woman doing her part to further the cause of suffrage.[20] Florida women were split between those who favored federal suffrage only and those who favored both state and federal suffrage, and this lack of agreement kept Florida suffragists from being more successful. In December 1918, May issued a "white paper" to refute Trammell's and Fletcher's argument that a vote for equal suffrage was an abdication of the principle of states' rights, denouncing this view as an excuse to oppose suffrage for women. She asked the senators if, since President Wilson and the national Democratic party had endorsed equal suffrage, this meant they were no longer Democrats and wanted to know how could they call the United States democratic if one-half the nation was "still without a voice." [21]

In January 1919, May, Dr. Jewett, Ivy Stranahan, and other suffragists met in Orlando to discuss the upcoming legislative session. In a speech, "The Two Roads to Victory," May again argued that women needed both the federal equal suffrage amendment and a state primary bill.[22] When the Florida legislature convened a few months later, she and the other women were ready to submit their primary bill. During the session they lobbied tirelessly, May working simultaneously for suffrage and for bills affecting conservation, park matters, and compulsory education. The lawmakers paid little attention to the desires of the suffragists. The primary measure failed even to reach the floor of either chamber. During that summer, however, Congress approved the nineteenth amendment, which was quickly ratified and made law. Neither Florida senator voted for the amendment, and it went unendorsed by the Florida legislature until 1969.

In 1920, May was appointed associate chairperson of the National Democratic Committee for Florida, a position whose responsibilities included organizing local Democratic women's clubs. May was never to hold an elected political office, although on several occasions she was offered a postmistress position and was urged by many Floridians to run for governor during the late 1920s. As she wrote a friend, "I am still having pressure brought to bear to run for Governor. It is quite flattering and compimentary but I can keep so busy without this. . . . I think I will just pursue the even tenor of my way." [23] Florida was soon to elect several female legislators, including Ruth Bryan Owen, daughter of William Jennings Bryan and May's relative by marriage. [24]

With the passage of the nineteenth amendment the women's movement throughout the nation underwent a fundamental change. As numerous organizations representing women's views emerged in the political arena, the Florida Federation of Women's Clubs, long the standard-bearer, was no longer the only organization to speak for the state's women. Indeed, the federation underwent a gradual retrenchment until by 1930 it would cede its place as one of the state's most progressive voices to the Florida League of Women Voters, which was informally organized in Palm Beach County in August 1920 amd officially incorporated at a state meeting in Jacksonville in April 1921. [25] A nonpartisan organization, the league's aim was the political education of women and the exercise of political participation to achieve its progressive goals. [26] The birth of the league coincided with the date set for the first drive to register American women as voters. In Duval County, May made speeches to publicize the registration drive and organized women to canvass neighborhoods. Her friend, Helen Hunt West, a member of the radical National Woman's Party which May still refused to join, was the first Duval County woman to register to vote. [27] While white women were the principal recipients of the new democracy, 7,309 Negro women and 8,709 white women registered in the county. [28]

May saw the League of Women Voters as an organization with a useful future, and she became a charter member. Indeed, the league's state officers recognized her political experience; May served as legislative chairperson from the organization's inception through 1927. Other federation members joined the league—Ivy Stranahan, Mary Jewett, and Lucy Blackman—but many clubwomen saw it as a competitor and opposed its aggressive stance. Not only did the league lack the air of gentility and tradition that had made the federation popular with southern women, but it differed from the federation in more concrete ways: for many years it was concerned almost exclusively with political matters; it established chapters only in Florida's largest cities; it never owned any clubhouses; it included more northern women newly arrived in Florida and more women from minority groups, including many Jewish women. In 1921 the league began publishing *The Florida Voter.* (The following year the Florida Federation of Women's Clubs established its own publication, *The Bulletin,* later titled *Florida Clubwoman.*) Besides May's legislation committee, the league organized committees on child welfare, education, the legal status of women, living costs, social hygiene, women in industry, political information, and international cooperation.

As head of the league's legislation committee, May organized the Florida Legislative Council in 1921. As May described this strategy being used in other states, "The plan is for each organization to submit its legislative program to the council which will decide on the measures to be presented and who and how many bills to be pushed during one session. . . . The elimination of divided interests and wasted effort, the concentration of the entire force of the womanpower of the state upon any measure will practically insure its enactment as a law." [29] Thus the Legislative Council, with May as president for nearly a decade, became a clearinghouse for more than ten state organizations, speaking at its peak for more than 25,000 Floridians. Eventually, the council would break apart because of the economic strains of the depression and because of the desire of many of these organizations to control their own legislative calendar.

The Legislative Council represented such disparate state groups as the Florida Federation of Women's Clubs, the Florida League of Women Voters, the Federation of Business and Professional Women's Clubs, the Florida Mothers' Clubs (PTAS), the Florida Education Association, the Florida Forestry Association, the Women's Christian Temperance Union, and the Florida Audubon Society. With May at its helm, the council lobbied in Tallahassee for legislative programs that tried to include something for everyone. In 1925, for example, the program called for stricter controls over the state board of education, required reading of the Bible in public schools, the selection of women as jurors, repression of prostitution, establishment of an industrial school for Negro girls, licensing of carnivals and traveling shows, creation of a board of forestry and a state game and freshwater fish commission, and local option stock laws. [30] The 1927 legislative shopping list included twenty-three items.

In addition to these issues, the League of Women Voters and the Legislative Council worked to promote state participation in the national Sheppard-Towner maternity-infancy program. They also urged a survey of conditions of Florida working women, the removal of common law disabilities on married women, and the elimination of the state's poll tax. May continued to urge Florida women to become involved in local and state political matters, and in April 1922 she outlined the achievements of fourteen of the state's organizations in "Women's Work in Florida" for *Florida Magazine,* describing the new Legislative Council and urging all Florida women to join in the political process. As head of the council, May Jennings became more well known than ever in the halls of government in Tallahassee.

Even after women received the vote May continued to promote women's rights, though she refused to join the National Woman's Party and opposed that organization's Mott bill (equal rights amendment), which was also rejected by the increasingly conservative Florida Federation of Women's Clubs. She wrote in 1923, "I am unquestionably opposed to the Amendment because it is a direct abridgement of states rights and would repeal all of the special protective legislation for women." [31]

Even though the 1917 legislature had passed a statewide prohibition bill, which was ratified by voters the following year, and the national eighteenth amendment had been enacted in 1919, it fast became apparent that prohibition had a precarious future. Late in 1919, when the National Anti-Saloon League organized groups in each state to counteract the growing disrespect for the new law, May was selected to chair the women's division of the Florida Educational and Temperance Campaign. Florida, near the "wet" Bahamas, quickly became a major smuggling route for those who sought to import illicit liquor. Citizens in Florida's coastal cities witnessed a series of battles between smugglers and state and federal enforcement officials. The campaign's objectives were to educate the public about prohibition, support police officials and raise money to oppose the liquor interests, which were workng to get the new amendment repealed. The organization was supported by many women who were also members of the FFWC and the Florida Equal Suffrage Association. [32] May was expected to call upon her vast talents and her network of friendships to find county chairwomen as she had so often done for other organizations. But the war, the bond campaigns, and the struggles over suffrage and prohibition had left the American public emotionally exhausted and cynical, uninterested in new moral causes. A conservative, probusiness mood permeated the country. Increased mobility and greater economic freedom had created a public which no longer supported progressivism. Many Americans resented prohibition as a prudish law which sought to regulate their personal behavior.

May found it difficult to secure the people needed for temperance education work. Previously cooperative clubwomen were now unwilling to help. One of May's stenographers wrote during the search for workers, "It

seems to me like this Education Temperance work is about the worst we
have ever tackled. I never saw the way the women are afraid to accept
chairmanships. . . . We will never get the state organized at the rate we
are going."³³ In addition, officials at the organization's state and regional
headquarters bickered among themselves over jurisdiction and expense al-
lotments. The decision to eliminate the women's division was one of May
Jennings's few failures.

During the autumn of 1919 Governor Jennings had an acute attack that
was diagnosed as severe indigestion but apparently was a heart attack. For
nearly a year he had complained of chest pains and fatigue, and after his
attack he continued to deteriorate. With her husband gravely ill and bedridden, May was forced to hire round-the-clock nurses to care for him. By
Christmas the prognosis was serious indeed, and May, accompanied by
friends, Dr. and Mrs. M. O. Terry, he the former surgeon general of the
state of New York, took the governor to the Breakers Hotel in Palm Beach
where it was thought that the warm weather would facilitate his recovery.
He did improve and in February 1920 was transferred from Palm Beach to
the Ponce de Leon Hotel in St. Augustine. On February 27 it was decided
that he was well enough to return to the Jennings home in Jacksonville. As
he was preparing for the trip, he suffered another massive attack and died
within minutes. Sherman Jennings was fifty-six.

Governor Jennings's funeral was held in the Main Street Baptist Church
in Springfield with Governor Catts, former Governor Gilchrist, and scores
of other state officials in attendance. All offices in Tallahassee were
closed, and flags across the state were flown at half-mast. Jennings was
buried in Evergreen Cemetery, not far from his and May's home.³⁴

Even the death of May's mother years before had not affected her so
deeply. She had spent twenty-nine years working alongside her husband,
sharing his many dreams and aspirations for Florida and its people. For
several months after her husband's death she remained at home in Jacksonville, closing out his affairs and using the time for quiet reflection. She
was forty-six years old, energetic and too young to retire from public life.
She knew that she would continue her work; there were too many things
yet to be done. She wrote, "I expect to dedicate the rest of my life to the
development of our beloved state to which my dear husband devoted so
much of his time and thought, and I hope in a measure to be instrumental
in bringing to realization some of the great things he started and dreamed
for Florida."³⁵

A few months after Governor Jennings's death, May as president of the
Springfield Improvement Association was asked to lead the fight against a

new city commission ordinance, passed without notice, calling for the paving of Main Street and the destruction of its palm-lined esplanade. Favoring the paving were realtors and local car dealers who organized themselves as the Main Street Improvement Association. May and other area residents, including Ion L. Farris, fought to retain the parkway. The Springfield Improvement Association even held a nonbinding referendum on the issue. May managed to get the city council to oppose the commission, a stand more symbolic than practical since real power lay with the commissioners. Mayor John W. Martin, who also opposed the paving plan, was equally unsuccessful. During the most critical period of the struggle May urged that the city remove the sidewalks, if necessary, but leave the scenic esplanade intact. She argued that Main Street was still a residential street and that "back of all the agitation was the real estate scheme perpetrated by those who have moved to palatial homes in Riverside . . . the people of Springfield not being willing to have Main Street's beauty destroyed in the interest of a few gentlemen who want to make money in real estate." [36] Despite a battle which was carried into the courts, Springfield lost; the picturesque, palm-lined esplanade was dug up along with many of the roadway's large oak trees, and Main Street became one of the city's busiest commercial thoroughfares. Next to the Jennings house there was soon a grocery store and across the street a saloon. [37]

During the same year, 1920, May was elected vice-president of the General Federation of Women's Clubs, having served as the organization's Florida director since 1918. Her campaign brochure for the position stated that she was a woman "born to an inheritance of big thinking and right acting who had fearlessly chosen what she believed right." It also stated that she was "a pioneer in every progressive movement in [Florida]." [38] Upon her election as vice-president, May was placed in charge of the federation's national home economics demonstration extension work, which operated in cooperation with the U.S. Department of Agriculture. She was a familiar figure to officials of that agency because of her work with the Smith-Lever and corn club programs years before. By late 1922 May could report that thirty-nine states and 2,500 counties in the nation had established rural extension programs.

During May's four years as vice-president she served the General Federation in many ways, including membership on the committee that located, purchased, and raised over $150,000 to renovate a headquarters building in Washington, D.C. On two occasions she and her colleagues were entertained at the White House. She also served as chairperson of the General's medical loan scholarship fund, raising money to support young women

who were interested in becoming doctors, and on a committee that urged
Congress to create a federal department of education, headed by a woman
with cabinet rank.[39]

In 1923 May became vice-chairperson of the General Federation's
Women's National Committee for Law Enforcement and was placed in
charge of the nine southeastern states, allowing her to continue her support for enforcement of national prohibition. Her appointment was the result of her work for the defunct Florida Educational and Temperance Campaign and of her presidency of an organization formed late in 1920, the
Duval County Law Enforcement Committee.[40] The following year, May's
name was put in nomination for president at the national 1924 biennial
convention of the General Federation.[41] Although she did not win, she was
made a honorary lifetime vice-president of the organization in recognition
of her years of service.

In Jacksonville, May continued her civic activities, helping to establish
the Springfield Garden Club and to organize movements to clean up
Springfield, beautify Hogan's Creek, and landscape Long Branch Creek
near Evergreen Cemetery. In March 1924, May became a charter member
of the Jacksonville chapter of the National Aeronautics Association,
which sought to further the growth of aviation in northeast Florida.[42] The
group was instrumental in helping Florida Airways to inaugurate mail
flights in 1926. In 1927 she attended a banquet honoring Charles
Lindbergh, but despite her interest in aviation she never flew in an air-
plane. During these years May served as chairperson of the endowment
fund for the new tubercular and crippled children's hospital built in Jacksonville at Panama Park on Trout Creek. She remained active on the board
of Daniel Orphanage, and she continued to help her old friend Marcus
Fagg raise money for the Children's Home Society.

In 1925 May worked to secure passage of the bill that created the Florida State Library in Tallahassee. As a past member of the War Library
Council and a former president of the FFWC she was familiar with the library needs of the state. At her urging, the federation donated as the new
library's nucleus its ancient but large traveling library which had criss-
crossed the state for so many years. May also helped to secure for the new
state library the private collection of books that had belonged to William
Jennings Bryan.

Also in 1925 May was appointed chairperson of the women's editorial
advisory committee of *Tropical America*. Though the magazine lasted
only two years, she managed to publish articles pertaining to Royal Palm
Park, home demonstration work, conservation of the state's natural re-

souces, and Florida's new park system.[43] She wrote the editor, "What I bring to the magazine in prestige, position, standing in the state, is a matter of long years of attainment, and I am not unmindful of the fact that, being as conversant with state affairs as I am . . . has its great value. At least it helps me to the accomplishment of things that otherwise would be impossible. . . . The articles, I dare say, have not possibly, as much literary merit as many others could bring, but I do feel that my information as to state affairs is possibly as far reaching as that of anyone else."[44]

CHAPTER 9

Doctor May

THROUGH THE years May Jennings never lost her interest in conservation. After she relinquished the presidency of the Florida Federation of Women's Clubs in 1917, she was appointed head of its conservation department, taking charge for nineteen years of the club's programs concerning Royal Palm Park, waterways, good roads, Seminole Indians, and bird protection. There were few conservation issues in Florida during this long period with which she was not in some way involved, from a drive to get a riparian rights bill passed to protect the state's rivers and estuaries to campaigns making the mockingbird and the Sabal palm symbols of the state and having February 14 declared "Bird Day" in Florida.

Royal Palm Park continued to demand much of her time because it was always in need of money, particularly during its early years. The site became not only a popular tourist attaction with thousands of annual visitors but also a setting for scientific studies. Improvements at the park continued; a well was dug and a water tower built. A pen on the premises held several Key Deer to entertain sightseers. In 1918 T. L. Mead of Oviedo willed his collection of several thousand hybrid orchids to the park. Private monetary gifts secured by Charles Simpson and David Fairchild helped to keep the park solvent, but by late 1918 funds were so low that drastic steps were needed. A part-time caretaker replaced the warden. The old "mile-of-dimes" cardboard strips were reissued to federation members, and clubs were urged to hold bake sales and bazaars to raise money for the park. Irritated by the perennial financial crisis at the park, some federation members became critical of May and began to insist that the park be sold.

Before the 1919 legislative session opened, May wrote an article about the park for *Mr. Foster's Travel Magazine,* a national monthly.[1] May and her committee sent a reprint of that article, which included pictures of the hammock, to each legislator; but despite intense personal lobbying and a park display the women set up in a Capitol corridor, the legislature failed to vote funds. May felt betrayed, for many of her friends among the legislators had assured her that the appropriation bill would pass. The original 1915 bill granting the park lands to the federation had provided a token $1.00 a year state appropriation; frustrated and angry, May wrote Comptroller Ernest Amos, demanding the $4.00 the state owed. It was sent. At that time May wrote a friend, "The work [conservation in Florida] is up hill and one gets dreadfully discouraged at times."[2]

Continuing her work for the park and for other conservation projects, May tried in 1920 to secure Rockefeller Foundation funds for the purchase of 10,000 acres adjacent to the park for a bird sanctuary. She was fearful that the land would be sold by the state to an industrial conglomerate interested in land speculation just as the Alligator Bay rookery land had been the year before, a sale May had tried but failed to prevent. When no Rockefeller Foundation funds were offered, later in 1920 and in 1921 May distributed copies of the articles "Natural History of Paradise Key and Nearby Everglades Florida" and "Birds of Royal Palm Hammock" to prominent individuals and legislators who might aid the park.[3] In 1920 she raised some money by renting the Arcade movie theater in Jacksonville to show slides of the park. She continued to write letters of protest to state and federal officials about the lack of enforcement of existing bird and wildlife laws. Governor Sidney J. Catts was particularly recalcitrant, opposing any type of conservation measures. May, undeterred, continued to campaign for newer and more stringent laws. When Governor Cary Hardee took office in 1921, May sent him a long letter about the conservation measures she felt that the state needed and urged him to create a state natural resources department. During these years May and her colleagues worked closely with the Florida Wildlife League, the Florida Audubon

Society, and the Florida Conservation Commission, a new organization
that worked for the establishment of bird sanctuaries and wildlife reservations within the state. She counted as friends many nationally known
naturalists and conservation officials.

During the years of World War I, May had become embroiled in one
conservation controversy that made headlines for months. Because of the
emphasis on conserving food, some Washington official wondered if in
some way sea birds might be prevented from eating fish. Florida shellfish
commissioner J. A. Williams then ruled that since pelicans were thought
to eat perhaps a million dollars' worth of fish a day in Florida, the species
should be controlled by robbing its rookeries of eggs and killing older
birds outright. The Florida Audubon Society and other naturalists severely
criticized Williams and other state officials who favored this plan. Feelings
ran high on both sides of the issue. Stanley Hanson, a Fort Myers Indian
agent and federal inspector of migratory birds, wrote May, "All this talk
about the pelican being responsible for the disappearance of food fish is a
lot of *rot*." [4] May and her conservation committee circulated petitions opposing the bird slaughter, and the National Audubon Society began to
exert pressure on the U.S. Food Administration, which was supporting the
shellfish commissioner.

May wrote for help to her friend E. W. Nelson, chief of the Bureau of
Biological Survey in Washington. He and employees of the bureau visited
Florida to study the situation. They prepared and sent May an official report, "The Truth about the Pelicans," defending the habits of the beleaguered birds. May gave the paper to William F. Blackman, president of the
Florida Audubon Society, and he had it retitled, reprinted, and distributed
throughout the state.[5] At the time May wrote the president of the FFWC, "It
seems we are in for a fight to save our birds." [6] And so they were.

Coastal newspapers such as the *St. Petersburg Independent* condoned
the destruction of the birds. May's views on behalf of the birds carried a
great deal of weight around the state: not only was she chairperson of the
federation's conservation committee, but she was an officer of the Florida
Audubon Society and a member of the State Food Commission, organizations on different sides of the issue. Her views were so well publicized and
she herself so well respected by the general public that at a meeting of the
State Food Commission, which was charged with promoting food conservation, she was able to get a resolution passed protesting the killing of
Florida's pelicans. The plans to exterminate the birds were dropped. One
fact that had made the whole episode so bizarre and incongruous was that
Florida was the site of the nation's first federal wildlife refuge, Pelican Is-

land in Indian River County, established in 1903 by President Theodore Roosevelt specifically to protect pelicans.

In 1921 May wrote E. W. Nelson in Washington to get the new caretaker at Royal Palm Park, Gordon T. Doe, appointed a deputy game warden. In the letter she acknowledged for the first time that her hard work was beginning to show results. She wrote, "About the middle of last month I visited Royal Palm Park and on the bridge where we go over the lily pond we stopped our car between 5 and 6 in the evening and saw to the north on a little island belonging to our property between two and three thousand water fowl go to roost. I am beginning to feel that our bird conservation work is well started, but you can readily realize how very carefully the warden has to guard this spot. He virtually has to put the birds to bed every night to keep the hunters from shooting into them." [7]

The year 1921 proved pivotal in the history of the park. For many years efforts by May and a few staunch supporters had permitted the park to stay open to the public. Now, whether because of May's campaign, sympathy for her because of Governor Jennings's death the year before, the park's popularity, or sheer exasperation, the 1921 legislature approved a $2,500 annual appropriation. The park's future was assured. While the federation retained ownership and managerial responsibility, the state took over most of the financial burden. Overjoyed, May wrote letters of thanks to each legislator who had voted for the appropriation bill. Through the years she continued to oversee the operation of the park as its popularity increased and Florida's 1920s real estate boom brought thousands of tourists to its vine-covered, palm-shadowed pathways. The hurricane of 1926 and several grass fires the next year caused severe damage, forcing the legislature to appropriate $10,000 for restoration. Before the decade was out additional acreage was acquired, increasing the park's size to nearly 12,000 acres. In 1929, acting on behalf of the federation, May offered Royal Palm to the proposed Everglades National Park if it should be created. This fortuitous gesture helped to promote the national park.

During these same years May continued to work with Ivy Stranahan on behalf of the Seminole Indians. After the 1917 legislature set aside 100,000 acres of state land in Monroe County for an Indian reservation, the women began to agitate to transfer the land to federal ownership when they learned that Washington would make no improvements on the reservation as long as the government did not hold title to it. In a memorial to this effect presented to the 1919 legislature, May wrote, "If this land was under Government control steps would be taken to drain portions of the tract that could then be made available to the Indians. The only Government Indian Reservation [in Florida] contains about 23,000 acres in Big Cypress Swamp, Lee County, with only about 5 percent of the land [arable]. . . . We appeal to you to give the Indians a permanent home and settle this question for all time."[8] During maneuvers to secure the land transfer May again clashed with the acerbic Minnie Moore Willson over the question of whether hunting or agricultural lands were more beneficial to the Indians. May favored the acquisition of dry, arable land, writing of Mrs. Willson, "I think she is more anxious for acres than for quality."[9]

The Indians were finding it increasingly difficult to sustain themselves and were seeing their traditional way of life destroyed. "Because of white hunters and the development of canals, drainage operations, and highways, the supply of wildlife had been reduced to a point where deer, bear, and turkey were rarely found. Some food and virtually all other articles had to be purchased at the trading post. Cash income came from the sale of furs, hides, dolls, baskets, and from occasional farm labor, and part-time work as hunting guides."[10]

The 1919 legislature was unresponsive to the request to cede the state lands to the federal government. For nearly twenty years, May, Ivy Stranahan, and other friends of the Seminoles continued to lobby on behalf of the Indians, until the Dania (Hollywood) Federal Reservation was established in 1931, and additional lands in Broward County were secured for the Indians in 1936. These women worked to obtain not only land but also medical care, jobs, and educational benefits for the Indians.

Other conservation issues occupied May Jennings during the 1920s and 1930s: reforestation, forest fire control, cattle tick eradication, and fencing. Because of the clubwomen's concern with conservation in general and because some prominent clubwomen, especially in South Florida, were married to naturalists, the federation had since its early years been interested in forestry matters. Governor Jennings had called for a state forestry board and the post of state forester in 1901. When Royal Palm Park was repeatedly threatened by forest fires, the federation's conservation committee launched an active program to get a forest fire control bill through the legislature.

The bill that eventually passed provided only weak ineffective county option control. May led the fight for a tougher law, helped by her son, Bryan, who, because of the Jennings family's large timber holdings, was interested in forestry matters and worked with his mother. In January 1919, May addressed the Conference of Southern Foresters in Jacksonville on the need for a state department of natural resources to oversee a forestry board and coordinate other conservation programs. She also outlined the federation's struggles for tough conservation laws. As a result of the speech, May was appointed to a committee charged with setting up a citizens' state forestry organization. Although there was not much time before the 1919 legislature convened, those committee members interested in forestry matters decided to lobby for the establishment of a state forestry board and stronger fire control measures. The legislature adjourned without attending to the forestry group's requests, and shortly after, the Florida Forestry Association was formally established with B. F. Williamson of Gainesville as president, Bryan Jennings vice-president, and May the special consultant on legislation.[11] Williamson later remembered that "Mrs. W. S. Jennings was a public spirited woman [who] realized the loss occurring the way forests were being handled. She at the time . . . conceived the idea of getting together a group to develop it into the forest service and she really sparked the flame that developed into the FFA." [12]

The new association dedicated itself to preserving Florida's forests and wildlife and to eliminating wildfires. Its bylaws stated that it intended "to represent the interest of all people, the sportsmen, and the wood-using, naval stores, agricultural and horticultural industries." [13] The bylaws purposely included these segments of the population because their support was needed if it were to achieve its goals. Chief among the organization's opponents was the cattle industry. Cattlemen had long believed that the periodic burning of range grass and undergrowth helped retard scrub vegetation, rejuvenated the soil, and produced tenderer, lusher grasses. According to B. F. Williamson, "The cattle man knew when the cattle were hungry that he could drop a match and have them luscious green food in a couple of weeks." [14] A contemporary stated, "The first people who started fire protection and tree planting had an awful uphill fight because in Florida widespread burning of the woods was an accepted thing. It was felt that the woods ought to be burned in order to kill the boll weevil, get rid of snakes, take care of cattle ticks and almost anything else. The woods were burned in order to clear the land and to keep the pasture growth from getting too high. It was an easy thing to do, and there was no regard for the other fellow's property." [15]

For years cattlemen and foresters had clashed in the halls of government over range burning to produce new vegetation and had argued whether "to burn or not to burn." [16] Appalled by the indiscriminate burning practices of the cattlemen, May frequently argued this question in speeches throughout Florida. She always advocated the proposed state department of natural resources and a forestry board and urged cooperation with the federal

government in establishing national forest reserves in Florida and in wildfire prevention programs. Eventually several large preserves were established, and Florida began participating in some fire prevention programs,
meager efforts in May's eyes.

In 1921 May and her colleagues pushed through the legislature a bill
creating fire districts in the Everglades. The following year Bryan Jennings ran for the legislature on a platform calling for the establishment of
a forestry board and a tick eradication program. He was defeated in the
primary but continued to work for the Florida Forestry Association,
which secured passage in 1925 of a bill supplementing the 1921 wildfire
measure. But both were county option laws and therefore not strong
enough to bring the problem under control. In 1925 the Forestry Association tried again to secure authority to establish a state forestry board,
without success. Conservationists did achieve some victories that year,
however. A bill protecting dogwoods, hollies, and mountain laurels was
passed, as was a bill creating a state park system under the auspices of the
trustees of the Internal Improvement Fund. It would be several years, however, before any parks other than the still privately owned Royal Palm Park
would be created.

In October 1925, May published an article in the *Christian Science
Monitor*, "Conservation in Florida," in which she described the successes
to date—a game and freshwater fish department, a park system, and the
protection of flowering trees. That same year she helped arrange a speaking tour among Florida's women's organizations for Lillian Taliaferro Con-
way, a federal forestry expert hired by the association to publicize the
need for state forestry laws.

From its inception the Florida Forestry Association worked to establish
local forest fire protective associations in each of Florida's counties. These
associations were nongovernmental groups of landowners who banded together to protect their areas from wildfires and voluntarily to fight such
fires should they arise. The association also lobbied in favor of the Clarke-
McNary Act enacted by Congress in 1924, which set up a system of national and state cooperation in fire prevention, reforestation, stream flow
maintenance, and forestry tax laws. The association published in 1925
a pamphlet entitled "Common Forest Trees of Florida" and the following year "Forest Fires in Florida." Statistics compiled by the association
showed fires in Florida to be a major problem: "In 1927, 15,646 fires were
recorded, of which 15,437 occurred in unprotected areas. . . . The total
number of acres burned rose to 13,260,820." [17]

In 1927 the Forestry Association returned to the legislature with a com-

Rep. Austin Mann of Hernando, ca. 1885

May, ca. 1878

St. Joseph's Academy, ca. 1884. May (about twelve years old) is in the first row, third from the left; Grace is in the front row, second from the right.

At St. Joseph's ca. 1888: May (about sixteen years old, at the right), Eunice Williams (left), and Mother Superior Marie Lazarus Lhostal

May in 1896

May in 1890

May at her graduation from
St. Joseph's in June 1889

May and Bryan in Tallahassee, ca. 1902

Courtesy, P. K. Yonge Library of Florida History

May in her inauguration dress, 8 January 1901

Lodge at Royal Palm Park, ca. 1920

Sherman, Bryan, and May, ca. 1920

May, ca. 1930

James E. Ingraham (driving), May (in middle of back seat), and William Jennings Bryan (back seat), ca. 1920; others are not identified.

May, ca. 1960

President Harry S Truman at Everglades City, 6 December 1947, to deliver keynote address at opening of Everglades National Park. May is at the far right, next to Claude Pepper.

prehensive bill that called for establishing a state forestry board. In later years, pioneer forester Clinton H. Coulter recalled that "several [association members] camped over at the legislature and pressed the legislators by personal contact, and got the bill introduced. . . . That early group beat the drums and did the spade work and lobbied up in Tallahassee to get over the bill." Mr. Williamson remembered that association members "realized the cattleman was not interested in our bill and we thought it dangerous to draw one law, so we drew two laws to cover forestry protection and another to cover fire protection. The matter was presented to the legislature. This required an appropriation so a committee was appointed to the House. The authorities that appointed this committee were not favorable to forestry. I was able to go to Tallahassee and see what could be done and from every important point to study forestry and see the main man on the committee on forestry in the Legislature. This man happened to be an old lawyer and when he got through misrepresenting the situation before the committee, the bill was killed in committee. Then the sparks began to fly. Mrs. W. S. Jennings got busy. George Pratt, President of the American Forestry Association had been down here and while he had no financial interests in the state, he did in forestry. . . . He gave us a truck and a moving picture to go all over the state and show people, so that the bill that the committee had turned down had to be accepted and was voted on by 2/3 of the Representatives of the Legislature . . . [and] the Department of Forestry was brought into being." [18]

At the time of the passage of the bill May wrote, "I handled the Forestry law entirely myself except for several days work done at different times during the session by my son, who is the author of the law. We are very proud of this big step in conservation for Florida." [19] Because of her leadership and lobbying and publicity work during the fight, May Jennings was referred to by newspaper reporters as the "Mother of Florida Forestry." She received from the American Forestry Association a bronze medallion in recognition of her activities. One friend wrote to her: "Bully for you in regard to the forestry laws. This is only one of the many things you have done. I wish Florida had a half a dozen of you." [20] May's friend, Governor John W. Martin, appointed Bryan Jennings to the newly created Board of Forestry. He served for ten years (1927–37), during which time the board established a reforestation program, worked to prevent forest fires and enforce wildfire legislation, organized the Florida Forest Service, worked with civic groups to publicize the work of foresters, and eventually helped establish a system of state parks. The creation of the Florida Board of Forestry was one of May Jennings's most significant accomplishments.

In addition to forestry matters, the Florida Federation of Women's Clubs had always shown an interest in the cattle industry and its problems. The federation's first legislative resolution, in 1895, had concerned itself with free-roaming livestock. Around 1900 the national and state governments began a public program to control the Texas cattle fever tick, which had invaded southeastern ranges. Florida's first tick eradication control bill, passed in 1899, gave all eradication authority to the counties. In 1913 the State Board of Health was authorized to lead the eradication program, but once again real power was left in the hands of county commissions, many of whom refused to participate. In 1915 the State Livestock Sanitary Board assumed the responsibility for the eradication program, but it too made little headway. The failure to eliminate the tick threatened to become a major political issue. Aware of the impending crisis, clubwomen at the 1916 federation convention endorsed a strong cattle tick eradication program. Their slogan, "Protect Our Babies' Milk," referred to the ticks' attack on the state's dairy herds, which affected the amount and quality of the usable cows' milk.

By 1917 the tick problem had become so severe that most of the state's cattle were under quarantine. In spite of an estimated $10 million annual loss to the range industry, not all cattlemen believed that the tick should or could be eliminated. The Florida Livestock Association, dominated by William F. Blackman and Mrs. Potter Palmer, of Sarasota, favored a strong eradication program, but the Florida Cattlemen's Association, controlled by F. A. Hendry, opposed it. Blackman, who was also president of the Florida Cattle Tick Eradication Committee, wrote May in 1918 requesting her help in the battle. The November 1918 election was approaching, and those in favor of tick control had managed to get a local-option dipping measure on all of the counties' ballots. Blackman's wife, Lucy, knew that the FFWC was well organized, and her husband turned to it for help in promoting the tick eradication program.

Cattle tick eradication was viewed by cowmen as a major economic issue; many felt dipping would drive them out of business. Joe Ackerman, in his history of the industry, says, "Time involved in the actual dippng forced part-time cattlemen and farmers with sizable herds to become full-time cattlemen or get out of the business altogether. One could no longer turn his herd loose on the open range and forget about them until round-up time. . . . It was a constant cycle of hunting cattle, driving them to the vats and dipping them twice a month. And, of course, the cattle were not the only carrier of the tick."[21] As election day approached, May hurried to organize the clubwomen and help Blackman's group. The women also favored two other issues on the ballot at that time, a statewide prohibition amendment and a ten-mill amendment to promote good roads. On election day clubwomen across the state took up posts outside the polling places to urge support for the three measures. Prohibition and the millage measures won handily, and compulsory cattle dipping was adopted by twenty-eight of Florida's fifty-four counties.

It was apparent that without a statewide compulsory dipping law Florida would never be free of the tick problem. Many citizens thought that a successful tick program also depended upon fencing ranges to control the movement of both infected and dipped cattle. Fencing was anathema to cattlemen, who regarded open ranges as an eternal and sacred right. As one historian writes, "Florida was the last cattle state still to have large range areas unfenced. Fences had been around a long time, but traditionally they had been used in Florida to keep cattle out rather than to keep cattle in. . . . Cattleman J. B. Starkey remembered fondly riding for nearly three weeks in the spring of 1914 without seeing a fence. 'There were no roads then between Alva and Sebring and the area we rode over was still for pioneers. Like all Florida cowmen, we rode by the sun, traveling over 325 miles. It was wild country with plenty of room for a man who wanted to raise stock.'" [22]

When the 1919 legislative session opened, the forces favoring tick eradication were prepared. Once again William Blackman solicited May's help. He sent a letter to each woman's club in the state: "I am writing you after consultation with Mrs. W. S. Jennings, chairman of the conservation committee of the Florida Federation of Women's Clubs, asking that a committee be appointed immediately in every club in the state, whose duty it shall be to urge this matter [statewide compulsory dipping of cattle] upon the attention of the members of the Senate and House, in personal interviews if possible, or by letter. May we not count on you to see that this is done without delay?" [23]

In addition to Blackman's group and the clubwomen, other organizations working for tick eradication were the Florida Development Board and the Florida No-Fence League, whose primary aim was to see that all free-range or no-fence laws were replaced by compulsory fence laws. Several clubwomen were officers in this league; May was listed as an advisory member. She also at this time joined the Florida Development Board (forerunner of the Florida Chamber of Commerce), of which she would be a member for the next forty years. However, May opposed linking tick eradication with fencing for she felt that to do so would only confuse the public further and thereby jeopardize the passage of a compulsory dipping bill.

Despite continued heavy lobbying by eradication proponents, the 1919 and 1921 legislatures refused to pass a compulsory law, thus setting the stage for an all-out confrontation between the cattlemen and their opponents at the next session. After weeks of frantic lobbying and horse-trading between the two factions, the 1923 legislature passed Florida's first compulsory statewide dipping bill, which authorized the state to pay one-half of each cowman's dipping expenses and placed the dipping program under a reorganized Livestock Sanitary Board. In some counties, when dipping actually began, violent skirmishes erupted between officials and irate, intractable cattlemen. Several persons were killed, and many dipping vats around the state were destroyed. During the early years of the dipping program over 70,000 head of cattle were sold so owners could avoid the dipping process. Eventually, dipping became commonplace and the tick was finally eliminated, but not before the state had spent millions of dollars, the cattlemen had undergone several more quarantine periods, and the Seminole Indians had threatened to go on the warpath to save their tick-carrying reservation deer from being exterminated. During this long struggle, May and the women of the federation strongly supported the authorities, although there was some wavering during the Seminole Indian crisis.

The no-fence proponents were not so fortunate, Despite their success at getting a bill on the 1922 ballot to prevent loose livestock, they were unable to rescind a single law allowing open ranges. Throughout her life May Jennings favored and worked for the passage of compulsory fence laws. At one point she got so agitated about the problem that she launched her own letter-writing campaign. She wrote to one official, "It is high time Florida ceased to make cow pastures of the highways."[24] (Florida would have no statewide compulsory fence law until 1947. Even then, some municipalities did not get around to adopting fence laws until the 1960s, despite the nuisance and safety hazard caused by the open ranges as the state expanded its road system and more and more cars took to its highways.)

In 1922, as a member of the Florida Historical Pageant Association, May became associated with John B. Stetson, Jr., and the Florida State Historical Society, which had been established in October 1921.[25] May wrote Stetson for some pictures for use in the pageant's program for its 1922 open-air Jacksonville extravaganza depicting the Ribault–Menéndez de Avilés conflict in drama, song, and dance.[26] Stetson complied with May's request, and in a long letter he outlined his plans for the new historical organization and urged her to join. May became an enthusiastic booster of the society, whose objectives were "to further interest in the history of the state of Florida, to form a library devoted to Florida history, to acquire and preserve historical documents and memorabilia and collections of any sort referring to Florida, to foster research in early records, to publish results of such research, to render accessible scarce historical materials by facsimile or reprint."[27] She wrote letters to forty-two prominent friends, asking them to join also. Many accepted her invitation; early members included Lincoln Hulley, Senator D. U. Fletcher, Peter O. Knight, Kirk Munroe, Dr. Prentice Carson, Dr. James A. Robertson, Cary Hardee, and A. A. Murphree. When the society's first publication appeared in late 1922, May's name and those of many of her friends appeared on the back flyleaf of the book as sustaining members of the organization.[28]

During this period May also became a friend of Jeanette Thurber Connor (Mrs. Washington E. Connor), a cofounder of the Florida State Historical Society and a resident of New York City who spent her winters in New Smyrna.[29] During one of her Florida sojourns, Mrs. Connor became interested in the ruins of an old sugar mill in Volusia County which she incorrectly identified as the remains of the Spanish mission erected in 1696, San Joseph de Jororo.[30] Mrs. Connor bought the property and began to restore it. The site was dedicated at elaborate ceremonies in February 1926, with May, DAR and Historical Society members, and other prominent Floridians in attendance.[31]

By 1927 May had become a vice-president of the historical society. At the society's annual meeting held at DeLand in February 1927, she was given the responsibility of raising the money to save Turtle Mound, an ancient Indian midden located on the Indian River near Titusville. Referred to by Mrs. Connor as a "monument to the ancient and popular institution of the picnic," the mound was nearly 100 yards long and over 80 feet high.[32] It was being destroyed by sightseers, roadbuilders seeking shell, and fishermen depleting the oyster beds at the foot of the mound. Mrs. Connor had been trying since 1921 to save the site but without success. In 1924 when she asked May for help, May told her, "All this about Turtle Mound is most interesting and as soon as I can get my breath I will see what can be done."[33] By 1928 May had raised the necessary money, and the mound was purchased and placed under the protective custody of the historical society. During the 1930s May frequently checked the fenced-off site. She also sought help from state authorities who had agreed to save the mound's oyster beds. By 1939, when the Florida State Historical Society had merged with the Florida Historical Society, Turtle Mound and the Connor "mission" had been placed under the auspices of the state park system and had been designated historic memorials. May, who had lobbied for a park system for years and for both the 1927 law that established the Internal Improvement Fund Trustees as the state's first park board and the 1935 bill that created an official park agency, became actively involved in the creation of the park system. By 1935, with help from the federal Fulmer-Copeland Bill, which financed state park land acquisitions, Florida had established Mayakka, Gold Head Branch, Hillsborough, and Torreya state parks, and officials were looking at twenty-seven other proposed sites. May was particularly interested in securing St. Johns Bluff, Suwannee River park, and Highlands Hammock Arboretum and putting under full state auspices the "old mission" and her beloved Turtle Mound. Her interest in the new park system became so intense that she boldly made application to Governor Sholtz to be appointed director of the new park agency. Despite much support and the endorsement of scores of friends and officials, she was passed over for the job, a disappointment that remained with her for many years.

On 17 March 1929, Stetson University announced that it was conferring upon May Austin Elizabeth Mann Jennings an honorary Doctor of Laws degree, the LL. D. She was now "the most widely known" woman in Florida.[34] Others honored that day by the university were Florida Governor Doyle E. Carlton and John B. Stetson, Jr., at that time U.S. minister to Poland. At ceremonies presenting the degrees, Stetson President Lincoln Hulley said of May that he was conferring "the degree for distinguished service to Florida upon one who had doctored more laws than anyone else in the state."[35]

CHAPTER 10

"Lover of Beauty"

M AY JENNINGS devoted most of the final three decades of her life to conservation and beautification work, although she maintained a high level of interest in politics. An ardent and lifelong Democrat, May was associate chairman of the National Democratic Committee for Florida in 1920 when blacks comprised nearly half of Duval County's newly registered women voters. Alarmed Florida party officials hastily urged the formation of whites-only county Democratic female clubs throughout the state. Because of May's position, her vast network of female friendships, and her demonstrated organizational skills, she was put in charge of establishing these.

May, who was to remain a loyal Democrat all her life, appointed fifty-four women from around the state to organize the clubs. The local Duval County League of Democratic Voters was organized by May and other Jacksonville women on 27 September 1920. At its first public meeting, the women heard a fiery address by Judge Dodge, a flamboyant local party official. The *Florida Times-Union* printed the speech the next day:

127

This White Women's Democratic League is about to take ship and sail into the political ocean of suffrage. . . . Some desire to lend their presence and aid in case of storm or disaster or political sea sickness. . . . In the South there can be but two political parties, a white Democratic party and a negro-split Republican party. You cannot afford to aid or encourage the party candidate who elevates the negro. . . . Is your party going to be a negro Republican office holding party or the party of the white men of the South who for fifty years past have done all in their power to protect you. . . . You know what it means to let the negro race once get an idea that they are equal or superior in any way to the white race. . . . Choose you this day who are your friends. I am sure your choice will be the Democratic party from top to bottom.

Although May had worked successfully with various black female leaders, she, like most southern whites, feared total black equality. While she and other southern women had scoffed at the charge by white males that female suffrage would lead to blacks controlling politics in the South, she now worried that their prediction might be coming true.

In Jacksonville, May helped to organize the Duval County League of Democratic Women, which the *Florida Times-Union* unabashedly reported was formed "in order that the county might be saved from negro domination."[1] Included among the county chairwomen whom she recruited to organize other clubs in the state were her old friends Ivy Stranahan, Florence Cay, Grace Whitford, Sudie B. Wright, and Rose Lewis, who all had served as officers in the Florida Federation of Women's Clubs.[2] Thousands of Florida women joined the clubs, the Duval League boasting more than 1,500 members at one time. The clubs held "voting schools" to familiarize the women with voting procedures, ballots, and candidates.[3] They also helped organize the women so that they could participate in the political process at the precinct level.

To the dismay of the Democrats, however, the 1920s witnessed a national political trend that favored the Republican party. The progressive era was over and the mood of the country had changed. Republicans Warren G. Harding, Calvin Coolidge, and Herbert Hoover followed one another as president. Membership in the Florida Democratic clubs gradually declined, and within the decade most of them had ceased to exist. Despite the clubs' demise and the end of her tenure as a national party official, May maintained her interest in politics, serving twice, in 1928 and 1932, as Ruth Bryan Owen's campaign manager. Ruth Owen represented South

Florida's 4th District as Florida's first female congresswoman, later serving as U.S. ambassador to Denmark.[4] While Owen served in Washington, May visited her frequently and served as a consultant on Florida matters. In 1935, when a dire economic climate and the controversies of the New Deal had revived people's political interest, May and other party regulars reorganized the defunct Duval club as the Duval County Democratic Women, Inc.[5] May was elected president, an office she held for over nineteen years, leading the organization as it opposed the use of "sweat boxes" in state prisons and jails, sought the updating of county registration lists, campaigned to secure voting machines, and promoted bills to prohibit politicking around polling places.[6] They also sponsored the "50/50 rule," which allowed women greater participation in the affairs of the Democratic party. At the time May expressed the hope "that every precinct and ward in every county and state committee would be filled by proper representatives of our best women citizens."[7] In 1936 May was among the dignitaries who escorted Mrs. Eleanor Roosevelt when she came to Jacksonville on a speaking tour.

At the end of the nineteen years as head of Duval's Democratic women, May noted in an interview with a local newspaper reporter that "women vote now and think nothing of it. But there was a day when they didn't and thought a great deal about it. . . . We must keep active, we stand for high class elections, but we don't endorse candidates. Instead, we endorse measures. We go out for something and fight for it." She also said that she had "fought for causes ever since I can remember."[8]

Through the years May's interest in state government never waned. In 1942 when officials threatened to change public health policy, she submitted a resolution to the FFWC: "whereas civilian health is a paramount consideration at the present time . . . and the state has announced the intention of discontinuing public health service and units in counties of less than 25,000 population, be it resolved that the FFWC protests the discontinuance . . . and that copies of this resolution be forwarded to Governor Holland, and State Board of Health and the press."[9] The resolution, along with protests which May solicited from other organizations, prevented the cancellation of the program.

From the 1930s on, however, politics took second place in May Jennings's life to conservation and beautification projects. Her association with Ruth Owen, an avowed conservationist, allowed her to continue to fight to preserve the Everglades. One of Mrs. Owen's first actions in the House of Representatives was to sponsor a bill for the creation of a national park in the Everglades. The idea was not new—many groups had called for it over the years—but Mrs. Owen was prepared to fight for it on the national level. Senator Duncan U. Fletcher sponsored the bill in the Senate.

With the concurrence of the federation, May offered Royal Palm Park as part of the proposed national park. She also worked with other interested groups to make the national park a reality, a struggle that would prove long and arduous. To lay the groundwork at the state level, May and her fellow conservationists pushed bills through the 1931 and 1935 state legislatures providing for the acquisition of 325,000 acres of state land in Dade, Monroe, and Collier counties and for the establishment of a state Everglades National Park Commission.

Many prominent Floridians and other Americans spoke out in favor of the proposed park, including U.S. Secretary of the Interior Ebert K. Furlew; Gilbert Pearson, president of the National Audubon Society; Roger Toll, superintendent of Yellowstone Park; H. C. Bumpus of the National Park Service; Gifford Pinchot, national conservationist; Mrs. Thomas A. Edison, a resident of Fort Myers; David Fairchild, Ernest F. Coe, and John K. Small, South Florida conservationists; and Fairchild's brother-in-law Gilbert H. Grosvenor, head of the National Geographic Society. When famed landscape architect Frederick Law Olmsted, Jr., and other dignitaries toured the Everglades on an official inspection trip, they were escorted by Coe, chairman of a citizens' group known as the Tropic Everglades National Park Association, and were flown over the area in the Goodyear blimp, which was stationed in Miami. The onset of the depression and the defeat of Ruth Owen in 1932 temporarily sidetracked the issue, and even though in 1934 President Franklin D. Roosevelt signed the bill authorizing the park, and the federation voted to give Royal Palm Park to the proposed national park, it would be many years before the national park came into existence.

During those years May continued to oversee operations at Royal Palm Park. The site registered over 20,000 visitors in 1930, but fires and devastating storms continued to wreak havoc. With the help of her son, Bryan, who was president of the State Board of Forestry, Arno B. Cammesen, director of the National Park Service, and Robert Fechner, a federal agent, May secured brigade 262 of the Civilian Conservation Corps for the park. They made extensive repairs to the lodge and grounds, accomplished much toward fire protection, planted one thousand trees and shrubs, and strung twelve miles of telephone wire from the park to Homestead, connecting Royal Palm Hammock with the outside world.

Govenror David Sholtz, a past president of the State Chamber of Commerce, appointed May to the state's Everglades National Park Commission, which had been inactive since its authorization in 1929. In 1937 the other commissioners chose her to lobby the legislature for an $87,000 appropriation to provide for the commission's work. Fred Cone, the new governor, who was opposed to the national park, agreed to sign the appropriation bill if the entire commission would first resign, assuring May that he would reinstate most of the members. Under threat of the governor's veto, May acceded to the demand, whereupon Cone appointed G. O. Palmer, a friend from Columbia County, as the new chairman of the commission. Palmer allowed the commission to remain in limbo, and it was claimed that he also allowed the funds to be expended on relatively unimportant activities. Feeling betrayed in what she thought was a fair political arrangement, May thereafter referred to Cone as a "double-dealer" and a dishonest man. Nevertheless, Cone's tactic effectively stymied the movement to establish the park, which was opposed by some recalcitrant local landowners and by many of the state's hunters and fishermen.

Despite such discouraging setbacks, May and the conservationists continued their work, temporarily eclipsed by World War II; but in 1945 Governor Millard Caldwell revived the defunct commission and named May as a member. The new commission was led by August Burghard from Fort Lauderdale and John D. Pennekamp from Miami, and among its twenty-five commission members were May's old friends Mrs. T. V. Moore, long-time federation worker from Miami, and Harold Colee, a state Chamber of Commerce official. Since May still owned land near Flamingo, the governor designated her as the commissioner representing the area's landowners. May immediately deeded her land to the state for the park. Pennekamp remembered May as "a most loyal commission member, who attended every meeting, took little or no part in the discussion, but invariably voted approval of all proposals." [10] When the Everglades National Park became the country's twenty-ninth national park, in the spring of 1947, the old federation lodge at Royal Palm Park served as the park's first visitors' center. Years before, May had written Governor Sholtz, "If we [the FFWC] had not conserved this beauty spot [Royal Palm Hammock] years ago there would not have been any talk of a National Park." [11] Park dedication ceremonies at Everglades City, Florida, on 6 December 1947 were attended by many national and state officials and dignitaries and by more than 8,000 of the general public.[12] May, seated on the speakers' platform, had worked to preserve the Everglades for more years than any other person present. John Pennekamp presided, and there were speeches by Ernest F. Coe, August Burghard, Senators Claude Pepper and Spessard

Holland, Governor Caldwell, and Secretary of the Interior Julius A. Krug.
President Harry S. Truman, who was wintering at Key West, flew to Everglades City to deliver the keynote address. May was on the program preceding the speeches; she and Mrs. L. J. McCaffery, president of the Florida Federation of Women's Clubs, presented a plaque to Newton Drury,
director of the National Park Service. The presentation was a symbolic act
giving Royal Palm State Park to the federal government. It culminated the
thirty-three-year fight May had waged to preserve the beauty and unique-
ness of Paradise Key and the surrounding Everglades.

   The *Florida Times-Union* that day published a long editorial summing
up May Jennings's life work:

   Everglades National Park is a permanent monument to the Florida
   Federation of Women's Clubs, for to this energetic organization
   must go most of the credit for the long and much of the time trying
   struggle that resulted in setting aside that portion of the Everglades
   area that now becomes Everglades National Park. . . . The part
   played by the Florida Federation of Women's Clubs is recognized by
   the Government, as indicated by a letter received by Mrs. W. S.
   Jennings . . . from Newton B. Drury, director of the National Park
   Service. "The donation by the Federation constitutes a major step
   toward the ultimate goal. . . . The State Park area has been property guarded from depredation and perpetually kept for Park purposes by the Federation as you pledged it would be in your speech
   of dedication on November 23, 1916." . . . All who are familiar
   with the work of Mrs. Jennings will agree that a large measure of
   credit is due her for determination and persistence which at times
   bridged wide gaps of disappointment in the progress of the program. Today Mrs. Jennings, who is attending the dedication at
   Everglades City, declared that "It has been a long hard fight, but
   the final outcome very gratifying"; with that there will be general
   agreement.[13]

   Since her early club days May had been interested in beautification
work, and from the 1920s until her death in 1963 she was the most prominent "beautifier" in Florida. Like many other movements this one seemed
to have a life of its own. Beginning around 1920, it grew rapidly, peaked
in the 1930s and 1940s, and gradually declined during the years after
World War II. Several organizations were established to accomplish the
movement's goals. The first formal garden club in Florida was organized

in Jacksonville in March 1922, at the Riverside Avenue home of Ninah Cummer.[14] Its membership was composed mainly of women from the Jacksonville Woman's Club. Two years later at the home of Grace Trout (Mrs. George W. Trout) the women organized the Florida Federation of Garden Clubs, listing three clubs in the charter—Jacksonville, Halifax, and Winter Park. Within a decade garden clubs had spread across the state, each with several subgroups called circles. Jacksonville counted eighteen circles. May belonged to the Springfield circle. The Rockledge club had a group of black women known as the Magnolia circle.[15]

The Federation of Garden Clubs became an invaluable ally of May Jennings, and her beautification efforts were also supported by the Tamiami Trail Association, Dixie Highway Association, Florida Branch of the National Association for Restriction of Outdoor Advertising, Florida Federation of Women's Clubs, and State Chamber of Commerce. May's introduction to the formal movement came at the chamber's third annual state Beautification Convention in Tampa in October 1924, where she spoke on the conservation movement in Florida.[16] But not until 1928, when she and a small group met on 19 June at the Jacksonville Mason Hotel, did May's beautification work begin in earnest. Out of this meeting came the Duval County Highway Beautification Association, which developed close ties with local garden clubs, the Chamber of Commerce, and other groups interested in beautification.[17]

The State Chamber of Commerce with which May worked had a long and complex history. There had been many Florida booster organizations over the years, but the immediate antecedent of the State Chamber was the Tick Eradication Board established in 1916, in turn an offshoot of the Southern Settlement and Development Association composed of growth-minded cattlemen and lumbermen. In 1921 the Tick Eradication Board changed its name to the Florida Development Board and in 1925 to the Florida State Chamber of Commerce. Through these formative years it was led by the same slate of officers: Jules M. Burguierres of West Palm Beach, William L. Wilson of Panama City, A. A. Coult of Fort Myers, and A. G. Cummer of Jacksonville. May Jennings began working with the organization when it was still known as the Tick Eradication Board. By the time it became the chamber and moved its headquarters to Jacksonville, she was one of its better known members.

For years the chamber, the garden clubs, and other organizations tried with little success to get beautification and highway standards upgraded. As president of the Duval County Highway Beautification Association, May attended the chamber's Eleventh Annual State Beautification Convention in November 1928 in Kissimmee and spoke to the meeting on "Legislation for Highway Beautification." [18] She had brought with her a bill on highway beautification, which she presented to the convention. It later was published in *Beautiful Florida*, the Florida Federation of Garden Clubs' official journal. She wrote, "It seems quite time, although years too late in some cases, but vital to the future of the state, for higher authorities to take a decided stand and declare a definite policy in regard to road beautification and plan for rights-of-way suitable to such need. I will recommend to the Legislative Council that a definite policy be fixed by law." [19] Drawn up with the help of Bryan Jennings, the bill had several sections: it mandated that a beautification expert be appointed to the State Road Department's governing board; that every Florida road have a right-or-way of not less than 100 feet; that all road construction be done from the center of the right-of-way outward and any widening of a roadbed be uniform in nature; that beautification and landscaping work reproduce the natural setting as closely as practicable; that at least 24 feet of the 100-foot right-of-way be reserved for conservation and beautification; that all wire-holding poles be set back to the outer edges of the right-of-way; and that county commissioners be allowed to authorize expenditures for beautification of county roads. The measure left little to conjecture or debate; like all of May Jennings's proposed bills, it was direct and to the point.

In 1929, with the endorsement of Governor Doyle Carlton, May submitted her bill to the state legislature. Although hours of lobbying convinced her that the bill would be passed, it was narrowly defeated. At the time she wrote to federation members, "You will recall that the Highway Beautification Bill was taken by me to Tallahassee with the full endorsement of the FFWC, by the Duval Highway Beautification Association, where it originated, by the State Chamber of Commerce, Gulf Coast Highway [Association] and Florida Federation of Garden Clubs. I have never handled legislation . . . that had such enthusiastic support, and still failed to become law. . . . I had two conferences with the Governor and several with Chairman Bentley. . . . It is needless to tell you that I also had to satisfy the wire, or pole using companies." [20] (Utility and outdoor advertising companies were to remain opponents of May's for many years.) The bill's defeat might also have been due to county officials' lukewarm support. May often had clashed with local officials over road policy, and in fact during the campaign to get the highway bill enacted she was involved in another confrontation. She wrote a friend, "Cresap [a Volusia County official] is not entirely my friend, I think, because it was he who cut down the cathedral oaks [on the road to] New Smyrna, and he knows we are after his scalp." [21] In 1931 she returned to Tallahassee with the bill. This time even more groups favored its passage, and it became law without much opposition. Despite the bill's easy passage, May wrote a supporter, "I worked on it for about five years and had to present three different [versions] before I could get it passed." [22] The following year, May was able to persuade the governor to use the bill and appoint the first landscape architect to the state road department.

The Duval County Highway Beautification Association grew to have local political clout. It was responsible for beautifying eighteen miles of Atlantic Boulevard from Jacksonville to the beach, Pearl Street, Saratoga Point, San Jose Boulevard, Trout River Bridge, Edgewood Avenue, Main Street, and Beach Boulevard. It oversaw the landscaping of city and county sites including Imeson Airport, the Duval County Courthouse, the Matthew Bridge entrances, and the downtown riverfront. It also was responsible for the acquisition of DeWees Park at Atlantic Beach and the right-of-way for the road that leads to St. John's Bluff, the site of Fort Caroline National Monument.

In conjunction with the Springfield Woman's Club, the Duval County Highway Beautification Association also turned an unsightly dump along Long Branch Creek and marsh in north Springfield into a fifty-acre park, named Jennings Park in May's honor. In addition the association, with the aid of local garden clubs, oversaw the planting of thousands of flowers, trees, and shrubs along county and city roadways. Many of the projects were completed with federal funds allocated to agencies such as the Works Progress Administration, the Civilian Conservation Corps, and the Federal Emergency Relief Administration, whose Florida director was May's longtime friend Marcus Fagg. Through the years the association received many accolades. In 1933, May received a "Resolution of Appreciation" from the Jacksonville City Council, and in 1952 she received a special citation from the Florida Federation of Garden Clubs. In addition, in 1958, her last year as president, the association was cited by the General Federation of Women's Clubs and the Sears-Roebuck Foundation as one of the nation's most successful beautification groups.

The Florida Federation of Women's Clubs and the Springfield Improvement Association continued to receive May's attention. In 1932 the SIA, later known as the Springfield Woman's Club, built a clubhouse only a few blocks from the Jennings' home. [23] Through the years the organization kept a vigilant eye on Springfield and took the lead in keeping the public buildings, schools, and parks in the area clean and in repair. The group also supported the efforts to beautify Hogan's Creek in Springfield Park.

As Lucy Blackman remembered: "Some years ago Mrs. Jennings represented the Springfield Improvement Association in a campaign to beautify unsightly muddy Hogan's Creek which divides the main part of downtown Jacksonville from Springfield. The Creek winds through the city for a mile and a half before it empties into the St. Johns River. The association under Mrs. Jennings's leadership worked eighteen years before they secured a bond election for a half million dollars for the work and it took two years more before they could persuade the city commission to sell the bonds for the work. Mrs. Jennings finally secured the engineer wanted for the work and it is now conceded the most outstanding work of its kind in the whole southeast—with its bulkhead, concrete walks and ballisters and lighting system. A bronze tablet bears the Springfield Improvement Association name and date. Mrs. Jennings was asked to dedicate the beautiful improvement and turn on the lights which she did." [24]

With the Hogan Creek–Springfield Park project and the passage of the highway beautification bill of 1931 behind her, May's reputation as the state's leading exponent of beautification was further enhanced when she succeeded Lorenzo A. Wilson as chairman of the State Chamber of Commerce's beautification committee in 1934. The committee was made up of prominent Floridians, among them Mrs. John Ringling of Sarasota, Rex Beach of Sebring, Harold Hume of Gainesville, and Mrs. Jessie Ball Du Pont and Mrs. Bion H. Barnett of Jacksonville. [25] May held this chairmanship for over twenty-five years, during which she organized beautification auxiliaries in each community that had a Chamber of Commerce. Over the years these local committees helped establish scores of local parks and beautified many buildings and roadways. In 1936 May served on the board of governors of the *Southern Woman's Digest*, a magazine devoted to women's interests, which was published in Jacksonville. During the one year the magazine was published, May wrote several articles pertinent to the conservation and beautification movement. In one, "God's Own Garden," she described Royal Palm Park. [26] In another she advocated opening all state beaches to the public: "Our beaches must be declared to be state reservations or parks under the protection of the state. . . . Florida women must realize the value of Florida's beaches . . . and through local Chambers of Commerce, civic and social groups strive for a 'closed season' on Florida's coastline (which is being fenced off for private use)." [27] Shortly after this article appeared May proposed that the state legislature enact a law calling for the protection and beautification of the state's waterways and beaches, but the measure did not pass. For years the Chamber of Commerce and May's various beautification organizations backed legislation to create a state intercoastal waterway system with public boat-launching facilities and park areas along its route. The groups' efforts were only partially successful. It would take World War II to convince state and federal officials of the strategic, commercial, and recreational benefits of such a system.

The outbreak of World War II forced the beautification movement to operate at a reduced pace. Most projects were geared to beautifying the grounds in and around Florida's many military installations. At Cecil Field in Jacksonville, May personally oversaw the erection and landscaping of a flagpole plaza on the quadrant in front of base headquarters. During the conflict she made her own personal contribution to the war effort by open-ing her Springfield home to roomers to help ease Jacksonville's critical housing shortage. Many contemporaries recall the small, neat sign, "JEN-NINGS," which hung from her front porch during those days. In 1943 she participated in the christening of the 10,500-ton Liberty ship, the S.S. *W. S. Jennings*. Members of the family and city officials attended the cere-mony, at which Thomas B. Adams, Sr., spoke about Governor Jennings's career. Then May christened the ship with the words "May this liberty ship prove as sea worthy, sturdy, strong, and dependable as the man was, whose name it is to bear." [28]

The end of the war brought a resurgence of the beautification program. With Americans more mobile than ever, thousands of tourists began to visit the state. Among the projects coordinated by May's State Chamber of Commerce beautification committee were the highways beautified in memory of the state's war dead, including a section of the old Spanish Trail (U.S. 90) from Monticello to Tallahassee, known as the Blue Star Highway; the highway between Tallahassee and Thomasville, Georgia; and a section of Highway 301 which began at Clermont and extended south through the Florida ridge for more than sixty miles.

During the 1950s Florida joined the national "Keep America Beautiful" campaign. For nearly a decade, each September was designated "Florida Beautification Month," during which May and her committee coordinated the effort that took place among hundreds of Florida garden and women's clubs, chambers of commerce, and beautification associations. Every few years, under the auspices of May's committee, these organizations met in convention. At one such meeting, in 1954, over 300 Floridians devoted a day to discussing antilitter campaigns, law enforcement problems, and public education issues.[29] That same year May's bill calling for the crea-tion of a division of landscaping within the State Road Department was rejected by the legislature.

In 1956 the State Chamber of Commerce dedicated a new headquarters building in Jacksonville. May supervised the landscaping, which included the installation of sabal palms and flowering trees on the grounds.[30] In 1959 she was a special guest when the William R. Kenan Floral Gardens were dedicated on the building's lawn.[31] In 1961, May, now eighty-eight years old, agreed to oversee one last Florida Beautification Month before she resigned as head of the committee. The *Florida Times-Union* wrote: "If while driving this month in the family car you see a lovely lady out planting flowers and shrubs along Florida's highways, it's a good bet her name will be Mrs. W. S. Jennings. . . . She is the hardworking chairman of the State Chamber's Beautification Committee. Since September is Beautification Month in Florida, Mrs. Jennings and her co-workers are extremely busy making the Sunshine State pretty for its winter guests. So when you see Mrs. Jennings out planting this month, stop and give her a hand to make Florida a more beautiful state." [32]

After May's retirement she received a plaque from the State Chamber of Commerce inscribed with a resolution of gratitude for her years of service.[33] She was made honorary member of the beautification committee and an honorary life member of the chamber. By now May had quite a collection of honors. In 1955 she had been named the Springfield Woman's Club's outstanding citizen, and the following year the Jacksonville branch of Soroptimist International had named her "Woman of the Year." [34] She had been honored at a University of Florida Centennial convocation program in Gainesville in 1953, with a medal for meritorious service as one of Florida's most outstanding leaders.[35] In 1961 the university named a women's residence hall in her honor. In the building hangs a bronze plaque upon which is inscribed the words "May Austin Mann Jennings/A civic leader and wife of William Sherman Jennings, made her own outstanding contributions to the life and growth of this state as a pioneer in highway beautification and park development. The progress of Florida forestry owes much to her dedicated interest."

In 1962 May Jennings contracted cancer and retired from all civic activities. Her son and daughter-in-law moved into her home to care for her and were at her bedside when she died on 24 April 1963, the day before her ninety-first birthday. Her funeral was held at Riverside Park Methodist church where friends, many blacks, including Eartha M. White, Chamber of Commerce officials, and members of the Springfield Woman's Club paid their respects. She was buried next to her husband in Evergreen Cemetery. The *Florida Times-Union,* in an editorial, noted her passing and asked, "Who will step forward to take her spade?" [36]

The legislature of the state of Florida issued that day a concurrent resolution expressing deep sympathy and regret over her passing: "The people
of the entire state of Florida mourn the loss of a warmly dedicated woman
of rare charm, intelligence and leadership of the highest order who built
an enviable record of good works, NOW THEREFORE, BE IT RESOLVED BY
THE HOUSE OF REPRESENTATIVES OF THE STATE OF FLORIDA, THE SENATE
CONCURRING: That on behalf of the people of Florida this legislature does
unanimously express its deep and earnest sense of regret and heartfelt sorrow at her untimely passing." [37]

In 1963, a few months after her death, May Jennings was awarded a
Chair of Business in the State Chamber of Commerce's Florida Hall of
Achievement. On 12 November 1966, the State Road Department in cooperation with the Florida Federation of Garden Clubs erected a highway
marker on U.S. Highway 17, near Yulee, where U.S. Highways 1 and 301
enter the state. The marker bears the inscription "In memory of MAY
MANN JENNINGS lover of beauty."

CHAPTER 11

A Life of Good Works Assessed

A FTER EXAMINING and evaluating both May Jennings's life and the vast legacy of good works that she left behind, an observer can draw only one conclusion: she stands alone as Florida's most impressive and successful female citizen. Few women have been recognized for having made lasting contributions to Florida's cultural, political, and civic institutions. There are few works about women in general and Florida women in particular,[1] yet recently scholars have shown that many women around the country were making impressive contributions to their local, state, and national communities. In Florida it was May Jennings, more than any other woman in the twentieth century, who contributed to the welfare and progress of the state.

Indeed, May Jennings's record of public service can be matched by few other figures in Florida history, male or female. Her list of achievements is staggering.[2] Hardly a single enterprise dedicated to the public welfare escaped her notice and support. In addition to her own achievements, for more than sixty years she inspired and provided ideas and leadership to the Florida women's movement, and part of what makes her so fascinating and her contributions so unique is her longevity. Her life spanned the whole of the women's movement, from its earliest stirrings to its modern phase. Born in 1872, when women were just beginning to put aside full-time domesticity and step into the public arena, she lived through some of the movement's most exciting and historically significant periods. She died in 1963, the year in which Betty Friedan published her classic, *The Feminine Mystique*,[3] a work that marks the beginning of the modern struggle for women's rights, a struggle that can be traced to the early suffragists but that differs radically in temper and circumstance.

May Jennings's accomplishments and interests were so vast that it is difficult to single out any one as more significant than any other. But it can be agreed that her conservation work, a lifelong avocation that included the saving of the Everglades, was her primary contribution to Florida and her single most impressive achievement. Her record of accomplishments makes one ask what accounts for her extraordinary record of good works? Were her achievements and abilities such that we should consider them (and her) an aberration, or was her career a supreme example of what was also happening elsewhere? What made May Jennings such a unique, charming, and endearing public figure?

There can be little doubt that heredity and background account for some of May's success. She seems to have taken after her father and to have inherited Austin Mann's zest for life, his tireless vitality, his sharp intellect, and his love of politics.[4] In addition, her exposure, from childhood, to a steady diet of public service and political wheeling and dealing by her father would account for much of her own practical political sense and astute legislative lobbying skills. Too, there can be little doubt that because her father treated her as a son, May Jennings did not always feel the public disapproval that other women did when they tried to participate in all-male activities. She seems not to have accepted the view that politics was a masculine endeavor. Her nature and her upbringing provided her the self-confidence to be herself, and the time she spent helping her father in his campaigns and legislative tasks prepared her for her own public career.

Too, her personal charisma should not be overlooked as a factor that contributed to her success. She could always walk into a room full of people and become at once the focal point. Her magnetism, her beauty, and her genteel nature were characteristics that aided her in her work. She brought a cheerful and dignified approach to all of her endeavors. She was not afraid to speak her mind or to stand up for her beliefs, and she had no axes to grind. That such a refined woman could also possess a calculating mind, extraordinary tact, and good intuitive judgment, and that she could

take on so many diverse activities and causes and keep her sunny disposition, must have puzzled many. She had many admirers and few detractors
during her lifetime.

Other factors in May Jennings's childhood contributed to her success.
Having spent most of her formative years at the family's orange grove
surely contributed to her lifelong interest in Florida's flora and fauna.
Those years, when she was surrounded by the sights, sounds, smells, and
beauty of tropical Florida, must have prompted her desire to conserve that
environment. Of course, like other progressives of her day, she desired to
see the state's resources developed to bring money and people and a better
life to what was then a poor state. Her father's and husband's interests in
drainage, cross-state barge canals, roads, and agricultural development
also played a part in her interest in Florida's environment. But, unlike
them, and unlike other developers who viewed Florida as a paradise await-
ing the hand of man, she tempered such exploitive dreams with a gentling
touch and an awareness that Florida's beauty and resources were priceless
assets to be appreciated and protected. In her defense of the pelicans, of
Turtle Mound, of Paradise Key, of the Seminole Indians, we see a woman
who understood that to develop Florida with no thought to the toll on its
resources would be too high a price to pay. The conservation efforts of
May and the small coterie in Florida who worked with her were stimulated
by and were a part of a larger conservation movement, spawned during the
Progressive era and led by John Muir, Gifford Pinchot, Theodore Roosevelt, and other national figures. This movement, on the national level, was
to culminate in the establishment of the U.S. Forest Service, the National
Park Service, and pioneering wilderness laws.[5] Floridians' efforts under
May Jennings's leadership seem to be one of the more successful and vigorous state offshoots of the national movement and the only one led by a
woman.

May's interest in conservation transcended the national movement because hers was a lifelong commitment. All her life she was guided by a
protective attitude toward people, nature, and things that needed special
care. Perhaps it stemmed from the fact that her mother had died when she
was young, and from an early age she felt the responsibilities of being the
eldest of four children. For years after her mother's death, she was solici-
tous toward her siblings and mothered them through many critical mo-
ments. Much of her public career—her work to protect children, working
women, the public's health, and the environment—reveals this nurturing
and compassionate spirit.

May's education at St. Joseph's also fitted her for a public career; it reinforced her protective attitude and strengthened the sense of public duty that she had received from her father. The genteel but sound academic training and the moral and emotional stability she received at the school inculcated characteristics important to her future. She never lost her composure in public, nor did she ever lose sight of her long-term goals. The public's perception of her remained positive throughout her life.

The influence of Sherman Jennings on May was incalculable. Kindred spirits in both intellect and outlook, they shared a mutual devotion to and aspiration for Florida's public welfare. They were well suited to one another, and like her father before him Sherman recognized, appreciated, and welcomed May's political talents. There is little doubt that his political reputation and past political positions aided May in her own public career and smoothed the way for many of her achievements. In the early years it was often Sherman who made the first contact with officials she was to deal with. He, like their son, Bryan, later, was to write much of the legislation that May submitted on behalf of her causes, and it was his financial success that allowed her to pursue her ambitions full-time and with such devotion. But, though he opened doors for her, it was May and the women with whom she worked whose day-to-day efforts must be given credit for achieving what they did. The mysterious but powerful entity known as the old-girl network, working first through the Florida Federation of Women's Clubs and later through other organizations, enabled May to achieve her most significant successes. Everglades National Park exists today because of the intrepid clubwomen who had the foresight and determination to preserve the Everglades and the leadership of May Jennings to achieve this goal. Likewise, May and her coworkers brought about other progressive programs, among them tick eradication, highway beautification, public health measures, child protection laws, and forestry legislation.

Other studies show that these Florida women were part of a larger movement in the nation.[6] Anxious to participate in the political and civic life in their communities and led by forceful leaders like May, women were being seen and heard across the land. In every state and territory, women were accomplishing wonders in public health, education, conservation, and government. Indeed, women elsewhere were involved in many of the same pursuits, though not on such a large and diverse scale, as was May Jennings, among them two southern contemporaries of May's: Laura Clay of Kentucky and Anna Pennybacker of Texas.[7] The trend that had begun with the abolition, missionary, and temperance societies of the late nineteenth century was to culminate in the women's clubs movement—the establishment of the General Federation of Women's Clubs and the found-

ing of the state federations—and, finally, suffrage for women, followed by
what modern scholars call "social feminism." May Jennings fits squarely
within the bounds of social feminism.[8]

Though women accomplished more in some parts of the country than in
others, usually because of a higher degree of local tolerance or exceptional leadership, all areas were affected by women who worked for progress and the public good. This study of May Jennings shows conclusively
that Florida was part of this trend, that women in the state were actively
pursuing an agenda of good works that would be of historical significance.
It shows that even without the vote during part of this period, women still
achieved many of their goals. Without the women's efforts and May Jennings's untiring leadership, the state would not have many of its parks,
beautification projects, libraries, and hospitals, and much of its progressive social legislation. Florida women went directly into the political
mainstream once they achieved the ballot, and we now know how they did
it: through the federation and the League of Women Voters, through the
Legislative Council, and through local Democratic party politics. We see
that Florida's earliest female politicians got started in local woman's clubs,
where they developed their leadership skills; they honed them in the federation and brought them to fruition on state boards and commissions and,
finally, in state and national elective offices.[9]

May Jennings, the most prominent exponent of social feminism in Florida, was unique to Florida but not to the nation; there were nearly a score
of women across the nation who, like her, led women in their states to
achieve some remarkable goals. This fact does not diminish May's contributions, for even among those talented few she stands out. And, the historian must ask, what if she had not appeared on the scene? There would
still have been a Florida Federation of Women's Clubs and a League of
Women Voters, and perhaps even a beautification movement, but surely
the accomplishments would not have been as impressive without the un-
matched energy and enthusiasm that May brought to those causes. That no
other women stepped forward to challenge her place or to lead the state's
women shows the rare blend of talents she brought to her public service
and the rare person she was. Finally, we must not overlook the positive
example she set for thousands of women in the state, many of whom must
have aspired to public careers of their own. While there is no way to calcu-
late the final effects of the positive influence that she asserted upon the
aspirations of Florida women, we know that she had few detractors and
many admirers throughout her life. And we know that her name and legacy will rest favorably in the memory of future generations.

For the author, part of the pleasure of writing about such a remarkable woman has been the knowledge that when May's story was finally told, it would erase for all time the generally held belief that Florida women had no history to tell, that they were merely passive bystanders in their state's history. Now we know that to be untrue, that there was a parallel story developing along with the traditional version of Florida's history. And while only a part of this exciting new history has been told in this biography, and while there remains much work to be done to uncover the rest of the women's story, it is hoped that this life of May Jennings will prove how rewarding the new historical findings will be.

Appendixes

1. "Beyond the Alps Lies Italy"

Kind Friends,

There are occasions when silence is more eloquent than words, when we are surrounded by circumstances in which it would seem mockery to attempt to give utterance to our feelings. Such are the emotions which arise in our souls, as we stand before you today, to take our final farewell.

We have been as wayfarers among you seeking for treasures in distant lands and in our search for knowledge we have been separated from those who are near and dear to us, but, in the gloom which, at times, overspread our days of search, we were encouraged by the thought that "Beyond the Alps Lay Fair Italy" our beloved home and that at a future day, the highest peak would be reached and laden with treasures we would return to our homes.

Ours has frequently been a weary struggle for, in the rugged paths, how often has the shadow of discouragement disturbed our efforts! How often

146

has the phantom of glory tried to lead us astray! How often, too, have we fallen when we thought ourselves secure, and with bleeding hearts lay amid the rocks; but, cheered on by the hope of one day arriving at the top of the Alps we arose and continued our work.

Having at last, climbed one by one the rocky cliffs, and having come in sight of our friends and home, we rejoice and fondly arranging the treasures sought and found, we look upon them and with the poet, consider them "things of beauty, hence, joys forever."

Among the rare and precious stones which we have gathered on our weary journey across the Alps, our labor has been rewarded by the possession of the Garnet, emblematic of constancy and fidelity; we have also found the Bloodstone, symbolic of wisdom, courage and firmness; procured the peerless Diamond of faith and innocence, and secured the Sapphire of virtue and truth: these are the most precious among our collections of gems; these complete our casket.

Although we were happy in finding our earnestly sought treasures, yet, we often grew sad and sighed for home, but, we were encouraged by the kind and reassuring words of our esteemed guides, for whom we have formed strong attachments. Our associates, too, have grown dear to us— as we greet each other today perhaps to meet no more, and as the blithesome notes of happy school day songs are echoed among the heights, the key notes of memory are touched, and their sweet but mournful strains force the tear drops to dim our eyes "ere we summon the courage to say farewell."

For looking backward from the craggy heights, the scene is well calculated to move every chord and to open up the vista of the past; we gaze with pleasure mingled with pain on the dear old classroom and recreation hall, where hand-in-hand we worked and played together, and "the social smile of every welcome face, will in fond memory ever hold a place."

Nor is the chapel hidden where low before our Lord we made known our little wants; to all these we must bid adieu, but in days to come happy memories will call forth the aspiration,

> Oh! friends regretted
> scenes forever dear,
> Remembrance hails you
> with her warmed tear!
> Drooping she bends o'er
> pensive Fancy's urn,
> To trace the hours
> which never can return

Yet with the retrospection
loves to dwell,
And soothe the sorrows
of her last farewell!

May A. Mann
26 June 1889

2. Presidents of Florida Federation of Women's Clubs, 1895–1920

1895–97
Mrs. P. A. Borden Hamilton
Village Improvement Association, Green Cove Springs
1897–98
Mrs. N. C. Wamboldt
Town Improvement Association, Fairfield (Jacksonville)
1899–1901
Mrs. J. C. Beckman
Woman's Town Improvement Association and Cemetery Association,
    Tarpon Springs
1901–3
Mrs. W. W. Cummer
Woman's Club, Jacksonville
1903–5
Mrs. Lawrence Haynes
Woman's Club, Jacksonville
1905–6
Mrs. Richard F. Adams
Woman's Fortnightly Club, Palatka
1906–8
Mrs. Charles H. Raynor
Palmetto Club, Daytona
1908–10
Mrs. Thomas M. Shackleford
Woman's Club, Tallahassee
1910–12
Mrs. A. E. Frederick
Woman's Club, Miami

1912–14
Mrs. William A. Hocker
Woman's Club, Ocala
1914–17
Mrs. W. S. Jennings
Woman's Club, Jacksonville; Springfield Improvement Association,
Springfield
1917–19
Mrs. Edgar A. Lewis
Woman's Club, Fort Pierce
1919–21
Mrs. J. W. McCollum
20th Century Club, Gainesville

3. Clubs in Florida Federation of Women's Clubs

PART 1: 1905

Date of Entry	
1895	Village Improvement Association, Green Cove Springs
	Village Improvement Association, Tarpon Springs
	(changed to Cycadia Cemetery Association)
	Village Improvement Association, Crescent City
	Village Improvement Association, Orange City
	Village Improvement Association, Fairfield
1896	——
1897	Palmetto Club, Daytona
	Literary and Debating Club, Melrose
	Avilah, Rockledge
1898	Woman's Club, Jacksonville
	Woman's Fortnightly Club, Palatka
	Village Improvement Association, Ormond
1899	——
1900	——
1901	Housekeepers, Coconut Grove
1902	——
1903	Village Improvement Association, San Mateo

1904   Current Events Club, Live Oak
              20th Century Club, Gainesville
              New Century Club, High Springs
              Village Improvement Association, Lake Como
              Woman's Club, Fort Myers
              Current Events Club, Tampa
              Married Ladies' Afternoon Club, Miami
1905   ——

PART 2: 1914

State Section 1: *Citrus, Sumter, Lake Hernando, Polk, De Soto,
Hillsborough, Manatee, and Lee counties*

Civic League, Arcadia
Woman's Club, Auburndale
Woman's Club, Bradenton
Woman's Club, Brooksville
Mother's Club, Clearwater
Woman's Club, Clearwater
Alpha Sorosis, Dade City
Woman's Civic Club, Dade City
Woman's Club, Eustis
Woman's Club, Fort Myers
Woman's Club, Lakeland
Woman's Club, Leesburg
Woman's Club, Manatee
Ladies Village Improvement
    Association, Ozona

Fortnightly Club, Punta Gorda
20th Century Club, Ruskin
Woman's Club, St. Petersburg
Woman's Town Improvement
    Association, St. Petersburg
Woman's Club, Sarasota
Civics Association, Tampa
Woman's City Club, Tampa
Woman's Club, Tampa
Civics Club, Tarpon Springs
Cycadia Cemetery Association,
    Tarpon Springs
Civic League, Wachula
Woman's Club, Wildwood
Civic League, Winter Haven

State Section 2: *Jefferson, Madison, Hamilton, Columbia, Baker,
Nassau, Taylor, Suwannee, Bradford, Lafayette, Alachua,
Levy, and Marion counties*

Woman's Club, Dunnellon
Ladies Civic League, Fernandina
20th Century Club, Gainesville
Village Improvement Club,
    Hawthorne
New Century Club, High Springs

Woman's Club, Lawtey
Woman's Club, Live Oak
Woman's Club, Madison
Woman's Club, Mayo
Woman's Club, Ocala
Woman's Club, Perry

Woman's Club, Jasper   School and Civic Club, Starke
Current Topic Club, Lake City

State Section 3: *Escambia, Santa Rosa, Walton, Holmes,*
Washington, Bay, Jackson, Calhoun, Liberty, Franklin,
Gadsden, Wakulla, and Leon counties

Woman's Club, Panama City   Woman's Club, Tallahassee
Civic League, Pensacola

State Section 4: *Duval, Clay, St. Johns, Volusia (part),*
and Putnam counties

Village Improvement Association,   Pan-Hellenic Association,
  Crescent City   Jacksonville
Palmetto, Daytona   Springfield Improvement
Woman's Club, DeLand   Association, Jacksonville
Village Improvement Association,   Woman's Club, Jacksonville
  Federal Point   Woman's Club, Orange Park
Village Improvement Association,   Village Improvement Association,
  Green Cove Springs   Ormond
Fairfield Improvement Association,   Woman's Club, Palatka
  Jacksonville   Woman's Civic League, St.
Ladies' Civic Improvement Club   Augustine
  of Riverview, Jacksonville   St. Cecilia Club, St. Augustine
Ladies' Friday Musicale,   Ladies Village Improvement
  Jacksonville   Association, San Mateo
New Springfield Woman's Club,   Book Club, South Jacksonville
  Jacksonville   Woman's Club, South Jacksonville
                                        Village Improvement Association,
                                          Welaka

State Section 5: *Volusia (part), Seminole, Orange, Brevard,*
Osceola, St. Lucie, Palm Beach, Dade,
and Monroe counties

Woman's Club, Boynton   Woman's Club, Miami
Public Library Association, Cocoa   Woman's Club, New Smyrna

The Folio, Coconut Grove
Housekeepers, Coconut Grove
Woman's Club, Fort Lauderdale
Woman's Club, Fort Pierce
Woman's Club, Homestead
Ladies Civic Association, Key
    West
Woman's Club, Lake Worth
Woman's Club, Melbourne
The Mothercraft Club, Miami

Village Improvement Club, Orange
    City
Sorosis, Orlando
Woman's Civic League, Orlando
Ladies Civic Improvement Club,
    Pompano
Woman's Club, Sanford
Woman's Club, Stuart
Progressive Culture Club,
    Titusville
Entre Nous, West Palm Beach

4. Annual Conventions of the FFWC, 1896–1919

Number	Date	Location
First organized	1895 (Winter)	Green Cove Springs
1st	1896 (Winter)	Green Cove Springs
2d	1897 (Winter)	Jacksonville
3d	1898 (Winter)	Daytona
4th	1899 (Winter)	Jacksonville
5th	1900 (Winter)	Palatka
6th	1901 (Winter)	Daytona
7th	1902 (Winter)	Crescent City
8th	1903 (Winter)	Ormond
9th	1904 (Winter)	Jacksonville
10th	1905 (Winter)	Miami
11th	1906 (Winter)	Tampa
12th	1906 (Autumn)	Tallahassee
13th	1907 (Autumn)	Gainesville
14th	1908 (Autumn)	Live Oak
15th	1909 (Autumn)	Palatka
16th	1910 (Autumn)	Ocala
17th	1911 (Autumn)	Jacksonville
18th	1912 (Autumn)	West Palm Beach
19th	1913 (Autumn)	Orlando
20th	1914 (Autumn)	Lakeland
21st	1915 (Autumn)	DeLand

22d	1916 (Autumn)	Miami
23d	1917 (Autumn)	Tampa
24th	1918 (Autumn)	Daytona
25th	1919 (Autumn)	St. Petersburg

5. The "Old-Girl" Network

The network was a group of women who worked with May on federation committees. Those on the all-important *legislation* committee during May's administration included Mary Wright Drane (Lakeland), wife of Herbert Drane, former member of the state house and a state senator during the 1913 and 1915 sessions; Allie Farris (Jacksonville), wife of Ion L. Farris, ex-speaker of the house and member of the senate during the 1915 and 1917 sessions; Ella Burford (Ocala), wife of Robert A. Burford, former member of the house and a Marion County official; Dycie Sweger (Live Oak), wife of Roy L. Sweger, who edited the *Gadsen County Times* and later served in both the Florida house and senate; Lena Shackleford, wife of Thomas Shackleford, who served on the state supreme court from 1902 until 1917; Ruby Whitfield (Tallahassee), wife of C. Talbot Whitfield, private secretary to Governors Gilchrist and Trammell; Minerva Jennings (Jacksonville), wife of Frank E. Jennings, member of the State Board of Control and later a member of the house; Margaret Young (Jacksonville), wife of William B. Young, the state's judge advocate general and later a house member; Jessie Hilburn (Palatka), wife of Samuel Hilburn, who served in the 1908 house and the 1911 senate; Bell Rood (New Smyrna), wife of Henry Rood, owner of the *New Smyrna News;* Rose Wilson (Sarasota), wife of C. V. Wilson, former member of the 1903, 1905, and 1907 house and owner of the *Sarasota Times;* Maggie Davis (Perry), wife of William B. Davis, Taylor County judge; Ida Dunn (Tallahassee), wife of Royal C. Dunn, state railroad commissioner; Lina L'Engle Barnett (Jacksonville), wife of Bion H. Barnett, founder of the Barnett banking empire; Catherine Phillips (Jacksonville), wife of Henry B. Phillips, circuit judge of Duval County; Eugenia Roberts (Key West), wife of E. O. Roberts, former house member and Monroe County state attorney; Ninah Cummer (Jacksonville), wife of Arthur G. Cummer, co-owner of the state's largest lumber mill and naval stores company; Frances Anderson (Jacksonville), suffragist and activist, daughter of prominent attorney Herbert L. Anderson; and Antoinette Frederick (Miami), widow of that city's first civil engineer, attorney, and land developer, John S. Frederick.

May's *major officers and board of directors* included: Mary Sorenson Moore (Miami), wife of T. Vivian Moore, developer, former legislator, and South Florida's "pineapple king"; Florence Cay (Tallahassee), wife of Charles A. Cay, Leon County legislator and civic leader ("Flo" Cay, a confidante of May's, ran a boardinghouse favored by legislators; she was therefore able to keep abreast of the public and not-so-public happenings in the capital); Ora Minium (Jacksonville), wife of Harry B. Minium, member of the State Board of Control; Kate V. Jackson (Tampa), daughter of John Jackson, one of the founders of that city; Elizabeth Hocker (Ocala), daughter-in-law of William Hocker, state supreme court justice from 1903 to 1915; Ella Brown (Green Cove Springs), wife of T. J. Brown, former legislator and civic leader; and Lucy Wamboldt (Jacksonville), wife of Nelson C. Wamboldt, city councilman.

Dollie Hendley (Dade City), wife of Jefferson A. Hendley, Pasco County pioneer and former legislator, served on the federation's *civics* committee, as did Mrs. John E. Avery (Pensacola), who was married to a member of the house. The federation's *publicity* committee was equally well staffed. It included Nelle Worthington (Tampa), wife of Justin E. Worthington, editor of the *Tampa Times*; and Marjory Stoneman Douglas (Miami), whose father was editor and co-owner of the *Miami Herald*.

The *conservation* committee, one of the federation's largest and most active committees, was concerned with bird protection, forestry, waterways, good roads, and Seminole Indians. The well-connected women who served on this committee included Julia Hanson (Fort Myers), wife of a pioneer doctor and mother of a state bird warden and Seminole Indian agent; Mrs. James Paul (High Springs), whose husband served in the 1915 house; Edith Gifford (Coconut Grove), wife of John Gifford, author and forestry expert; Maria Ingraham (St. Augustine), wife of James E. Ingraham, president of Flagler's Model Land Company; Mary Barr Munroe (Coconut Grove), author and wife of Kirk Munroe; Elizabeth McDonald (Stuart), wife of Jackson McDonald, mayor of Stuart; Ethelyn Overstreet (Orlando), wife of Moses Overstreet, banker and future state senator; Mrs. W. J. Tweedell (Homestead), wife of a Dade County commissioner; Ivy Stranahan (Fort Lauderdale), wife of Frank Stranahan, a pioneer developer and Seminole Indian trader; Minnie Moore Willson (Kissimmee), wife of James Willson, president of the Florida Waterway Association and a cofounder, along with his wife, of the Friends of Florida Seminoles; Ella Dimick (Palm Beach), wife of Captain Elisha N. Dimick, former house and senate member and a pioneer banker and developer; Eugenia Davis (Tallahassee), whose husband, George I. Davis, Leon County's postmaster, had played a prominent role at the 1885 Constitutional Convention; and Jane Fisher (Miami), wife of Carl G. Fisher, entrepreneur and developer of Miami Beach.

The federation's *education* committee was composed of Sudie B. Wright (Lakeland), whose husband, George Wright, had founded the Wright Coffee Importing Company; Mrs. T. J. McBeath (Jasper), whose husband was past editor of the *Florida School Exponent;* Allison Locke (Jacksonville), daughter of Judge James W. Locke of the Fifth Circuit Court of Appeals; Mrs. Walter Corbet (Jacksonville), whose husband headed Prudential Insurance Company; and Virginia Darby Trammell (Lakeland-Tallahassee), wife of Park Trammell, governor of Florida.

Iva Sproule-Baker (Miami), who with her husband owned a prominent music academy, served on the federation's *music* committee along with Lucretia Mote (Leesburg), a graduate of the New England Conservatory of Music and wife of E. H. Mote, former legislator and central Florida citrus tycoon. The *public health* committee contained three physicians, Dr. Ellen Lowell Stevens (Jacksonville), Dr. Grace Whitford (Ozona), and Dr. Sarah E. Wheeler (Lakeland), and one dentist, Dr. Emma Dickinson (Orange City). Members of the federation's *home economics* committee were Pattie Monroe (Miami), wife of A. Leight Monroe, prominent doctor and civic leader, Mrs. W. T. Gary (Ocala), whose husband served in the state senate; Agnes Ellen Harris (Tallahassee), dean of the home economics department at Florida State College for Women; and Mrs. A. W. Young (Vero), whose husband served in both the state house and senate.

Additional members of the network included Lucy Blackman (Winter Park), wife of William F. Blackman, president of Rollins College; Katherine B. Tippetts (St. Petersburg), owner of the Belmont Hotel and a well-known author; Annie Broward (Jacksonville), wife of Napoleon Bonaparte Broward, former governor and head of a large tugboat company; Soledad Safford (Tarpon Springs), widow of the former governor of Arizona; Dorothy Conradi (Tallahassee), wife of Edward Conradi, president of the Florida State College for Women; Lula Paine Fletcher (Jacksonville), wife of U.S. Senator Duncan U. Fletcher; Eloise Hulley (DeLand), wife of Lincoln Hulley, president of Stetson University; Elizabeth Skinner (Dunedin), daughter of Lee Skinner, west coast pioneer and owner of the state's largest citrus grove; Edna Fuller (Orlando), who was to be Florida's first female legislator; and Halle Warlow (Orlando), wife of Picton Warlow, judge of the Orange County criminal court.

6. Campaign Song for May Mann Jennings

Sung at the GFWC biennial convention Los Angeles, June 1924.

"May Mann Jennings"
(to the tune of "Auld Lang Syne")

Should work and merit be unsung
or unrewarded stay?
Then praise the splendid
    worthiness
And merits of our May.

May Jennings for our President
Achievement, charm and cheer
To carry on the Winter's work
The fruitful Maytime's here.

Her record stands for all to read
Performance through and through
A tale of work and victory
Of lofty dreams made true.

May Jennings for our President
Achievement, charm and cheer
For every law and plan we need
Make her the engineer.

North and South and East and West
One womanhood we stand
And loyally uphold the best
For home and native land.

May Jennings then for President
Achievement, charm and cheer
Her splendid service let us crown
With faith and vision clear.

In her our hopes and dreams are
    safe
Our seeking meets an end
Her past is ours, our future hers
Hail, Champion and Friend.

May Jennings then for President
Achievement, charm and cheer.
From coast to coast we pledge our
    faith
To the Maytime of the Year.

From *Florida Bulletin* 3(8) (May 1924).

7. Women Appointed by May Jennings
to Organize Democratic Women's Clubs
in Florida Counties, October 25, 1920

County   *Names*

Alachua   Mrs. M. E. Edwards, Gainesville
Baker   Mrs. J. C. Hodges, Macclenny
Bay   Mrs. William L. Wilson, Panama City
Bradford   Mrs. F. A. Scott, Starke
Brevard   Mrs. J. J. Parrish, Titusville
Broward   Mrs. Frank Stranahan, Ft. Lauderdale
Calhoun   Miss Marie Yon, Blountstown
Citrus   Miss Nellie Miller, Inverness
Clay   Mrs. T. J. Brown, Green Cove Springs
Columbia   Mrs. Roy Chalker, Lake City
Dade   Mrs. W. S. Pratt, Miami
De Soto   Mrs. J. H. Hancock, Punta Gorda
Duval   Mrs. Florence Cooley, Mrs. G. C.
               Bucci, Jacksonville
Escambia   Mrs. Lois K. Mays, Pensacola
Franklin   Mrs. G. F. Wedag, Apalachicola
Flagler   Mrs. G. C. Vara, Bennett
Gadsden   Mrs. Maude Love, Quincy
Hamilton   Mrs. C. L. Adams, Jasper
Hernando   Mrs. Harry Mickler, Brooksville
Hillsborough   Mrs. Amos Norris, Tampa
Hardee   Mrs. W. A. Sassoms, Bonifay
Jackson   Mrs. C. L. Wilson, Marianna
Jefferson   Mrs. R. J. Mays, Monticello
Lafayette   Mrs. O. B. Dees, Mayo
Lake   Mrs. Cora Peet Hammond, Tavares
Lee   Mrs. William S. Gwynn, Fort Myers
Leon   Mrs. Charles A. Cay, Tallahassee
Levy   Mrs. Preston King, Williston
Liberty   Mrs. T. E. Shuler, Bristol
Madison   Mrs. A. W. Vann, Madison
Manatee   Mrs. Josiah Varn, Bradenton
Marion   Mrs. W. T. Gary, Ocala

Monroe	Mrs. Allen B. Clear, Key West
Nassau	Mrs. A. S. Allen, Fernandina
Okaloosa	Mrs. W. C. Pryor, Camp Walton
Okeechobee	Mrs. George F. Parker, Okeechobee
Orange	Mrs. A. B. Whitman, Orlando
Osceola	Mrs. Willa Steed, Kissimmee
Palm Beach	Mrs. J. B. O'Hara, Palm Beach
Pasco	Mrs. J. A. Hendley, Dade City
Pinellas	Dr. Grace Whitford, Ozona; Mrs. J. C. Blocker, St. Petersburg
Polk	Mrs. George M. Wright, Lakeland
Putnam	Mrs. Rena Brown, Palatka
Santa Rosa	Mrs. D. R. Reed, Milton
St. Johns	Mrs. Noble Calhoun, St. Augustine
St. Lucie	Mrs. Edgar Lewis, Fort Pierce
Seminole	Mrs. John Leonardy, Sanford
Sumter	Mrs. J. C. Getsen, Webster
Suwanee	Mrs. T. J. Redford, Live Oak
Taylor	Mrs. W. B. Davis, Perry
Volusia	Mrs. M. L. Stanley, Daytona
Wakulla	Mrs. A. B. Winn, Sopchoppy
Walton	Mrs. R. E. F. McKaskill, DeFuniak Springs
Washington	Mrs. W. C. Lockey, Chipley

8. Florida State Chamber of Commerce, Beautification Committee, 1934

Mrs. William S. Jennings, Jacksonville, chairwoman
Lorenzo A. Wilson, Jacksonville
J. Ray Arnold, Groveland
Irwin A. Yarnell, Lake Wales
Mrs. John Ringling, Sarasota
W. E. Sexton, Vero Beach
Mrs. George M. Wright, Lakeland
Mrs. W. L. Wylie, St. Petersburg
Rex Beach, Sebring
Sen. J. E. Larson, Keystone

Judge J. B. Stewart, Fernandina
Sen. M. O. Overstreet, Orlando
Dr. W. H. Huniston, Vero Beach
Mrs. M. L. Stanley, Daytona Beach
Mrs. Jack Pryor, Tampa
Irving Batchelor, Winter Park
J. D. Rahner, St. Augustine
Mrs. A. G. Cummer, Jacksonville
Mrs. August Hecksher, Anastasia Island
H. Harold Hume, Gainesville
Mrs. A. B. Whitman, Orlando
J. B. Prevatt, State Road Department, Tallahassee
Mrs. S. B. Rohrer, Miami Beach
Thomas J. Pancoast, Miami Beach
J. D. Ingraham, Jacksonville
H. E. Wood, Department of Education, Tallahassee
Virginia P. Moore, Tallahassee
Mrs. Meade A. Love, Quincy
Mrs. Jessie Ball Du Pont, Jacksonville
Mrs. Bion H. Barnett, Jacksonville
Mrs. C. E. Johnson, Orange Park
Mrs. William L. Wilson, Jacksonville
E. P. Green, Sr., Bradenton
Hon. John Shepherd, Jr., Palm Beach
Mrs. C. A. Miles, Tampa

9. May Mann Jennings's Achievements and Awards

Florida Federation of Women's Clubs

1912–14   State chairman, Education Committee
1914–17   President, FFWC
1917–36   State chairman, Conservation Committee and Royal Palm
           Park Committee

General Federation of Women's Clubs

1914–19   Chairman, Florida, Joint Committee GFWC and NEA
           School Patrons Department

1917–18	State chairman, Army Cantonments
1918–20	Florida director of GFWC
1920–24	1st vice-president, GFWC
1920–22	National chairman, Home Economics Demonstration Work, GFWC, in conjunction with U.S. Department of Agriculture
1920–24	Member, committee to purchase and endow GFWC headquarters in Washington, D.C.
1923–24	National chairman, Medical Loan Scholarship Fund
1923–24	Vice-chairman, Woman's National Committee for Law Enforcement

Local Women's Clubs

1891–1901	Whittier Club (renamed Village Improvement Association; Woman's Club), Brooksville
1905–14	Jacksonville Woman's Club, chairman of legislation, civics, conservation, Jacksonville
1905–	Ladies' Friday Musicale, Jacksonville
1912–14	President, Springfield Improvement Association (renamed the Springfield Woman's Club), Jacksonville
1917–	Founder-president, Duval County Federation of Women's Clubs, Jacksonville
1920–22	President, Springfield Improvement Association (renamed the Springfield Woman's Club), Jacksonville

Legislative and Political Work

1905–7	Chairman, Legislation Committee, JWC
1921	Cofounder, Florida League of Women Voters
1921	Founder, Democratic Women's Club, Jacksonville
1921–27	President, Florida Legislative Council
1928–30	Campaign manager, Ruth Bryan Owen congressional campaigns
1935–62	Founder-president, Duval County Democratic Women, Inc.

Legislative Lobbying Achievements—State Level (partial list)

Renovation and funding of Boys' Industrial School, Marianna
Establishment and funding of Girls' Industrial School, Ocala
Constitutional amendment for school bonds
Ten-mill school tax

State acceptance of Smith-Lever funds from federal government
Compulsory education law
Women as school board members, jurors, members of boards and
    commissions
Establishment of a commission for the feeble-minded
Good-roads laws
Constitutional amendment for road bonds
Establishment of Royal Palm Park
Establishment of State Board of Forestry
Compulsory dipping of cattle for tick eradication
Stock fence laws
Acceptance of Sheppard-Towner funds from federal government
Abolishment of county convict lease system
Penal camp and jail inspection laws
Substitution of electrocution for hanging as capital punishment
Public school teaching of nature study, bird life, and humane treatment
    of animals
Constitutional amendment for state reapportionment
Laws for conservation and protection of specific wildlife, trees, shrubs,
    and plants
Establishment of State Park Service
Creation of state Everglades National Park committee
Use of mechanical voting machines in elections
State reservation for Seminole Indians
Establishment of Florida State Library, Tallahassee

Legislative Lobbying Supported at National Level (partial list)

Smith-Lever Bill (agricultural extension work)
Prohibition amendment
Susan B. Anthony amendment (women's suffrage)
Appropriations for home economics demonstration work
Sheppard-Towner Bill (infant-maternal health care)
Establishment of Everglades National Park
Protection of Indian claims on government reservations

World War I Work

1915   State chairman, Belgian Relief
1917–18   State chairman, Army Cantonments (for GFWC)
1917–18   Member, Executive Committee, State Food Commission
                and Council of Defense

1917–18   Member, Executive Committee, State Library War Council
1918–19   Member, Executive Committee, National War Savings
           Council
1918–19   State chairman, Woman's Division, five Liberty Loan cam-
           paigns (organized 54 counties, directed 2,000 women,
           sold $17,140,897)
1918–19   Member, Executive Committee, United War Work
1918–19   Member, Executive Committee, Armenian-Syrian Relief
1918–19   State chairman, Woman's Land Army

Conservation and Beautification Achievements

1910   Chairman, Conservation Committee, Jacksonville Woman's
           Club
1915   Establishment of Royal Palm Park (director of its operations
           1915–36)
1917–36   Chairman-member, FFWC Conservation Committee
1919–24   Member, Executive Committee, State Audubon Society
1919–   Cofounder-member, Florida Forestry Association
1920s   Member, Florida branch of National Association for Re-
           strictions on Outdoor Advertising
1923–   Founder-member, Springfield Garden Club
1927–35   Protection of Turtle Mound and Sugar Mill (near New
           Smyrna)
1927–61   State chairman, Beautification Committee, Florida Cham-
           ber of Commerce
1928–61   Founder-president, Duval County Highway Beautification
           Association
1929–47   Member, Everglades Park Committee (established by
           governor)
1930s   Chairman, renovation and beautification of Hogan Creek
           and Springfield Park, Jacksonville

Miscellaneous Organizations (partial list)

1911–   Member, Daniel Memorial Orphanage Association and
           Children's Home Society, Jacksonville
1912–   Member–vice-regent, Katherine Livingston Chapter,
           DAR, Jacksonville; state chairman, Old Trails and
           Road Committee; state chairman, State Library
           Committee
1914–   Founder-member, Jacksonville Federation of Mothers'
           Clubs (forerunner of PTA)

1911–15	Cofounder-director, Young Women's Christian Association, Jacksonville
1917–19	Director, state Anti-Tuberculosis Association
1920	Chairman, Women's Division, Florida Educational and Temperance Campaign
1921–23	Member, Woman's Advisory Board, Georgia State Fair, Atlanta
1921–24	Founder-president, Duval County Law Enforcement League, Jacksonville
1922–23	Member, Forum Committee (speakers' bureau), Jacksonville
1922–24	Member, Executive Committee, Citizens' Memorial Committee, Inc., Jacksonville (World War I monuments)
1922–39	Charter member–vice-president, Florida State Historical Society
1923–	Founder-member, Springfield Garden Club
1923–24	Member, American Legion Auxiliary
1924–	Charter member, National Aeronautical Association of USA, Jacksonville chapter

Honors and Awards

1927	Gold Medal of Achievement, American Forestry Association
1929	Honorary Doctor of Laws, Stetson University
1930	Jennings Park (Long Branch Creek near Evergreen Cemetery), City of Jacksonville
1933	Resolution of Appreciation, Jacksonville City Council, for beautification work
1947	Citation for Everglades National Park work, Newton B. Drury, director, National Park Service
1952	Citation from FFGC for beautification work
1953	Medal and citation for Outstanding Service to the State, University of Florida Centennial Convocation
1954	"Mother of Forestry" citation from the Florida Forestry Association
1955	"Outstanding Citizen of the Year" Award, Springfield Woman's Club
1956	"Woman of the Year" Award, Jacksonville chapter, Soroptimist International
1958	"Citation for Beautification Work," GFWC and Sears-Roebuck Foundation

1961   "Certificate of Achievement" and lifetime membership,
        State Chamber of Commerce
1961   Jennings Hall, women's dormitory, University of Florida,
        Gainesville
1966   Commemorative highway marker, U.S. 71, Yulee, Florida,
        State Road Department and Florida Federation of Garden
        Clubs

Notes

Chapter 1. Crystal Grove and Papa

1. John Q. Langford, Jr., "Senator Austin S. Mann."
2. Interview with Dorothy Brown Jennings, 27 July 1978.
3. *Florida Legislative Directory 12th Session*, 1883, p. 59. Austin Mann was born 14 January 1847; there is evidence that he was christened Austin Shuah but as an adult changed his name to Austin Shuey.
4. Elizabeth Bell Hightower to author, 2 July 1978. Rachel Kline was born on 11 September 1852.
5. Lucy Worthington Blackman, *The Women of Florida*, 2:92.
6. Langford, "Senator Austin S. Mann."
7. Ibid.
8. Richard J. Stanaback, *A History of Hernando County, 1840–1975*, p. 47.
9. Daniel G. Brinton, *A Guidebook of Florida and the South for Tourists, Invalids, and Immigrants*, p. 107.
10. J. M. Hawks, *The Florida Gazeteer*, p. 45.
11. R. A. Divine, "The History of Citrus Culture in Florida, 1565–1895."
12. Hawks, *Florida Gazetteer*, p. 45.
13. Hampton Dunn, *Back Home: A History of Citrus County, Florida*, p. 74.
14. Ibid., p. 67.
15. George M. Barbour, *Florida for Tourists, Invalids and Settlers*, p. 53.
16. Hernando County landownership certificates for 79.8, 119.7, 40, 41.6, 80.7,

165

and 40.1 acres, 1882: Austin Shuey Mann Papers, box 1 (hereafter cited as ASM Papers).

17. Hawks, *Florida Gazetteer*, p. 46.

18. Langford, "Senator Austin S. Mann."

19. Interview with Dorothy Brown Jennings, 27 July 1978.

20. A. S. Mann to May M. Jennings, 5 October, 4,14 December 1903, May Mann Jennings Papers, box 1 (hereafter cited as MMJ Papers); A. S. Mann to William S. Jennings, 22 August 1899, William S. Jennings Papers, box 3 (hereafter cited as WSJ Papers).

21. A. S. Mann to May Jennings, 9 August 1906, 10 December 1903, MMJ Papers, box 2.

22. Langford, "Senator Austin S. Mann."

23. S. S. Harvey to A. S. Mann, 5 June 1902, ASM Papers, box 1.

24. A. S. Mann to May Jennings, 22 December 1903, MMJ Papers, box 2.

25. A. S. Mann to Marietta Staples Kline, 22 December 1903, to May Jennings, 11 October 1904, ibid.

26. Langford, "Senator Austin S. Mann."

27. *United States Census*, 10th, Florida, Hernando County, 1880.

28. Interview with Dorothy Jennings Sandridge, 8 June 1978.

29. May Jennings, speech, "What Brooksville and Hernando County Can Be If Her People Will," 1915, MMJ Papers, box 16; May Jennings to Mrs. Louis Thompson, 18 May 1917, MMJ Papers, box 10.

30. Mann-Jennings Family Bible, in possession of Dorothy Jennings Sandridge.

31. Undated and unidentified newspaper clipping, in possession of Dorothy Jennings Sandridge.

32. May Jennings to Dr. Grace Whitford, 7 September 1917, MMJ Papers, box 11.

33. Interview with Dorothy Brown Jennings.

34. Two months after his wife's death the following item appeared in a Tampa paper: "The Democrats of Hernando County have succeeded in getting their local politics into a terrible tangle. It seems the Mann nominated for the Senate was not the man they wanted at all, so another 'Conservative Democrat' has come out Independently against him." *Tampa Sunland Tribune*, 20 October 1882.

35. Biographical sketch of May Mann Jennings, 1919, MMJ Papers, box 16.

36. Austin Mann, Jr., was born in Tallahassee on 20 December 1886.

Chapter 2. "Beyond the Alps Lies Italy"

1. St. Joseph Academy Roll, 1883, located in St. Joseph's archives. The Mann girls' ages were erroneously listed as twelve and eight.

2. Sisters of St. Joseph, *Living Waters*.

3. Sister Thomas Joseph McGoldrick, "The Contribution of the Sisters of St. Joseph of St. Augustine to Education, 1866–1960."

4. Sister Mary Alberta, "A Study of the Schools Conducted by the Sisters of St. Joseph of the Diocese of St. Augustine, Florida, 1866–1940."

5. May Jennings to Carrie McCollum, 30 April 1915, MMJ Papers, box 5.

6. Jane Quinn, *The Story of a Nun: Jeanie Gordon Brown*, p. 68.

7. *Prospectus of St. Joseph's Academy*.

8. Ibid.

9. Quinn, *Story of a Nun*, p. 85.

10. Florida Latimer, "Convent Life," *Pascua Florida*, February 1903, quoted in Quinn, *Story of a Nun*, pp. 86–87.
11. Edward Nelson Akin, "Southern Reflections of the Gilded Age: Henry M. Flagler's System, 1885–1913."
12. *St. Augustine City Directory*, 1884.
13. *Pascua Florida*, May 1889, p. 9.
14. Biographical sketch of May Mann Jennings, 1919, MMJ Papers, box 16.
15. *Prospectus of St. Joseph's Academy*.
16. *Pascua Florida*, June 1891, flyleaf. One such advertisement read, "The Florida Orange and Vegetable Auction Company of Jacksonville, Florida. Over one-hundred dealers represented, A. S, Mann, President and Manager."
17. Valedictory address; see Appendix 1.
18. *Pascua Florida*, June 1891, p. 10.
19. Edward C. Williamson, "Independentism: A Challenge to the Florida Democracy of 1884," p. 147.
20. Edward C. Williamson, "The Constitutional Convention of 1885," p. 116.
21. Edward C. Williamson, *Florida Politics in the Gilded Age, 1887–1893*, p. 137.
22. Ibid., p. 183.
23. Judge E. C. May, *Gators, Skeeters, and Malary: Recollections of a Pioneer Florida Judge*, p. 58.
24. Ibid., p. 57.
25. The newspaper was the *Brooksville Register*, whose editor was Cash Thomas. According to Stanaback's *A History of Hernando County*, the paper was well written and won prizes at state fairs (p. 171).
26. Lloyd Walter Cory, "The Florida Farmers' Alliance, 1887–1892," p. 41.
27. James O. Knauss, "The Farmers' Alliance in Florida."
28. Stanaback, *History of Hernando County*, p. 129.
29. *Tallahassee Daily Floridian*, 12 April 1891.
30. *Jasper News*, 13 August 1892.
31. Arnold M. Pavlovsky, "We Busted Because We Failed: Florida Politics, 1880–1908," p. 151.
32. *Tallahassee Weekly Floridian*, 8 April 1891.
33. Ibid., 27 May 1891.
34. Biographical sketch of May Mann Jennings, 1919, MMJ Papers, box 16.
35. *Tallahassee Daily Floridian*, 14 May 1891.
36. *Pascua Florida*, June 1891, p. 10.

Chapter 3. Sherman

1. A. B. Caldwell, ed., *Makers of America: Florida*, 4: 252.
2. Cadet certificates, in the possession of Dorothy Jennings Sandridge.
3. Mary Bryan to May Jennings, 28 February 1920, in the possession of Dorothy Jennings Sandridge.
4. *Brooksville Sun*, 27 June 1952.
5. Louis W. Koenig, *Bryan: A Political Biography of William Jennings Bryan*, p. 39.
6. Florida Bar certificates, in the possession of Dorothy Jennings Sandridge.
7. James H. Jones, *History of Brooksville City Government*.
8. James H. Jones, "Genealogical Record of Legal Marriages in Hernando County for the Period 1877–1890."
9. Barbour, *Florida for Tourists*, p. 58.

10. Oliver Marvin Crosby, *Florida Facts*, p. 101.
11. Brooksville Board of Trade, *A Book of Facts for Those Seeking New Locations in the South*, p. 6.
12. *Sunnylands: A Florida Monthly Magazine*, August 1901, p. 109.
13. Brooksville, *The Hernando News*, 25 July 1891.
14. Undated and unidentified newspaper clipping, Jennings scrapbook no. 1, 1901, WSJ Papers.
15. *Gainesville Daily Sun*, 11 June 1901.
16. Biographical sketch of May Mann Jennings, 1919, MMJ Papers, box 16.
17. Florida Sunday School Association, *Minutes of the Eighth Annual Convention*, p. 24.
18. Harry C. Garwood, *Stetson University and Florida Baptists*, p. 78; Jack P. Dalton, "A History of Florida Baptists."
19. *Brooksville Sun*, 28 November 1952.
20. Brooksville, *The Hernando News*, 25 July 1891.
21. Stanaback, *History of Hernando County*, p. 62.
22. Brooksville, *The Hernando News*, 22 August 1891.
23. Blackman, *The Women of Florida*, 1:130.
24. William T. Cash, *The Story of Florida*, 2: 520.
25. Undated and unidentified newspaper clipping, Jennings scrapbook no. 1, 1901, WSJ Papers.
26. Williamson, *Florida Politics in the Gilded Age*, passim. The phrase "the great American barbecue" was coined by Vernon L. Parrington in his classic work *Main Currents in American Thought*, vol. 3, to describe the social, economic, and political exploitation that characterized the Gilded Age.
27. Ibid., p. 187; V. O. Key, Jr., *Southern Politics in State and Nation*, p. 82; Pavlovsky, "We Busted Because We Failed," p. 215.
28. The book, costing $1.25, was ordered from Drew and Co., Jacksonville, 17 June 1899; WSJ Papers, box 3.
29. Pavlovsky, "We Busted Because We Failed," p. 230.
30. Undated and unidentified newspaper clipping, Jennings scrapbook no. 1, 1901, WSJ Papers.
31. *Jacksonville Florida Times-Union*, 9, 15, 29 April, 6 May 1900.
32. *Palatka Advertiser*, 30 April 1900; *Tampa Times*, 10 May 1900.
33. DeLand, *Volusia County Record*, 17 May 1900.
34. *Jacksonville Florida Times-Union*, 27 May 1900.
35. *Tampa Tribune*, 28 May 1900.
36. *Jacksonville Florida Times-Union*, 24 June 1900.
37. Samuel Proctor, *Napoleon Bonaparte Broward: Florida's Fighting Democrat*, p. 161.
38. *Jacksonville Florida Times-Union*, 19 June 1900.
39. Ibid., 18, 19 June 1900.
40. Ibid.
41. David Colburn and Richard K. Scher, "Florida Gubernatorial Politics in the Twentieth Century," p. 104.
42. *Jacksonville Florida Times-Union*, 12 June 1900.
43. Ibid.
44. Ibid.
45. Proctor, *Broward*, p. 163.
46. *Jacksonville Florida Times-Union*, 22 June 1900.
47. Ibid., 24 June 1900.

48. J. D. Beggs to William S. Jennings, 5 July 1900, WSJ Papers, box 4.
49. John M. Barrs, *Some A.D. 1900 Democratic Platforms in Florida*.
50. Herbert Drane to William S. Jennings, 25 June 1900, WSJ Papers, box 4.
51. Colburn and Scher, "Florida Gubernatorial Politics," p. 104.
52. John H. Lee to William S. Jennings, 23 June 1900, WSJ Papers, box 4.
53. E. R. Russell, *Brooksville as I First Knew It*.
54. A. S. Mann to William S. Jennings, 22 August 1899, WSJ Papers, box 3.
55. Barrs, *Some A.D. 1900 Democratic Platforms*.
56. *Jacksonville Florida Times-Union*, 4 October 1900.
57. Ibid., 20 September 1900.
58. Ibid., 21 September 1900.
59. Ibid., 5 September 1900.
60. William Jennings Bryan to William S. Jennings, 15 October 1900, WSJ Papers, box 5.

Chapter 4. The Governor's Lady

1. Proctor, *Broward*, p. 174.
2. *The Weekly Tallahassean*, 10 January 1901.
3. Ibid., 17 January 1901.
4. Ibid.
5. *Lake City Citizen-Reporter*, 11 January 1901.
6. The handwritten original copy of the address is in the possession of Dorothy Jennings Sandridge.
7. *The Weekly Tallahassean*, 10 January 1901.
8. Ibid., 1 August 1902.
9. Interview with Dorothy Brown Jennings, 27 July 1978.
10. Blackman, *The Women of Florida*, 2: 92.
11. Eustis, *Lake Region*, 5 September 1901.
12. *Florida Legislative Directory*, 1903, p. 43.
13. Elizabeth Bell Hightower to author, 2 July 1978.
14. For an assessment of William S. Jennings's gubernatorial abilities, see Colburn and Scher, "Florida Gubernatorial Politics."
15. For an overview of public land policies see J. E. Dovell, "The Railroads and the Public Lands of Florida, 1879–1905."
16. William S. Jennings, "Florida's Public Lands," p. 50.
17. Ibid., p. 54. Napolean Broward, Sherman's successor, would make the map even more famous in his gubernatorial campaign of 1904.
18. R. F. Rogers to William S. Jennings, April 1901, WSJ Papers, box 8.
19. Gordon N. Carper, "The Convict-Lease System in Florida, 1866–1923," p. 186.
20. Unidentified newspaper clipping, 18 October 1901, WSJ Papers, box 9.
21. Photographs of Jennings and Flagler together are in the possession of Dorothy Jennings Sandridge.
22. *New York American*, 18 December 1902.
23. C. H. Dickinson to William S. Jennings, 11 June 1901, WSJ Papers, box 9
24. Tallahassee, *The Daily Capital*, 5 December 1901.
25. Ibid., 13 May 1903.
26. Ibid.
27. *The Weekly Tallahassean*, 17 July 1903.

28. Ibid., 7 August 1903.

29. Alice Strickland, "Florida's Golden Age of Racing," p. 259.

30. *Florida School Exponent*, December 1900, p. 6.

31. *Daytona Gazette-News*, 22 June 1901.

32. *Jacksonville Florida Times-Union*, 13 September 1901.

33. *El Figaro*, June 1902.

34. The Moro Castle flag is in the possession of Dorothy Jennings Sandridge.

35. For a description of May 20 Emancipation Day celebrations, see Susan Bradford Eppes, *The Negro of the Old South*, p. 115.

36. E. Warren Clark to William S. Jennings, May 1901, WSJ Papers, box 9.

37. Ibid.

38. Proctor, *Broward*, p. 189.

39. Unidentified newspaper clipping, 25 August 1903, Jennings scrapbook no. 2, WSJ Papers.

40. Letterhead on campaign stationery, November 1903, WSJ Papers, box 16.

Chapter 5. Jacksonville, the Federation, and Other Matters

1. Jennings was a director of the Leesburg State Bank and the State Bank of Ybor City. An income statement for 1905 shows that the family spent $5,957 on living expenses, $2,866 on law office expenses, and $30,733 on investments: WSJ Papers, box 20.

2. *Jacksonville Florida Times-Union*, 23 May 1964.

3. Governor Jennings's desk is in the possession of Dorothy Jennings Sandridge.

4. *Jacksonville Florida Times-Union*, 23 May 1964.

5. A. S. Mann to W. S. Jennings, 30 June 1907, WSJ Papers, box 22.

6. *Jacksonville City Directory*, 1912.

7. *Jacksonville Florida Times-Union*, 23 May 1964.

8. Interview with Dorothy Brown Jennings, 27 July 1978.

9. Ibid.

10. *Jacksonville Metropolis*, 20 April 1908.

11. For a description of Jennings's role in resolving the legal problems that threatened the drainage project, see W. S. Jennings, "Florida's Public Lands," pp. 55–78.

12. *Jacksonville Metropolis*, 13 April 1907.

13. W. S. Jennings to William Jennings Bryan, 20 November 1908, WSJ Papers, box 22.

14. Itemized list of trip supplies, WSJ Papers, box 24. For additional details about the trip see Alfred J. Hanna and Kathryn A. Hanna, *Lake Okeechobee, Wellspring of the Everglades*, pp. 159–61.

15. *Miami City Map*, 1918; *Miami City Directory*, 1919.

16. For the story of the Everglades project and Jennings's, Broward's, and Bolle's roles in it, see Hanna, *Okeechobee*, pp. 118–72; *Jacksonville Metropolis*, 28 February 1906.

17. Arch Frederic Blakey, *Parade of Memories, History of Clay County, Florida*, pp.187–88. The majority of the Clay County land was still in the hands of the Jennings family in 1980.

18. *Jacksonville Metropolis*, 16 March 1907.

19. *Souvenir zum Verbandsfest*, 1907. May Jennings's copy of the Saengerfest program can be seen in the Haydon Burns City Library, Jacksonville.

20. For a short history of the women's movements of the nineteenth century and the role played by southern women, see Anne F. Scott, *The Southern Lady: From Pedestal to Politics, 1830–1930.*
21. Ibid.
22. Jennie June Croley, *The Woman's Club Movement in America*, p. 155. Green Cove Springs is designated the site of Florida's first woman's club.
23. Margaret Nell Price, "The Development of Leadership by Southern Women through Clubs and Organizations."
24. Croley, *The History of the Woman's Club Movement in America*, p. 55.
25. Blackman, *The Women of Florida*, 1: 129.
26. Ibid.
27. Florida Federation of Women's Clubs hereafter referred to as the Federation or the FFWC; the General Federation of Women's Clubs hereafter referred to as the General or the GFWC.
28. Blackman, *The Women of Florida*, 1: 130.
29. For a list of clubs in the FFWC, 1914, see Appendix 2.
30. For a list of presidents of FFWC, see Appendix 3.
31. For the location of first twenty-five FFWC conventions, see Appendix 4.
32. Blackman, *The Women of Florida*, 1: 131.
33. Ibid., p. 130.
34. Ibid.
35. Ibid., p. 153. The two women who introduced the resolution were Mary Barr (Mrs. Kirk) Munroe and Edith (Mrs. John) Gifford.
36. Ibid., p. 130.
37. Ibid., pp. 132–33.
38. Ibid., p. 136.
39. *Jacksonville Sun*, 2 December 1905.
40. *Florida Magazine*, November 1900, p. 105.
41. *Ladies Home Journal*, quoted in *Florida Magazine*, March 1902.

Chapter 6. "An Enthusiastic Clubwoman"

1. Woman's Club of Jacksonville, *Yearbook 1897–98*. For a history of the club see Mrs. Fred Noble, *The Woman's Club of Jacksonville, Golden Jubilee Issue, 1897–1947.*
2. Ibid.
3. Blackman, *The Women of Florida*, 1: 128.
4. *Sanford Herald*, undated, quoted in biographical sketch of May Mann Jennings, 1919, MMJ Papers, box 16.
5. *Jacksonville Dixie*, 8 November 1912.
6. "Railroad Resolution." Jacksonville Woman's Club, July 1906, MMJ Papers, box 3.
7. *Jacksonville Metropolis*, 24 July 1906.
8. Ibid., 23 November 1907.
9. Janie Smith Rhyne, *Our Yesterday.*
10. "Memorial to the Legislature," April 1907, MMJ Papers, box 3.
11. *Laws of Florida*, 1907, Chapter 5686, No. 91. The 1901 legislature had passed a child labor bill, but it was weak and ineffective.
12. Jacksonville clubwomen began work to secure a juvenile court system in the state in 1906. See *Jacksonville Metropolis*, 15 November 1906.

13. "Resolution," Jacksonville Woman's Club, 20 March 1909, MMJ Papers, box 3.
14. Gilchrist, a bachelor, and his mother were frequent guests in the Jennings's Jacksonville home. At his inaugural ball Gilchrist danced the first dance with May Jennings. It was noted that she wore the same gown she had worn to her husband's inaugural ball: *Jacksonville Metropolis*, 6 January 1909.
15. "Memorial on the Child Labor Law," Jacksonville Woman's Club, MMJ Papers, box 3.
16. Blackman, *The Women of Florida*, 1: 139.
17. Telegram, May Jennings to Mrs. Charles A. Cay [1911], MMJ Papers, box 3.
18. *Jacksonville Metropolis*, 22 November 1907.
19. Ibid., 27 November 1907.
20. Ibid., 10 February 1908. Also see Paul S. George, "A Cyclone Hits Miami: Carrie Nation's Visit to the Wicked City."
21. *Jacksonville Metropolis*, 19 December 1908.
22. Ibid., 27 January 1909.
23. "Report of Jail Committee," 22 May 1911, MMJ Papers, box 3.
24. *Jacksonville DAR* (n.d., n.p.).
25. Charter, Jacksonville YWCA, 11 February 1911, MMJ Papers, box 3.
26. May Jennings to W. S. Jennings, 19 February 1911, ibid.
27. Letty M. Fifield, *History of Jacksonville YMCA*, p. 17.
28. Young Women's Christian Association, *Yearbook, 1912–13*; for short histories of the Jacksonville YWCA see *Jacksonville Florida Times-Union*, 12 February 1950, 25 March 1951.
29. Speech, "Personal Service," MMJ Papers, box 3.
30. *Jacksonville Florida Times-Union*, 13 December 1912.
31. Susan Wight to May Jennings, [1913], MMJ Papers, box 3.
32. Blackman, *The Women of Florida*, 1: 141.
33. Edna Fuller to May Jennings [1913], Lucretia Mote to May Jennings, 15 May 1913, MMJ Papers, box 3.
34. Mothers' Clubs, organized during the first decade of the twentieth century, were the forerunners of Parent-Teacher Associations.
35. *Florida School Exponent*, June 1910, p. 12.
36. The 1914 Smith-Lever Act placed rural extension work high among the nation's domestic priorities.
37. "Education Committee Report," FFWC, February 1913, MMJ Papers, box 3.
38. Agnes E. Harris to May Jennings, 15 February 1913, ibid.
39. "Education Committee Report," FFWC, February 1913, ibid.
40. Elizabeth Hocker to May Jennings, 27 August 1913, ibid.
41. Mary Brownell to May Jennings, 19 October 1913, ibid.
42. Katherine Boyles to May Jennings, 6 December 1913, ibid.
43. *Jacksonville Florida Times-Union*, 30 March 1913.
44. "Memorial," Jacksonville Woman's Club, April 1913, MMJ Papers, box 3.
45. Emily Howard Atkins, "The 1913 Campaign for Child Labor in Florida."
46. "Legislative Committee Report," Jacksonville Woman's Club, May 1913, MMJ Papers, box 3.
47. *Miami Herald*, 7 August 1913.
48. Lena Shackleford to May Jennings, 20 October 1913, MMJ Papers, box 3.
49. Speech, "Practical Politics," 12 February 1914, MMJ Papers, box 4.
50. Speech before the Florida Education Association annual convention, 12 March 1914, ibid.
51. Program, GFWC, Biennial Convention, Chicago, 1914, ibid.

Chapter 7. Madam President and the Old-Girl Network

1. For a list of the federation's old-girl network, see Appendix 5.
2. Kate V. Jackson to May Jennings, 10 December 1914, MMJ Papers, box 4.
3. Florence (Cay) to May Jennings, 4 December 1914, ibid.
4. *Tallahassee Weekly True Democrat*, 11 December 1914.
5. May Jennings to Mrs. William Hocker, 8 January 1915, MMJ Papers, box 5.
6. May Jennings to Elizabeth Hocker, 5 April 1915, ibid.
7. Lucy Lock to May Jennings, 9 April 1915, ibid.
8. J. A. Hendley, *History of Pasco County, Florida*, p. 15.
9. May Jennings to Mrs. John McGriff, 30 April 1915, MMJ Papers, box 5.
10. Lena Shackleford to May Jennings, [May 1915], ibid.
11. Telegrams, Bryan Jennings to May Jennings, 2 June 1915; William S. Jennings to May Jennings, 3 June 1915, MMJ Papers, box 6.
12. "Florida Federation of Women's Clubs," 1915, MMJ Papers, box 5.
13. May Jennings to Mary Coogler, 9 February 1915, ibid.
14. L. B. E. [Mrs. R. A. Ellis] to May Jennings, 28 August 1915, MMJ Papers, box 6.
15. May Jennings to Mrs. T. V. Moore, 8 September 1915, MMJ Papers, box 4.
16. Kenneth R. Johnson, "The Woman's Suffrage Movement in Florida," lists twenty-eight leagues in Florida between June 1912 and November 1930 (p. 55).
17. Edith Stoner to May Jennings, 11 July 1915, MMJ Papers, box 6.
18. Speech, "Woman's Opportunity," FFWC, *Yearbook, 1915–16*, pp.26–31.
19. May Jennings to Charles Mosier, 23 February 1916, MMJ Papers, box 8.
20. May Jennings to Mary Munroe, n.d., MMJ Papers, box 9.
21. May Jennings to Charles Mosier, 3 April 1916, MMJ Papers, box 4.
22. *Miami Herald*, 24 November 1916.
23. Ibid.
24. *Woman's Journal*, April 1917, quoted in Johnson, "Woman's Suffrage," p. 87.
25. Sidney J. Catts to May Jennings, 8 May 1917, MMJ Papers, box 10.
26. "WCTU rally song," ibid.
27. May Jennings to Mrs. E. C. Loveland, 3 May 1917, ibid.
28. Johnson, "Woman's Suffrage," p. 210.
29. Ibid., p. 214.
30. May Jennings to Mrs T. V. Moore, 15 May 1917, MMJ Papers, box 10.
31. May Jennings to Mrs. Mary (William Jennings) Bryan, 25 May 1917, ibid.
32. May Jennings to Marie Randall, 30 May 1917, to Florence Cay, 29 May 1917, ibid.
33. May Jennings to Mrs. John D. Sherman, 21 May 1917, ibid.
34. Woodrow Wilson to FFWC, 21 November 1917, MMJ Papers, box 11.
35. Carrie McCollum to May Jennings, 27 November 1917, ibid.
36. May Jennings to Florence Cay, 26 May 1917, MMJ Papers, box 10.
37. May Jennings to Mrs. William Hocker, 5 June 1917, ibid.
38. "Report of President of FFWC," November 1917, MMJ Papers, box 11.

Chapter 8. A Dedicated Life

1. Steve Jantzen, *Hooray for Peace: Hurrah for War. The United States during World War I.*
2. T. Frederick Davis, *A History of Jacksonville, Florida and Vicinity, 1513–1925*, p. 270.

3. May Jennings to Kate Jackson, 25 May 1918, MMJ Papers, box 13.

4. Pamphlet, July 1917, MMJ Papers, box 10.

5. Edith Gray, *The History of the Jacksonville Chapter of the American Red Cross, World War I Period: 20 March 1914*, p. 30.

6. May Jennings to Mrs. George Bass, 1 February 1918, MMJ Papers, box 12.

7. "National Woman's Liberty Loan Committee Recommendations to County Chairmen," pamphlet, ibid. The European war began November 1914. The United States entered the conflict in April 1917. An armistice was signed by all parties in November 1918. The five Liberty Loan drives occurred May–June 1917, October 1917, April–May 1918, September–October 1918, and May 1919.

8. May Jennings to Fannie D. Williams, 11 February 1918, ibid.

9. May Jennings to Mrs. D. E. Austin, 1 February 1918, ibid.

10. May Jennings to Mrs. M. L. Stanley, 20 July 1917, MMJ Papers, box 10.

11. Sarah E. Sweat to May Jennings, 21 September 1919, MMJ Papers, box 13.

12. May Jennings to Mary McLeod Bethune, 20 July 1917, MMJ Papers, box 10.

13. John P. Ingle, Jr., *Aviation's Earliest Years in Jacksonville, 1878–1935*, p. 14.

14. The Duval County Federation of Women's Clubs was disbanded on 14 May 1965; see *Jacksonville Florida Times-Union*, 15 May 1965.

15. J. D. Privett to May Jennings, 5 April 1918, MMJ Papers, box 12.

16. May Jennings to Mary Jewett, 11 April 1918, ibid.

17. Mary Jewett to May Jennings, 15 April 1918, ibid.

18. Postcard, Anna H. Shaw to May Jennings, October 1918, MMJ Papers, box 14.

19. May Jennings to Elizabeth Skinner, 24 May 1918, MMJ Papers, box 13.

20. "What It Would Mean to the Cause If Each Suffragist Did Her Part," November 1918, speech, ibid.

21. May Jennings, "States' Rights," December 1918, ibid.

22. "The Two Roads to Victory," speech, 1919, MMJ Papers, box 14.

23. May Jennings to General M. O. Terry, 16 February 1926, MMJ Papers, box 18.

24. In 1928, Edna (Mrs. John) Fuller of Orange County became Florida's first female state representative. Lena (Mrs. C. E.) Hawkins became mayor of Brooksville in 1928. Ruth Bryan Owen became Florida's first congresswoman and served the Fourth District (Miami) from 1928 to 1932.

25. Blackman, *The Women of Florida*, 1: 152.

26. "The National League of Women Voters: What It Is, How It Works," pamphlet, [1921], MMJ Papers, box 17.

27. James R. McGovern, "Helen Hunt West: Florida's Pioneer for ERA."

28. Davis, *A History of Jacksonville*, p. 277.

29. May Jennings, "Women's Work in Florida," p. 14.

30. "The Florida Legislative Council Endorses Measures," *The Florida Voter*, April 1925, p. 11.

31. *The Southern Clubwoman*, December 1923, pp. 7–8.

32. For an explanation of the symbiotic relationship between Prohibition and women's rights movements, see James H. Timberlake, *Prohibition and the Progressive Movement, 1900–1920*.

33. Mrs. [?] Woods to May Jennings, 30 January 1920, MMJ Papers, box 16.

34. At the time of Jennings's death he was general counsel for the Everglades Sugar and Land Company; president of Jennings Artesian Farm Land Company, Dade Muck Land Company, Furst-Clark Construction Company, Everglades Contractors, Bowers Southern Dredging Company; vice-president and general counsel for the Florida State Drainage Land Company; chairman of the Ways and Means Committee of the Naval Stores Association of Florida; president of the Leesburg State Bank, Depositors Trust

Company; director of Barnes and Jessup Company; and a proprietor of extensive real estate holdings in Jacksonville, Brooksville, and Miami.

35. "Florida Director's Reports to the General Federation of Women's Clubs," March 1920, MMJ Papers, box 16.

36. "Arguments in defense of Main Street esplanade," ibid.

37. After the removal of the Main Street esplanade, Springfield gradually lost its original elegance. By the 1950s it had become a rundown neighborhood. Presently the area is enjoying a renaissance; many of its old, spacious and genteel homes have kindled the interest of architectural preservationists and young professionals who have begun to move back into the area.

38. "Florida Presents a Candidate for First Vice-President," pamphlet, June 1920, MMJ Papers, box 16.

39. This suggestion became a reality in 1977 when President Jimmy Carter appointed Shirley M. Hufstedler to head the newly created federal Department of Education.

40. The Duval County Law Enforcement Committee was established in December 1920. Scores of prominent Jacksonvillians were members, including Reverend W. A. Hobson, Mrs. J. D. Alderman, Annie Broward, Charles E. Jones, Marcus Fagg, W. F. Coachman, and Mrs. J. A. Corbet. This organization promoted the enforcement of Prohibition and other types of moralistic legislation; it disbanded in 1923.

41. Campaign song, "May Mann Jennings"; see Appendix 6.

42. Ingle, *Aviation*, p. 16.

43. *The Hollywood Magazine*, published by the Florida Society of America, first appeared in November 1924. In 1925 it changed its name to *Tropical America* and in 1926 became *South* magazine. May Jennings joined the magazine in December 1925.

44. May Jennings to O. E. Behymer, 6 February 1926, MMJ Papers, box 17.

Chapter 9. Doctor May

1. [May Jennings], "Royal Palm State Park."

2. May Jennings to E. W. Nelson, 15 September 1919, MMJ Papers, box 15.

3. W. E. Safford, "Natural History of Paradise Key and Nearby Everglades of Florida": Arthur T. Howell, "Birds of Royal Palm Hammock."

4. W. Stanley Hanson to May Jennings, 22 April 1918, MMJ Papers, box 12.

5. Florida Audubon Society, pamphlet, "A Defense of the Pelican," ibid.

6. May Jennings to Rose Lewis, 9 March 1918, ibid.

7. May Jennings to E. W. Nelson, 18 February 1921, MMJ Papers, box 17.

8. Memorial, FFWC, "To the Honorable Members of the Florida Legislature, Session 1919," MMJ Papers, box 13. For the history of Florida's Seminole Indian reservation, see James Covington, "Formation of the State of Florida Indian Reservation."

9. May Jennings to Ivy Stranahan, 9 February 1918, box 12.

10. James Covington, "Trail Indians of Florida," p. 40.

11. Williamson, a botanist and graduate of North Carolina State University, later served as vice-president of the U.S. Forestry Association. After long service on behalf of the state's forests, he is remembered as the "father of the Florida tung oil industry." For a sketch of his life, see *Jacksonville Florida Times-Union*, 10 August 1952.

12. B. F. Williamson, "Sketch and Reminiscences," p. 6.

13. Florida Forestry Association, pamphlet, "Forest Fires in Florida," December 1926.

14. Williamson, "Sketch," p. 6.

15. Forest History Society, "Oral Interview with Clinton H. Coulter, State Forester, Florida Forest Service," p. 6.

16. George H. Dacy, *Four Centuries of Florida Ranching*, p. 149.

17. A. Stuart Campbell, "Timber Conservation," p. 57.

18. Forest History Society, "Interview with Clinton H. Coulter," p. 5; Williamson, "Sketch," p. 6.

19. May Jennings to Paul G. Redington, 21 July 1927, MMJ Papers, box 18.

20. J. A. Robertson to May Jennings, 30 July 1927, ibid.

21. Joe Ackerman, Jr., *Florida Cowman, a History of Florida Cattle Raising*, p. 237.

22. Ibid., pp. 227–29.

23. William Blackman to "The Presidents of Women's Clubs of Florida," 22 March 1919, MMJ Papers, box 15.

24. May Jennings to Harold Colee, 29 July 1936, MMJ Papers, box 20.

25. For an explanation of why Stetson organized a new historical society and did not join the Florida Historical Society, see Watt Marchman, "The Florida Historical Society, 1856–1930," p. 28.

26. Florida Historical Pageant, *Program, April 20–22, 1922*.

27. Florida State Historical Society, *Charter and By-Laws*.

28. Ales Hrdlička, *The Anthropology of Florida*, flyleaf.

29. Jean E. Little, "The Life and Work of Jeanette T. Connor."

30. In 1941, Charles H. Coe, in *Debunking the So-Called Spanish Mission near New Smyrna Beach*, established conclusively that the "mission" was a sugar mill built about 1830 by the New York firm of Cruger and DePeyster. He attributed Connor's error to "an honest mistake" in judgment.

31. *New Smyrna News*, 20 February 1926. In addition to speeches and prayers by notables, the Glee Club of Stetson University sang patriotic songs.

32. Little, "Jeanette T. Connor," p. 26.

33. May Jennings to Jeanette Connor, 21 March 1927, MMJ Papers, box 18.

34. *Jacksonville Florida Times-Union*, 17 March 1929.

35. Blackman, *The Women of Florida*, 2: 92.

Chapter 10. "Lover of Beauty"

1. *Jacksonville Florida Times-Union*, 28 September 1920, p. 13.

2. Ibid., 25 October 1920, p. 9. For a complete list of the fifty-four women appointed by May to form Democratic clubs, see Appendix 7. These partisan clubs should not be confused with the nonpartisan League of Women Voters clubs organized in the state in 1921.

3. Ibid., 2 November 1920, p. 5.

4. Ruth Bryan Owen was defeated in the 1926 primary by Congressman W. J. Sears. She was elected in 1928 and reelected in 1930 but was defeated in 1932 by J. Mark Wilcox.

5. Alma Taylor, Secretary of DCDW, Inc., to author, 9 December 1976. The organization was incorporated 29 June 1935.

6. *Florida Times-Union*, 21 June 1945.

7. *Southern Woman's Digest*, April 1936, p. 2.

8. *Florida Times-Union*, 21 June 1945.

9. Mrs. Fred Noble, *Florida Federation of Women's Clubs: Jubilee Issue*, p. 85.

10. John D. Pennekamp to author, 27 August 1974.

11. May Jennings to Governor David Sholtz, 28 October 1933, MMJ Papers, box 19.

12. *Miami Herald*, 7 December 1947.

13. *Jacksonville Florida Times-Union*, 6 December 1947.

14. Jacksonville Garden Club, Founder's Circle, *Yearbook, 1926–27*.

15. Ella G. Alsop, *History of the Florida Federation of Garden Clubs*. In 1958, Jacksonville Garden Club, with 146 circles, was the largest club in the United States.

16. *Beautiful Florida*, November 1924, p. 3.

17. Duval County Highway Beautification Association, Constitution and By-Laws. 1928.

18. *Beautiful Florida*, November 1928, p. 4.

19. Ibid., March 1929, p. 15.

20. *The Florida Bulletin*, August 1929, p. 4.

21. May Jennings to J. A. Robertson, 20 March 1929, MMJ Papers, box 19.

22. May Jennings to J. A. Robertson, 20 July 1931, ibid.

23. In 1954 the Springfield Woman's Club celebrated its fiftieth anniversary. May Jennings was honored at this celebration.

24. Blackman, *The Women of Florida*, 2: 96.

25. For a complete list of committee members, see Appendix 8.

26. *Southern Woman's Digest*, April 1936, p. 6.

27. Ibid., p. 4.

28. Unidentified newspaper clipping dated 26 July 1943, in possession of Dorothy Jennings Sandridge.

29. *Florida Business Review and Outlook*, August 1954, p. 1.

30. Ibid., December 1956, p. 1.

31. Ibid., February–March 1959.

32. Quoted ibid., September 1961, p. 4.

33. Ibid., February 1962, p. 1.

34. *Jacksonville Florida Times-Union*, 24 October 1956.

35. University of Florida, "Centennial Convocation, Recipients of Awards, Program."

36. *Jacksonville Florida Times-Union*, 26 April 1963.

37. "House Concurrent Resolution, No. 1196, Expressing Deep Sympathy and Regret over the Passing of May Austin Mann Jennings," in possession of Dorothy Jennings Sandridge.

Chapter 11. A Life of Good Works Assessed

1. When research for this book was begun in 1975 there were fewer than fifteen entries under the subject heading "women" in the card catalogue of the P. K. Yonge Library of Florida History. In 1985, there were about fifty entries.

2. For a list of May Jennings's achievements and awards, see Appendix 9.

3. New York: W. W. Norton & Co., Inc.

4. Recent studies have shown that successful women most often have had strong father figures whom they have emulated and with whom they have identified. These women also appear usually to be either single children or firstborns. For a discussion of this phenomenon see Caroline Bird, *Enterprising Women* (New York: W. W. Norton & Co., 1976), and Ruth B. Kundsin, ed., *Women and Success: The Anatomy of Achievement* (New York: William Morrow & Co., 1974).

5. For a history of the conservation movement during the Progressive Era, see Samuel P. Hays, *Conservation and the Gospel of Efficiency: The Progressive Conservation Movement, 1880–1920*, 2d ed. (New York: Atheneum, 1974), and Albert Guttenberg, *Environmental Reform in the United States: The Populist-Progressive Era and the New Deal* (Monticello, IL, 1969).

6. For an overview of the women's movement, past and present, see Sophonisba P. Brackinridge, *Women in the Twentieth Century: A Study of Their Political, Social and Economic Activities* (New York: McGraw-Hill Book Co., 1933); Aileen S. Kraditor, *The Ideas of the Woman Suffrage Movement, 1890–1920* (New York: Columbia University Press, 1965); William O'Neill. *Everyone Was Brave: A History of Feminism in America* (Chicago: Quadrangle, 1971).

7. See Paul E. Fuller, *Laura Clay and the Women's Rights Movement* (Lexington: University of Kentucky Press, 1975); Rebecca L. Richmond, *A Woman of Texas: Mrs. Percy V. Pennybacker* (San Antonio: Naylor Co., 1941).

8. For a history of social feminism see J. Stanley Lemons, *The Woman Citizen: Social Feminism in the 1920s* (Urbana: University of Illinois Press, 1973); Dorothy E. Johnson, "Organized Women and National Legislation, 1920–1941" (Ph.D. diss., Case Western Reserve University, 1960).

9. Both Edna Fuller, Florida's first female legislator, and Ruth Byan Owen, its first female representative, took this route.

Bibliography

Papers

Jennings, May Mann. Papers. 23 boxes. P. K. Yonge Library of Florida History, Gainesville, Florida.
Jennings, William Sherman. Papers. 29 boxes. P. K. Yonge Library of Florida History, Gainesville, Florida.
Mann, Austin Shuey. Papers. 3 boxes. P. K. Yonge Library of Florida History, Gainesville, Florida.

Newspapers

Brooksville, *The Hernando News*, 1891.
Brooksville News Register, 1895.
Brooksville Sun, 1952.
Daytona Gazette-News, 1901.
DeLand, *Volusia County Record*, 1900.

179

Eustis, *Lake Region*, 1901.
Gainesville Daily Sun, 1901.
Jacksonville Dixie, 1912.
Jacksonville Florida Times-Union, 1900–1965.
Jacksonville Metropolis, 1906–9.
Jacksonville Sun, 1905.
Jasper News, 1892.
Lake City Citizen-Reporter, 1901.
Miami Herald, 1913–47.
New Smyrna News, 1926.
New York American, 1902.
Palatka Advertiser, 1900.
Sanford Herald, undated.
Tallahassee Daily Capital, 1901–3.
Tallahassee Daily Floridian, 1891.
Tallahassee Weekly Floridian, 1891.
Tallahassee Weekly True Democrat, 1914.
Tallahassee, *The Weekly Tallahassean*, 1901–3.
Tampa Sunland Tribune, 1882.
Tampa Times, 1900.
Tampa Tribune, 1900.

Periodicals

Beautiful Florida, vol. 1 (November 1924), vol. 5 (November 1928, March 1929).
El Figaro, vol. 18 (June 1902).
The Florida Bulletin, vol. 9 (August 1929).
Florida Business Review and Outlook, vol. 13 (August 1954), vol. 15 (December 1956), vol. 18 (February–March 1959), vol. 20 (September 1961), vol. 21 (February 1962).
Florida Magazine, vol. 1 (November 1900), vol. 4 (March 1902).
Florida School Exponent, vol. 3 (December 1900), vol. 17 (June 1910).
The Florida Voter, vol. 1 (April 1925).
Mr. Foster's Travel Magazine, vol. 11 (January 1919).
Pascua Florida, vol. 2 (May 1889, June 1891), vol. 14 (February 1903).
The Southern Clubwoman, vol. 12 (December 1923).
Southern Woman's Digest, vol. 1 (April 1936).
Sunnylands, A Florida Monthly Magazine, vol. 3 (August 1901).
Woman's Journal, vol. 18 (April 1917).

Municipal, State, and Federal Records

Florida Legislative Directory, 12th Session. 1883.
Florida Legislative Directory. Tallahassee, 1903.

Jacksonville City Directory, 1912. Jacksonville: R. L. Polk and Co., 1912.
Laws of Florida, 1907, Chapter 5686, No. 91.
Miami City Directory, 1919.
Miami City Map, 1918.
St. Augustine City Directory. St. Augustine: Chapin and Co., 1884.
United States Census, 10th, Florida, Hernando County, 1880.

Secondary Sources

Ackerman, Joe, Jr. *Florida Cowman, A History of Florida Cattle Raising*. Madison, Florida: Jimbob Printing, Inc., 1976.
Akin, Edward Nelson. "Southern Reflections of the Gilded Age: Henry M. Flagler's System, 1885–1913." Ph.D. dissertation, University of Florida, 1975.
Alberta, Sister Mary. "A Study of the Schools Conducted by the Sisters of St. Joseph of the Diocese of St. Augustine, Florida, 1886–1940." Master's thesis, University of Florida, 1940.
Alsop, Ella G. *History of the Florida Federation of Garden Clubs*. Jacksonville, 1943.
Atkins, Emily Howard, "The 1913 Campaign for Child Labor in Florida." *Florida Historical Quarterly* 35 (January 1957): 223–40.
Barbour, George M. *Florida for Tourists, Invalids and Settlers*. New York: D. Appleton and Co., 1882.
Barrs, John M. *Some A. D. 1900 Democratic Platforms in Florida*. Jacksonville: East Florida Printing Company, 1900.
Bennett, Congressman Charles. Interview, 5 November 1979, Jacksonville, Florida.
Bird, Caroline. *Enterprising Women*. New York: W. W. Norton & Co., 1976.
Blackman, Lucy Worthington. *The Women of Florida*. 2 vols. Jacksonville: Southern Historical Publishing Associates, 1940.
Blair, Karen Jane. "The Clubwoman as Feminist: The Woman's Culture Club Movement in the United States, 1868–1914." Ph.D. dissertation, State University of New York at Buffalo, 1976.
Blakey, Arch Frederic. *Parade of Memories, A History of Clay County, Florida*. Jacksonville: Clay County Bicentennial Steering Committee, 1976.
Bogart, Ernest Ludlow. *War Costs and Their Financing*. New York: D. Appleton and Co., 1921.
Brackinridge, Sophonisba P. *Women of the Twentieth Century: A Study of Their Political, Social and Economic Activities*. New York: McGraw-Hill Book Co., 1933.
Brinton, Daniel G. *A Guidebook of Florida and the South for Tourists, Invalids, and Emigrants*. Jacksonville: Columbus Drew, 1869.
Brooksville Board of Trade. *A Book of Facts for Those Seeking New Locations in the South*. Chicago: J. P. Black and Co., 1909.
Caldwell, A. B., ed. *Makers of America: Florida*. 5 vols. Atlanta: Florida Historical Society, 1911.
Campbell, A. Stuart. "Timber Conservation." *Studies in Forestry Resources in Florida* 1 (May 1932): 5–113.
Carper, Gordon N. "The Convict-Lease System in Florida, 1866–1923." Ph.D. dissertation, Florida State University, 1964.
Carver, Joan S. "Women in Florida." *The Journal of Politics* 41 (1979): 941–55.

Cash, William T. *The Story of Florida*. 4 vols. New York: American Historical Society, Inc., 1938.

Coe, Charles H. *Debunking the So-Called Spanish Mission near New Smyrna Beach*. Daytona Beach: Fitzgerald Publications, 1941.

Colburn, David, and Scher, Richard K. "Florida's Gubernatorial Politics in the Twentieth Century." Manuscript, 1980, in possession of the authors, University of Florida, Gainesville. (Published in 1981 by University Presses of Florida.)

Cory, Lloyd Walter. "The Florida Farmers' Alliance, 1887–1892." Master's thesis, Florida State University, 1963.

Covington, James. "Formation of the State of Florida Indian Reservation." *Florida Historical Quarterly* 64 (July 1985): 62–75.

_____. "Trail Indians of Florida." *Florida Historical Quarterly* 58 (July 1979): 35–57.

Croley, Jennie June. *The History of the Woman's Club Movement in America*. New York: Henry G. Allen and Co., 1898.

Crosby, Oliver Marvin. *Florida Facts*. New York: Oliver Marvin Crosby, 1887.

Dacy, George H. *Four Centuries of Florida Ranching*. St. Louis: Britt Printing Co., 1940.

Dalton, Jack P. "A History of Florida Baptists." Ph.D. dissertation, University of Florida, 1952.

Davis, T. Frederick. *A History of Jacksonville, Florida and Vicinity, 1513–1924*. St. Augustine: Florida Historical Society, 1925.

_____. *The Narrative History of the Orange in the Florida Peninsula*. Jacksonville: T. Frederick Davis, 1941.

Divine, R. A. "The History of Citrus Culture in Florida, 1565–1895." Manuscript, P. K. Yonge Library of Florida History, Gainesville, 1952.

Douglas, Marjory Stoneman. *The Everglades: River of Grass*. Coconut Grove: Hurricane House Publishers, Inc., 1947.

Dovell, J. E. "The Railroads and the Public Lands of Florida, 1879–1905." *Florida Historical Quarterly* 34 (January 1956): 236–58.

Dunn, Hampton. *Back Home: A History of Citrus County, Florida*. Inverness: Citrus County Bicentennial Steering Committee, 1978.

Duval County Highway Beautification Association. *Constitution and By-Laws*. N.p., 1928.

Eppes, Susan Bradford. *The Negro of the Old South*. Chicago: Joseph G. Branch, 1925.

Fifield, Letty M. *History of Jacksonville YMCA*. Jacksonville: Miller Press, 1950.

Florida Federation of Women's Clubs. *Yearbook, 1915–16*. Jacksonville, 1915.

_____. *Some Laws of Interest to Women*. Jacksonville, 1914.

Florida Historical Pageant. *Program, April 20–22, 1922*. Jacksonville: Community Pageant Association, 1922.

Florida State Historical Society. *Charter and By-Laws*. DeLand, 1922.

Florida Sunday School Association. *Minutes of the Eighth Annual Convention*. Ocala: Banner Steam Printing and Publishing House, 1889.

Forest History Society. "Oral Interview with Clinton H. Coulter, State Forester, Florida Forest Service," 6 February 1958. Manuscript, P. K. Yonge Library of Florida History, Gainesville.

Friedan, Betty. *The Feminine Mystique*. New York: W. W. Norton & Co., Inc., 1963.

Fuller, Paul E. *Laura Clay and the Women's Rights Movement*. Lexington: University of Kentucky Press, 1975.

Garwood, Harry C. *Stetson University and Florida Baptists*. DeLand: Florida Baptist Historical Society, 1962.

George, Paul S. "A Cyclone Hits Miami: Carrie Nation's Visit to the Wicked City." *Florida Historical Quarterly* 58 (October 1979): 150–59.

Gray, Edith. *The History of the Jacksonville Chapter of the American Red Cross, World War I Period: March 20, 1914–November 16, 1920*. Jacksonville: Edith Gray, n.d.

Guttenberg, Albert. *Environmental Reform in the United States: The Populist-Progressive Era and the New Deal*. Monticello, Ill., 1969.

Hanna, Alfred J., and Hanna, Kathryn A. *Lake Okeechobee, Wellspring of the Everglades*. Indianapolis: Bobbs-Merrill, 1948.

Harrison, Benjamin. *Acres of Ashes*. Jacksonville: J. A. Holloman, 1901.

Hawks, J. M. *The Florida Gazetteer*. New Orleans: Bronze Pen Steam Book and Job Office, 1871.

Hays, Samuel P. *Conservation and the Gospel of Efficiency: The Progressive Conservation Movement, 1880–1920*. 2d ed. New York: Atheneum, 1974.

Hendley, J. A. *History of Pasco County, Florida*. Dade City: J. A. Hendley, [1941].

Hightower, Elizabeth Bell. Personal communication to author, 2 July 1978.

Howell, Arthur T. "Birds of Royal Palm Hammock." *The Auk*, April 1921, pp. 5–10.

Hrdlička, Ales. *The Anthropology of Florida*. DeLand: Florida State Historical Society, 1922.

Ingle, John P., Jr. *Aviation's Earliest Years in Jacksonville, 1878–1935*. Jacksonville: Jacksonville Historical Society, 1977.

Jacksonville Garden Club, Founder's Circle. *Yearbook 1926–27*. N.p., n.d.

Jantzen, Steve. *Hooray for Peace: Hurrah for War. The United States during World War I*. New York: Alfred A. Knopf, 1971.

Jennings, Dorothy Brown. Interview, 27 July 1978, Penney Farms, Florida.

Jennings, May (Mrs. W. S.). "Conservation in Florida." *Christian Science Monitor*, 18 October 1925.

_____. "Royal Palm State Park." *Mr. Foster's Travel Magazine*, January 1919.

_____. "Woman's Work in Florida." *Florida Magazine*, April 1922, pp. 13–18.

Jennings, William S. "Florida's Public Lands." In *Legislative Bluebook, 1917*. Compiled by Pat Murphy. Tallahassee: T. J. Appleyard, 1917.

Johnson, Dorothy E. "Organized Women and National Legislation, 1920–1941." Ph.D. diss., Case Western Reserve University, 1960.

Johnson, Kenneth R. "The Woman's Suffrage Movement in Florida." Ph.D. dissertation, Florida State University, 1966.

Jones, James H. "Genealogical Record of Legal Marriages in Hernando County for the Period 1877–1890."

_____. *History of Brooksville City Government*. Brooksville: James H. Jones, 1965.

Key, V. O., Jr. *Southern Politics in State and Nation*. New York: Random House, 1949.

Knauss, James O. "The Farmers' Alliance in Florida." *The South Atlantic Quarterly* 25 (July 1926): 300–315.

Koenig, Louis W. *Bryan: A Political Biography of William Jennings Bryan*. New York: G. P. Putnam's Sons, 1971.

Kraditor, Aileen S. *The Ideas of the Woman Suffrage Movement, 1890–1920*. New York: Columbia University Press, 1965.

Kundsin, Ruth B., ed. *Women and Success: The Anatomy of Achievement*. New York: William Morrow & Co., 1974.

Langford, John Q., Jr. "Senator Austin S. Mann." Manuscript, P. K. Yonge Library of Florida History, Gainesville, 1950.

Lawrence, David L. "The Women's Rights Movement in Florida: From Suffrage to Equal Rights." Master's thesis, University of South Florida, 1980.

Lemons, J. Stanley. *The Woman Citizen: Social Feminism in the 1920s.* Urbana: University of Illinois Press, 1973.

Little, Jean Edkin. "The Life and Work of Jeanette T. Connor." Master's thesis, Stetson University, 1933.

McGoldrick, Sister Thomas Joseph. "The Contribution of the Sisters of St. Joseph of St. Augustine to Education, 1866–1960." Master's thesis, University of Florida, 1960.

McGovern, James R. "Helen Hunt West: Florida's Pioneer for ERA." *Florida Historical Quarterly* 57 (July 1978): 39–53.

Marchman, Watt. "The Florida Historical Society, 1856–1940." *Florida Historical Quarterly* (July 1940): 3–65.

May, Judge E. C. *Gators, Skeeters, and Malary: Recollections of a Pioneer Florida Judge.* New York: Vantage Press, 1953.

Noble, Mrs. Fred. *Florida Federation of Women's Clubs: Jubilee Issue.* Jacksonville, 1947.

————. *The Woman's Club of Jacksonville, Golden Jubilee Issue, 1897–1947.* Jacksonville, 1947.

O'Neill, William. *Everyone Was Brave: A History of Feminism in America.* Chicago: Quadrangle, 1971.

Paisley, Clifton. *From Cotton to Quail: An Agricultural Chronicle of Leon County, Florida, 1860–1967.* Gainesville: University of Florida Press, 1968.

Pavlovsky, Arnold M. "We Busted Because We Failed: Florida Politics, 1880–1908." Ph.D. dissertation, Princeton University, 1973.

Pennekamp, John D. Personal communication to author, 27 August 1974.

Price, Margaret Nell. "The Development of Leadership by Southern Women through Clubs and Organization." Master's thesis, University of North Carolina, 1945.

Proctor, Samuel. *Napoleon Bonaparte Broward: Florida's Fighting Democrat.* Gainesville: University of Florida Press, 1950.

Prospectus of St. Joseph's Academy. St. Augustine, 1890.

Quinn, Jane. *The Story of a Nun: Jeanie Gordon Brown.* St. Augustine: Villa Flora Press, 1978.

Rhyne, Janie Smith. *Our Yesterday.* Marianna, Florida, 1968.

Richmond, Rebecca L. *A Woman of Texas: Mrs. Percy V. Pennybacker.* San Antonio: Naylor Co., 1941.

Russell, E. R. *Brooksville as I First Knew It.* Brooksville: W. R. Russell, 1962.

Safford, W. E. "Natural History of Paradise Key and Nearby Everglades of Florida." *Smithsonian Journal* (1917): 377–434.

Sandridge, Dorothy Jennings. Interview, 8 June 1978. Orange Park, Florida.

Scott, Anne F. *The Southern Lady: From Pedestal to Politics, 1830–1930.* Chicago: University of Chicago Press, 1970.

Sisters of St. Joseph. *Living Waters.* St. Augustine, Florida, 1966.

Souvenir zum Verbandsfest, 1907.

Stanaback, Richard J. *A History of Hernando County, 1840–1975.* Brooksville: Action '76 Steering Committee, 1976.

Strickland, Alice. "Florida's Golden Age of Racing." *Florida Historical Quarterly* 45 (January 1967): 253–68.

Timberlake, James H. *Prohibition and the Progressive Movement, 1900–1920.* Cambridge: Harvard University Press, 1963.

University of Florida. "Centennial Convocation, Recipients of Awards, Program."
   Gainesville, 1953.
Williamson, B. F. "Sketch and Reminiscences." Manuscript, P. K. Yonge Library of
   Florida History, Gainesville, undated.
Williamson, Edward C. "The Constitutional Convention of 1885." *Florida Historical
   Quarterly* 41 (October 1962): 116–26.
_____. *Florida Politics in the Gilded Age, 1877–1893*. Gainesville: University of
   Florida Press, 1976.
_____. "Independentism: A Challenge to the Florida Democracy of 1884." *Florida
   Historical Quarterly* 27 (July 1948): 131–56.
Woman's Club of Jacksonville. *Yearbook, 1897–98*. Jacksonville, 1897.
Young Women's Christian Association. *Yearbook, 1912–13*. Jacksonville, 1912.

Index

Ackerman, Joe, 122
Acosta, St. Elmo, 69, 75
Adams, Mrs. C. L., 157
Adams, Mrs. Richard F., 148
Adams, Thomas B., Sr., 137
Addams, Jane, 78, 103
Alderman, Mrs. J. D., 175n
Alexander, James E., 96
Allen, Mrs. A. S., 158
Alliance. *See* Farmers' Alliance
Alligator Bay Rookery, 93, 115
Alva, 123
American Social Hygiene Assn., 102
Amos, Ernest, 115
Anastasia Island, 159
Anderson, Frances, 153
Anderson, Herbert L., 153
Anthony, Susan B., 97, 105–6
Antituberculosis movement, 79, 85,
    87–88, 93, 95, 100, 105, 112
Apalachicola, 96, 157

Arcadia Civic League, 150
Armenian-Syrian Relief Committee, 101
Arnold, J. Ray, 158
Artesian Farm Company, 52, 174n
Auburndale Woman's Club, 150
Audubon Society, 53, 77, 108, 115–
    16, 130
Avery, Mrs. John E., 154

Baker, William H., 78
Baptist Convention, Florida, 23
Baptists, 10, 19, 23, 40–41, 43, 71.
    See also Stetson University
Baptist State Board of Missions, 23
Baptist State Missionary Union, 71
Barnes and Jessup Co., 48, 175n
Barnett, Bion H., 92, 153
Barnett, Lina L'Engle (Mrs. Bion H.),
    61, 70, 92, 102, 136, 153, 159
Barrs, J. M., 25, 30
Batchelor, Irving, 159

186

Dees, Mrs. O. B., 157
DeFuniak Springs, 31, 96, 158
DeLand, 77, 89, 96, 125, 152, 155
DeLand Woman's Club, 151
Democratic Committee, National, 106–7
Democratic party, 15–16, 18, 21–26, 28, 30, 32, 43, 45–46, 50, 52, 106–7, 127, 129, 144, 176n
Depositors Trust Company, 175n
De Soto County, 26
Dickinson, Charles H., 37, 41
Dickinson, Dr. Emma, 155
Dimick, Elisha N., 154
Dimick, Ella (Mrs. Elisha N.), 154
Disston land sale, 15
Dixie Highway, 88, 92, 133
Dodge, Judge —, 127
Doe, Gordon T., 117
Dorman, J. F., 26
Douglas, Marjory Stoneman, 96, 154
Drainage of the Everglades, 38–39, 51–52
Drane, Herbert, 26, 30, 86, 153
Drane, Mary Wright (Mrs. Herbert), 153
Drury, Newton B., 132
Dunedin, 155
Dunn, Ida (Mrs. Royal C.), 153
Dunn, Royal C., 153
Dunnellon Woman's Club, 150
DuPont, Mrs. Jessie Ball, 136, 159
Durkee, Cordelia (Mrs. J. H.), 61
Duval County, 28, 45, 67–68, 71, 75–76, 94, 102, 105, 107, 112, 127–29, 133–35, 137–38, 153. See also Jacksonville
Duval County Democratic Women, Inc., 129
Duval County Federation of Mothers' Clubs, 72
Duval County Federation of Women's Clubs, 94, 105, 174n
Duval County Highway Beautification Assn., 133–35
Duval County Law Enforcement Committee, 175n
Duval County Law Enforcement League, 112
Duval County Prohibition League, 68

Duval County School Board, 76
Duval High School, 48
Dye, Charlotte, 91

Edison, Thomas Alva, 36, 77, 88
Edison, Mrs. Thomas Alva, 130
Education. See Public education
Edwards, Mrs. M. E., 157
Egan, Katherine Livingston (Mrs. Dennis), 61, 69
Eustis Woman's Club, 150
Everglades, 38–39, 51–52, 58, 80–84, 91, 115, 120, 129–32, 143. See also Conservation; Everglades National Park; Jennings, May Mann; Royal Palm Park
Everglades City, 131–32
Everglades Contractors, 174n
Everglades National Park, 84, 117, 129–32, 143
Everglades Sugar and Land Co., 174n

Fagg, Marcus, 66–67, 75, 77, 112, 135, 175n
Fairchild, David, 81, 90, 115, 130
Fairfield Town Improvement Assn. (Jacksonville), 148
Fairfield Village Improvement Assn. (Jacksonville), 149, 151
Farmers' Alliance, 6, 17–18, 30; Ocala Demands, 17
Farquahar, N. H., 43
Farris, Allie (Mrs. Ion L.), 153
Farris, Ion L., 75, 95–96, 111, 153
Fechner, Robert, 130
Federal Emergency Relief Administration, 135
Federal Point Village Improvement Assn., 151
Fencing livestock, campaign for. See Livestock
Fernandina, 103, 158–59
Fernandina Ladies Civic League, 150
Fisher, Carl G., 88, 155
Fisher, Jane (Mrs. Carl G.), 88, 155
Flagler, Henry, 13, 25, 29, 40, 92
Flagler, Mary Kenan, 40, 82, 88, 92
Flamingo, 81, 88, 131
Fletcher, Duncan U., 25, 91, 105–6, 125, 130, 155